Dialogue and Technology:
Art and Knowledge

The Springer Series on
ARTIFICIAL INTELLIGENCE AND SOCIETY

Series Editor: KARAMJIT S. GILL

Bo Göranzon and Magnus Florin (Eds.)

Dialogue and Technology: Art and Knowledge

Springer-Verlag
London Berlin Heidelberg New York
Paris Tokyo Hong Kong

Bo Göranzon, PhD
Mathematician and Researcher,
The Swedish Center for Working Life,
PO Box 5606, S-11486, Sweden

Magnus Florin
Dramaturg, The Royal Dramatic Theatre,
PO Box 5037, S-10241 Stockholm, Sweden

Cover illustration: Lennart Mörk, *School of Athens* (after Raphael)

ISBN-13: 978-3-540-19574-0   e-ISBN-13: 978-1-4471-1731-5
DOI: 10.1007/ 978-1-4471-1731-5

British Library Cataloguing in Publication Data
Dialogue and technology: art and knowledge. – (Artificial intelligence and society)
1. Human. Applications in artificial intelligence
I. Göranzon, Bo, *1941* – II. Florin, Magnus III. Series
001.3028563

Library of Congress Cataloging-in-Publication Data
Dialogue and technology: art and knowledge/Bo Göranzon and Magnus Florin, eds.
p.   cm. – (Springer series on artificial intelligence and society)
Papers originally presented at a conference held at Stockholm in May–June 1988.
Includes index.
1. Artificial intelligence.
I. Göranzon, Bo, 1941–   II. Florin, Magnus, 1955–   III. Series.
Q335.5.D53 1991
0063–dc20
                                                                90-48634
                                                                    CIP

Typeset by Best-set Typesetter Ltd, Hong Kong
2128/3830-543210 Printed on acid-free paper

Preface

This book springs from a conference held in Stockholm in May–June 1988 on Culture, Language and Artificial Intelligence. It assembled more than 300 researchers and practitioners in the fields of technology, philosophy, history of ideas, literature, linguistics, social· science, etc. The conference was an initiative from the Swedish Center for Working Life, based on the project *AI-Based Systems and the Future of Language, Knowledge and Responsibility in Professions* within the COST 13 programme of the European Commission. Participants in the conference, or in some cases researchers in areas related to its aims, were chosen to contribute to this book.

It was preceded by *Knowledge, Skill and Artificial Intelligence* (ed. B. Göranzon and I. Josefson, Springer-Verlag, London, 1988) and *Artificial Intelligence, Culture and Language* (ed. B. Göranzon and M. Florin, Springer-Verlag, 1990). The latter book springs, as this one, from the 1988 conference, and one further book will follow: *Skill and Education: Reflection and Experience* (Springer-Verlag, planned autumn 1991).

The philosophical and aesthetic interest of the contributions in the present volume is in large part due to the framework of the Dialogue Seminar, held regularly at the Royal Dramatic Theatre in Stockholm, in which several of the contributors have participated.

The contributors' thinking in this field varies greatly; so do their styles of writing. For example, contributors have varied in their choice of "he" or "he/she" for the third person. No distinction is intended, but chapters have been left with the original usage to avoid extensive changes. Similarly, individual contributors' preferences as to notes or reference lists have been followed.

Stockholm   *Bo Göranzon*
July 1990   *Magnus Florin*

Contents

Contributors

Susan Bassnett
Doctor, University of Warwick, Woodstock House, The Square,
Wolvey, Leicestershire LE10 3LJ, UK

Horace Engdal
Doctor, Department of Culture, Dagens Nyheter, Trädgårdsgatan
5, S-111 31 Stockholm, Sweden

Magnus Florin
Dramaturg, The Royal Dramatic Theatre, Box 5037, S-102 41
Stockholm, Sweden

Lars Gyllensten
Author, The Swedish Academy, Chairman of Nobel Prize
Foundation, Karlavägen 121, S-115 26 Stockholm, Sweden

Bo Göranzon
Doctor, Mathematician and Researcher, The Swedish Center for
Working Life, Box 5606, S-114 86 Stockholm, Sweden

Julian Hilton
Professor, Director of the Audio-Visual Centre, University of East
Anglia, Norwich, NR4 7TJ, UK

Allan Janik
Professor, Brenner Archive, Innsbruck University,
Speckbacherstrasse 17, A-6020 Innsbruck, Austria

Erland Josephson
Actor, Author, The Royal Dramatic Theatre, Box 5037, S-102 41
Stockholm, Sweden

Herbert Josephs
Professor, Department of Romance and Classical Languages,
Michigan State University, East Lansing, MI 48824-1027, USA

Lars Kleberg
Culture Attaché, Swedish Embassy, Ulitsa Rossolimo 8, Moscow,
USSR

Iurii Lotman
Professor, Russian Literature, University of Tartu, Estonia, USSR

Lennart Mörk
Artist, Scenographer, The Royal Dramatic Theatre, Box 5037,
S-102 41 Stockholm, Sweden

Agneta Pleijel
Author, Tantogatan 45, S-117 42 Stockholm, Sweden

Henrik Sinding-Larsen
Researcher, Department of Social Anthropology, University of
Oslo, Skedsmogata 6, N-0655 Oslo 6, Norway

Pehr Sällström
Assistant Professor, Department of Physics, University of
Stockholm, Norra Järnvägsgatan 13, S-153 00 Järna, Sweden

Thomas Tempte
Craftsman, Flintbacken 4, S-117 42 Stockholm, Sweden

Stephen Toulmin
Professor, Department of Philosophy, Northwestern University,
Bretano Hall, Evanston, IL 60208, USA

Clas Zilliacus
Professor, Department of Comparative Literature, Åbo Academy,
SF-20500 Åbo, Finland

Summaries

Chapter 2. A Dwelling Place for Past and Living Voices, Passions and Characters

Erland Josephson

This short piece focuses on the world of the theatre, where an astonishing number of human, technical and artistic components may be brought together in splendid harmony without the use of squared paper, computer networks and other common means of communication. Actors learn about the theatre's thousand years of experience and carry with them knowledge of the ancient practice of play-acting: how to reach truth by representation, how to communicate with crowds and individuals, with the individual in the crowd, and with a crowd of individuals. The technologist may see the theatre as a framework of learning from old knowledge and experience.

Chapter 3. Reflections on Dialogue

Allan Janik

The re-emergence of dialogue is seen as part and parcel of an attempt by some AI scientists to place information technology, "expert systems", etc., into some sort of proper perspective. This dramatic re-emergence is rooted in the need to understand the role of thought and experience in working life, particularly in Sweden with its commitment to industrial democracy. One of the most significant implications of the Dialogue Seminar is that it demonstrates to those of us who are not content to be passively "postmodern" the central position of dialogue in a *critical* appropriation of the fruits of modern science and technology.

Chapter 4. The Dialogue Seminar

Magnus Florin, Bo Göranzon and Pehr Sällström

The Dialogue Seminar is held on a regular basis at the Royal Dramatic Theatre, Stockholm, and publishes the quarterly magazine *Dialoger*. The Seminar approaches, directly and indirectly, various aspects of dialogue, applying a broad basis of philosophy, aesthetics and the history of ideas. Particular attention is given to the relationship between occupational knowledge and technology. The people behind the Dialogue Seminar are Magnus Florin, Bo Göranzon and Pehr Sällström, who exemplify here the concept of dialogue from sources which include Raphael, Plato, Shakespeare, Rousseau, Diderot, Offenbach and Goethe.

Chapter 5. The Essence of Dialogue

Pehr Sällström

Is there any sense in which a human can have a dialogue with a machine? In common usage dialogue means conversation, talk, discussion. However, the term is deliberately chosen here to signify a search for a certain quality in discourse, a quality not found in all conversations, some being nothing more than an exchange of empty words. A true dialogue does not persuade, delude or dumbfound another person, it is a process of finding something out together with another person. It has no pre-set goal, it has no end, and it is pure movement, movement which cannot be frozen and translated into a formula, a rule or a programme. Whether resulting in agreement or disagreement, dialogue helps to achieve clarity. Socrates used dialogue to demonstrate the falsity of the conviction that being able to state something is the same as possessing real knowledge. Dialogue is a means of gaining insight through inner reflection. "Intuition" places dialogue in a meaningful context, a "presence of mind" which gives it life and depth. Dialogue is not a particular behaviour or attitude; only something purely factual which, whether in the form of words, art or music, involves both parties in their total historical experience.

Chapter 6. The Dream of an Exact Language

Stephen Toulmin

In the twentieth century there has been a debate on whether natural language is adapted to its human tasks or whether it has essential defects which make it unsuitable as a medium for expression and the communication of thought. Why did such questions arise? Russell et al. dreamed of a language which would serve as a mirror, reproducing and reflecting the eternal structure of Reality and Truth. Why was there this desire for an eternal language of permanent, universal meanings? The dream of an exact language, which goes back to Plato, was at its most powerful in seventeenth-century Europe, during the time of religious warfare and the need for religious toleration. A renewed dialogue was needed among theologians with contrasting views. Leibniz et al. believed there had to be a universal language to serve as an instrument of reason. The period from the Renaissance to the present time has also been one of great uncertainty in the religious, cosmological and social spheres – hence a further appeal for rationality in science and language. Today the problem is less one of religious toleration than of racial and cultural diversity. Today's project concerns the building of compatible transnational television and computer links. The obstacles, such as cultural conflicts and a lack of international understanding, are greater. Moreover, it must be borne in mind that it is one thing to perfect an instrument and quite another to ensure that it is put to just, virtuous or even rationally discriminating use. An exact language, rational method and a united science are the three dreams of rationalism. They are still dreams. Why? The move from science of matter and energy towards that of information means that the distinction between pure and applied science is blurring as theory and praxis merge. The increase in technical interventions in the natural world is giving rise to an increasingly uncertain world in which we are less confident in our ability to forecast or limit their effects.

Chapter 7. Dialogue and Enlightenment

Horace Engdahl

Plato's dialogues found an influential interpreter in H.-G. Gadamer, who sees dialogue as a vehicle of truth, involving transformation. The utopian character of Gadamer's thought has been questioned by J. Habermas, who submits "true" dialogue with "noncoercive communication" which can be described as a democratic decision-making process on commonsense grounds leading to consensus rather than to truth and knowledge. However, when this modern Philosophy of Enlightenment is compared with the literary dialogues of Diderot, the encyclopaedist, we become aware of an enormous gap: here, dialogue is the opposite of consensus. An alternative tradition of dialogue is found in the Jewish tradition, with a contemporary exponent in Emmanuel Levinas, who describes the relationship of the "I" to the "Other".

Chapter 8. Theatricality and Technology: Pygmalion and the Myth of the Intelligent Machine

Julian Hilton

Can machines think? The Cartesian test lays down that to be deemed intelligent the machine must be independent of the programmer, otherwise it is merely imitating. One way of considering the issue of the simulation of human behaviour is to look at the theatre. The theatre is both simulated and real because the actors have to convince the audience that they are real. The theatre has been exploring the representation and simulation of people's behaviour for thousands of years. AI could learn from it. In the theatre art is enabled by technology – by staging, sets, lighting, costumes, effects and so on. It is a complex aesthetic machine. The effectiveness of simulation therefore depends on the imagination of the audience. The same may apply to the knowledge-based machine. The story of Pygmalion and the myth of the intelligent machine highlights the discrepancy between surface mimicry and depth. The myth included ideals which Pygmalion mistakenly held about women. The later work, in which Higgins taught Eliza to speak like him and assumed that he had taught her to think like him too, illustrates the danger of divorcing words from meaningful context. The teaching of Eliza took place from a linguistic knowledge base. The implication for AI of not considering the context and environment within which knowledge gains meaning is that the knowledge – engineering approach may fail to deal with the complexity of knowledge transfer.

Chapter 9. Humans and Automatons

Magnus Florin

This comment on Julian Hilton's article discusses two of his examples: the writings of Georg Büchner, and Heinrich von Kleist's *On Marionette Theatre*. While Hilton finds Büchner's parallel between people and automatons to be positive and constructive, Florin sees it as helpless and constrained. While Hilton sees in Kleist a connection between utopian dance and artificial intelligence, Florin focuses on the aspects of Kleist which do not permit a given conclusion or moral to be arrived at.

Chapter 10. Turing's Paradox

Bo Göranzon

Two important articles by Alan Turing are discussed: *On Computable Numbers with an Application to the Entscheidungsproblem* (1936) and *Computing, Machinery and Intelligence* (1950). The second article demonstrates the conviction of the unlimited possibilities of the "universal machine" to imitate human intelligence. But, paradoxically, the first article points out the limitations of such machines. The distance between the ability of machines and the intelligence of humans is to be found throughout the development of computer technology.

Chapter 11. Parody and Double-Voiced Discourse: On the Language Philosophy of Mikhail Bakhtin

Lars Kleberg

In his studies of literature and the philosophy of language Mikhail Bakhtin sees parody not as a criticism of an original but a "dialogical" dimension in literature closely related to intertextuality. The parody is not seen as a "form"; it is a function – a relation

between one text and another. All language is related to other
language and the deeper consequences of Bakhtin's thinking brings
one face to face with the impossibility of monological, monolithical
approaches to literature and other human expression – to all forms
of culture. Man is characterized by ambivalence, dialogue and
multiplicity.

Chapter 12. Notes on Metrical and Deictical Problems in Shakespeare Translation

Clas Zilliacus

Taking examples from Shakespeare's *The Taming of the Shrew, As
You Like It* and *Hamlet*, Clas Zilliacus gives practical evidence of the
degree of difficulty in a translation into Swedish which can claim to
be similar to the source. Both syntactic and metrical problems are
involved, added to which is the difference between Swedish and
English blank verse. The deictical function (referral, indication,
reference) is dealt with separately. How, for example, should the
difference between "you" and "thou" be treated in a translation to
a language which does not have corresponding forms? This may be
a very important issue in a translation. Hamlet first says "you" to
Horatio but he dies saying "thou". This kind of difference in
language may be used with powerful dramatic effect.

Chapter 13. The Translator's Knowledge

Susan Bassnett

Translation studies have emerged as a new discipline in the last
20 years. What is becoming increasingly obvious – and what
Bassnett argues for – is the degree to which the work of a translator
involves criteria that transcend the purely linguistic. One example
given here is the translation of knitting patterns from Danish
into English, which involve highly complex translation problems
because the conventions that operate between English and Danish
knitters are so different. A text belongs to its culture, its language,
and its world and is changed when transferred to another culture
and another language. Thus the task of the translator is to create a
text in a target culture which in its context fulfils a similar function
to that of the original. There can be no ideal "equivalence" between words and phrases in different languages, between text and
translation. Translating is a highly skilled and highly creative
activity.

Chapter 14. Information Technology

Henrik Sinding-Larsen

The development of information technology is approached here
through the concept of "externalization". Computer programming

Is seen as a step in the human history of externalization which can only be compared with the invention of speech and writing. But what happens to human knowledge when it is externalized as computer programs? Sinding-Larsen uses the development of the system of musical notation as a comparison. He finds complex relationships between the notation system and the music, as he does between computer technology and humankind's knowledge. As musical notation transformed music, computer technology transforms our knowledge.

Chapter 15. Intelligence and Creativity

Lars Gyllensten

This chapter is concerned with the question of intelligence which has implications for developments in the area of the intelligent machine. Does the speed of a calculation belie intelligence? Surely finding a simple way to a solution – something a computer cannot do – shows more intelligence. Compare computer memory and human memory: we may not have a computer's memory for fine detail, but this is because we select what we feel is relevant to us. A computer cannot perform this function. Consider the computer and intuition. At the age of 12, Gauss discovered by intuition the formula for the sum of an arithmetical sequence. Could a computer ever do this? Intelligence is more than the ability to calculate and build up complicated scenarios using data and a given strategy. This is a reductionist and defeatist definition. An element of creativity is essential in the concept of intelligence. In its turn creativity must include elements of systematic intelligence: critical consolidation, attempts to incorporate creative ideas in a standardized whole and to assess their relevance. The fascination with AI lies in the hidden paths along which the brain moves when it proceeds without really knowing what is happening and what it is up to.

Chapter 16. On the Views on Labour Reflected in Chekhov and the Bible

Agneta Pleijel

In earlier industrial societies work in industry was closely linked to a morality of duty which was both individual and social. But the status of work today and the moral system which gave it its status have undergone considerable change. The Book of Genesis can be seen as the first gospel of labour, but what is our view of the meaning of work today? In *The Three Sisters* Chekhov has shown with both tender irony and deep seriousness that the meaning of work cannot be separated from the meaning of life, and attempting to arrive at a new view of work therefore always involves attempting to arrive at a new view of man.

Chapter 17. *Rameau's Nephew:* A Dialogue for the Enlightenment

Herbert Josephs

Diderot's body of writings – including his translation of Shaftesbury, his biography of Seneca and his dialogues – is described as a persistent search for the vital interlocutor, for that other who might stimulate his imagination and onto whom he could project his ideas. To Diderot the dialogue was far more than a narrative strategy or a component of rhetorical technique: he had an aversion to literary speech limited to a single voice. None of his writing is farther removed from monologue than *Rameau's Nephew*, and it belongs to the dimension of the ambiguous, the uncertain and the paradoxical. It offers a world where new questions are generated and where isolated thought is changed into genuine dialogue.

Chapter 18. Literature, Reflection and the Theory of Knowledge

Allan Janik

Both humanists and scientists may think it absurd to suggest that literature can play a role in epistemology. But this is because literature has been consigned to a nebulous, non-cognitive realm of values, leading in the "fact"-worshipping twentieth century to the trivialization of studies which should illuminate the character of human life. The manifold nature of experience can only be captured significantly in narrative form, and by reflection, a mode of knowledge that involves epistemological pluralism. Literature has this ability and, through its capacity for concrete portrayal, it can also move us. Janik gives four examples: Aeschylus' *Orestia*, Shakespeare's *King Lear*, Diderot's *Rameau's Nephew* and the poetry of G. Trakl. His statement is: without literary reflection, the essential problematic character of human experience can only be superficially explored.

Chapter 19. The Chair of Tutankhamun

Thomas Tempte

Craftsmanship involves values, technical reasoning and a tradition that has changed little over the centuries. It can never be placed in opposition to new technologies. Craftsmen have used existing machines and designed new ones. In fact, the craftsman makes technical advance possible. However, the craftsman's workshop is not controlled by machines. His approach is different to the industrial approach. He applies all his faculties to performing a given task, and the work is not fragmented. The tradition of the craftsman is determined by aesthetics, tradition and taking the time the job needs. This is only possible when the craftsman is in control of his means of production. The integrity of the craftsman lies in the tools and machines he makes himself. To a craftsman a tool is an object that mechanically shapes the raw materials of nature into a desired form for a particular purpose. Therefore the computer cannot be regarded as a tool, but it could be a useful data machine.

Chapter 20. Semiotics and the Historical Sciences

Iurii Lotman

Lotman says that the science of history has been caught in an unfortunate position between the description of Hegel's idealism of the logical movement of history through great events on the one hand and the new school's picture of immobile history rooted in the practice and mentality of the collective on the other.

The latter school reacts against the former but they are fundamentally reunited in denying history and mankind the possibility of non-predictability, chance and freedom. Lotman argues against this kind of determinism and by using examples from film, mathematics and physics attempts to find the place of open change in the system. In particular, he discusses Prigogine's analysis of dynamic processes which, when equilibrium is disturbed, give rise to critical points – points of bifurcation – with different possibilities for development. Such points of non-predictability also exist in history. A basic error of current historical science is the rejection of non-predictability. But the development of science is, according to Lotman, characterized by a high degree of predictability, decidability, while the history of art is characterized by non-predictability.

Chapter 21. Working Memory

Julian Hilton

This chapter discusses the difference between human memory and computer memory, and the effects of this difference. There is a tendency to confuse memory capacity – dramatically expanded in computer technology – with understanding and competence. The latter qualities of the human working memory are connected with forgetfulness and fantasy – two qualities that are often seen as disturbing the potential causes of unreliability. But should they not be seen instead as positive properties of the human active memory?

On the basis of, among other things, Bacon's *The Advancement of Learning* and from the Art of Memory's emblematic relationships between memory and language, the question is posed whether the development of computer memory cannot better approximate human memory capacity. Sophisticated memory has the ability to forget – a characteristic linked to judgement. But present-day computer technology is not solely devoted to the gathering and storing of data.

Section I:

Introduction

Chapter 1

Introduction

Bo Göranzon and Magnus Florin

"Dialogue" and "technology" – what is the connection between these two concepts? We have observed that these two terms often occur together in discussions of what we call "artificial intelligence", "knowledge-based systems", etc. These two terms are sometimes used together in a superficial and careless way in, say, product advertisements or user documentation, and sometimes their juxtaposition has been more inspired inasmuch as it presents to us an attractive challenge to see in the new technology more than a mere collection of effective instruments; to see it as a means for people's linguistic and cognitive interaction.

There is a simple, pragmatic side to this. The tools of new technology develop rapidly, and as a result the relationship between man and technology becomes less mute and circumscribed and more dynamic and flexible. In this conditional sense we may assert that people are in a dialogue with machines. But then there is a dimension to the concept of "dialogue" which prevents us from accepting such a pragmatic view as universally applicable. "Dialogue" is one of the keystones in the development of philosophical and ethical thinking which we can trace back to ancient times in our culture. To Socrates and Plato dialogue is the very means by which knowledge develops. But it is more than that. In their work, dialogue emerges as a natural feature of human life. We can trace the development of the content of this term throughout the development of our culture.

Paradoxically, the word now appears to be in more frequent use than ever before, while the meaning it conveys is so often trite and diminished.

This book aims to demonstrate the breadth and complexity of the concept of "dialogue" – in particular in relation to new technology and what follows in its wake: the effects it has on the development and the preservation of occupational knowledge and skills, and its effects on society, on culture and on language.

As with *Artificial Intelligence, Culture and Language* (Springer, 1990) the starting-point of this book is the conference held in Stockholm in May–June 1988. This conference was a gathering place for a large number of the world's more prominent researchers in this field, and many of the contributions in this book were presented or prepared at the Stockholm conference. We do not see this book as a summary of something which has been brought to a close but as a continuation, or even as an introduction. Today, the effects of the new technology are to be studied not only in the field of technology, but in the entire cultural and social field – a field where there

are no limits to the viewpoints that may be relevant: philosophical, epistemological, linguistic or anthropological.

Erland Josephson, the actor and author, sets the pattern for the collection
of voices in this book with his article on the theatre's stewardship of its store
of ancient truths and experience, an article which ultimately applies to the
passing on of all knowledge and experience. The reader will find that this
link between aesthetics and technology, explicit or implicit, recurs throughout the book. Contributions in the field of drama and literature include
Julian Hilton's study of the significance of the myth of Pygmalion for the
"intelligent machine". Magnus Florin comments on Hilton's presentation of
the views of the nineteenth-century authors Büchner and Kleist on mechanical life – "automatons". Agneta Pleijel discusses the view of "work" and
"the value of work" in Chekhov's drama *The Three Sisters*.

The field of aesthetics is also represented by Henrik Sinding-Larsen's
article on music. Thomas Tempte's description of his reconstruction of
Tutankhamun's chair is central to the theme of this book. His work played a
crucial part in Bo Göranzon's project on "Education – Work – Technology"
at the Swedish Center for Working Life. It touches on the most important
aspect of all: the relationship of craft knowledge and skills to tools and
memory. This chapter also expresses the care and respect of a master
craftsman of our times for the work of his predecessors who lived over 3000
years ago.

Lars Kleberg discusses Mikhail Bakhtin's philosophy of language – a
central source for all discussions of the modern concept of dialogue. Allan
Janik describes the relationship between literature and the theory of knowledge; two things normally kept apart which we attempt to bring together in
this book.

Our interest in language is represented by the chapters on translation by
Clas Zilliacus and Susan Bassnett. The transfer of meaning between languages
is of great interest in the context of new technology, and in our view translators'
perceptions of the actual nature of language are of great significance here.

Aspects of philosophy and the history of ideas come to the fore in
Stephen Toulmin's article, which reminds us that the technological culture
of our times has its roots in the seventeenth-century thinkers' dream of a
rational, exact and universal language. In the final chapter, Julian Hilton
examines Francis Bacon's ideas on the advancement of learning in the light
of present-day technological change. Horace Engdahl examines the concept
of dialogue on the basis of, among others, Plato, Gadamer, Habermas and
Levinas and finds in Diderot's *Rameau's Nephew* a mobile dialogue which
does not result in a synthesis and conclusion, but which retains its force as a
dialogue.

Rameau's Nephew is a key text for those of us who are involved with the
Dialogue Seminar and the magazine *Dialoger* (see Allan Janik's article).
Herbert Josephs interprets *Rameau's Nephew* as Diderot's portrayal of a meeting of different traditions of knowledge in the Encyclopedia Project. This
interpretation became a metaphor which pointed to the way forward in our
research on occupational knowledge.

Iurii Lotman's contribution on semiotics and the historical sciences was
clearly written in the spirit of *glasnost* and *perestroika*. It is an exciting and

thought-provoking article for everyone who is receptive to periods of change in human history and to a discussion of the nature of change.

The development of new technology will continue, characterized by contradictory impulses and by both unlimited faith in its possibilities and awareness of its limitations – see Bo Göranzon's emphasis on Turing's paradox.

Despite our efforts to programme them, creativity and intelligence go their own ways. This is the essence of the contribution by Lars Gyllensten – who opened the Stockholm conference – and it is the essence of this book.

Translated by Struan Robertson

The Concept of Dialogue

Chapter 2

A Dwelling-Place for Past and Living Voices, Passions and Characters

Erland Josephson

This short piece focuses on the world of the theatre, where an astonishing number of human, technical and artistic components may be brought together in splendid harmony without the use of squared paper, computer networks and other common means of communication. Actors learn about the theatre's thousand years of experience and carry with them knowledge of the ancient practice of play-acting: how to reach truth by representation, how to communicate with crowds and individuals, with the individual in the crowd, and with a crowd of individuals. The technologist may see the theatre as a framework of learning from old knowledge and experience.

When some students of technology, in the early 1970s, asked to be allowed to study the work of the Royal Dramatic Theatre (*Dramaten*), in Stockholm, everyone naturally imagined that they were out to demonstrate how irrationally, wastefully and unsystematically the theatre went about things.

This turned out not to be the case at all. In fact, they were curious as to how people could achieve, in such a short time, such an incredibly complicated product as a theatrical production. The technologists, the community planners, experts on rationalization, programmers, compilers of timetables, directors general of post offices and other confused and imprecise creatures found they had a great deal to learn from Dramaten. An incredible number of human, technical and artistic components could within the space of a few short weeks be brought together in splendid harmony, without the use of squared paper, networks, flip-overs and sophisticated discussions of objectives.

To one question of how these things could be, the then director of the theatre had no answer. Perhaps, he thought, it might be due to thousand-year-old experience, to a stored and communicated knowledge; this, also, frequently acquired in a process of agonizing pleasure, active doubt, and just as active enthusiasm.

The actors carry with them ancient experiences of the terms of play-acting, and a knowledge, just as ancient, of how to reach truths by representation, how to communicate with crowds and individuals, with the individual in the crowd, and with a crowd of individuals.

And around these miracles of communication, people raise and lower curtains, backdrops and sets, write texts of transient or eternal value, create

ingenious lighting, arrange properties, build stages, smear gold on prosce-
nium arches, decorate the public spaces with monumental paintings to
underline the glory of the theatre, or serve soup in plastic bowls to empha-
size its ties with the common people.

Around the actors, directors weave their interpretations and visions, audiences their dreams. The actors are given their lines and instruction, and they
retrieve an insight. They serve as midwives to the innermost structures of
the spectator, sorting out confusions, or raising important questions. In a
few brief months, a complicated internal and external machinery allows us
to undergo or renew the experiences of Lear, or Hamlet, or Medea, to take
some of the most breath-taking examples. Alternatively, we take to the
streets and squares, exulting in the voices all around, and lending the
stopped mouths a voice, the tired bodies movement.

In the live theatre, the actor is thus surrounded not by "viewers" or
"listeners" but by spectators. The theatre audience must never be seen in
terms of figures, or as a market. Treacherous and borrowed words like
"marketing" and "sales department" are now creeping insidiously into the
language of the theatre, and can disrupt the ancient and existential agreements that exist between the theatre and its public.

Dramaten is an institution two centuries old, housed in an eighty-year-old
building. The building at once contains and expresses the institution. It is a
dwelling place of past and living voices, passions and characters. No one
can work there without feeling weighed down, challenged, encouraged,
threatened, deflated and pumped up by the past. The walls are full of
voices. You are forced to open a dialogue with the past, a dialogue that also
forces you into a discussion with the future.

An actor or actress engaged for his first year, straight from some academy
of drama, will soon find himself involved in a fruitful dispute with Anders
de Wahl (1864–1956), without, perhaps, having even heard of him. An older
colleague will try, with no clear awareness of the source, to inoculate a trace
of Hanson into a younger actor. Anders Henrikson (1886–1965) admired
Ivan Hedqvist (1880–1935), Mathias Henrikson admires Anders Henrikson,
Erland Josephson plays against Mathias Henrikson, and is infected by some
remarkable, naked intonations; a common harmony arises, and suddenly it
is Ivan Hedqvist who is delivering Lars Norén's text. This is probably true of
all theatre, but in a theatre like Dramaten it is clearer than elsewhere.

There are still actors today, vigorously active, who have stood on the same
stage as actors who played pages in *Hamlet* with Edvard Swartz in the title
role. Swartz was alive between 1826 and 1897, and probably lives on still in
some strange phrasing or sudden outburst on the part of a contemporary
interpreter. You can see this either as a burdensome tradition, or as a
liberating opportunity to test and exploit an intuitive knowledge that was
mastered long, long ago. Every age has its intonations, but they will be
more human, deeper, if they are played against a wider sounding-board.

There is a danger that the "national stages", such as Dramaten, will
husband the opportunities of tradition so poorly as to become its prisoners.
The trouble in that case is often that their perspective has been too short;
they seek their way back, but not sufficiently far, and not sufficiently deep.

The rejuvenators of dramatic art, and the avant-grade, have often drawn
their inspiration and their starting-points from the truly old and original

rites, the masques, the art of telling a story in the market. Basically, no people are more conservative than the avant-gardistes of the theatre.

It thus looks as if the basis of radical drama is an insight into the past. This is why Dramaten is such an important gauge of the health of Swedish theatre as a whole, and why it is more fiercely watched over and criticized than any other theatre in the country. The sign of Dramaten's vitality is the expectations that it excites. Even disappointment is a sort of recognition.

During the greater part of its short life-span, Dramaten has acted in a capital city without a university. This has sometimes contributed to promote a sort of artificial boundary between art and science. There have been times when actors have used the terms "academic" and "intellectual" as words of abuse. The academics, for their part, have devoted themselves to an old stout and avid content of actors; if they have felt admiration, then it has been an admiration from above, a reflection of liberal generosity.

Today, even natural scientists speak of art as a source of knowledge. Painters and sculptors, musicians, dancers and actors are necessary to formulate new and astounding insights, to create a language also for the researchers themselves, so that they can move forward. Actors are being assigned a role not just as the providers of an abbreviated chronicle of the times, but also as the keen-eyed explorers of the future. In an age in which people are speaking, as usual, of the crisis in the theatre, its task, its obligations and its opportunities are in fact being broadened.

In Dramaten, then, and in its actors, is stored an ancient knowledge of the future. Perhaps it was this that the young technologists saw, or sensed, when they sought their way to the threatre.

Translated by Keith Bradfield

Chapter 3

Reflections on Dialogue

Allan Janik

The re-emergence of dialogue is seen as part and parcel of an attempt by some AI scientists to place information technology, "expert systems", etc., into some sort of proper perspective. This dramatic re-emergence is rooted in the need to understand the role of thought and experience in working life, particularly in Sweden with its commitment to industrial democracy. One of the most significant implications of the Dialogue Seminar is that it demonstrates to those of us who are not content to be passively "post-modern" the central position of dialogue in a *critical* appropriation of the fruits of modern science and technology.

It is surprising, not to say shocking, that the concept of dialogue, so important in Central Europe in the inter-war years as well as during the heyday of "existential" thought in the 1950s and early 1960s throughout the West, should suddenly and strikingly re-emerge as the focal point for understanding both social relations and intellectual enterprises in the way that the Dialogue Seminar indicates that it has. The surprise results largely from the fact that the re-emergence of dialogue is part and parcel of an effort to come to set new technology, especially information technology, so-called expert systems and the like, into some sort of proper perspective; for the earlier philosophy of dialogue was principally religious in orientation and highly sceptical, when not outright hostile, to science and technology. Nevertheless, it is just this scepticism, liberated from the blinding character of hostility, which makes the dialogical perspective crucial for our contemporary efforts to raise the question of the human significance of technology. Thus, astonishment at the revival of dialogue as an integrating concept in current debates about the social implications of new technology rests upon a superficial understanding of the intellectual and moral resources of that tradition – a tradition which most certainly itself profits from this new challenge. Thus, the radical claims of technocrats, according to which there are no significant differences between human beings and machines, present dialogical thinkers with an opportunity to re-establish the importance of their perspective for understanding of human activity. The latent resources of the seemingly other-worldly religious thought of an Ebner or a Buber (as well as the seemingly arid theory of knowledge of the later Wittgenstein) here come to be seen anew in a socially relevant way that would hardly have seemed possible, say, fifteen years ago. No small part of this dramatic change has arisen from the need to understand the role of thought and experience in working life. For that reason, it is doubtful that all of this could have happened anywhere else than in Sweden.

Swedish commitment to industrial democracy makes the sorts of questions that a purely theoretical critique of, say, the enormous gap between promise and performance in the development of artificial intelligence programs a most pressing practical social consideration. In short, the perspective of working life is the perspective of practice: one that does not permit the luxury of abstract speculation in the way that theoretical debate does. In an industrial democracy advertisements like "Have a dialogue with a computer" or "Get three years experience in one week" cannot go ignored; for they have enormous implications for working life which can in no case be ignored. Thus, it should not be surprising that the founders of the Dialogue Seminar should set out to *test* these claims by raising basic questions about the role of dialogue within experience. It seems doubtful that this could have happened anywhere other than in Sweden, since it is only in Sweden that there is sufficient empirical evidence in the form of case studies of the social insurance system, the nursing profession, weather forecasting and surgical instrument making to make a strong case that the claims of computer marketing are vastly overstated. These studies have provided plenty of empirical grounds for suggesting that there is something uncompromisingly and disturbingly *monological* about the way machines "think". More than that, they suggest that we pay a huge price in the form of loss of skill (e.g. the experience of the social insurance system) when we ignore the difference between monological and dialogical discourse. The Dialogue Seminar has proved to be a way of exploring *why* this should be so.

It should not be surprising, then, that the Dialogue Seminar has, in the course of exploring this concept, touched upon several of the most pressing problems relating to modern life in a way that is accessible to an educated public but also with considerable depth with respect to the theory of science. Indeed, it is one of the most significant implications of the Seminar that those of us who are not content merely to be passively "post-modern" but want to appropriate *critically* the fruits of modern science and technology must place dialogue at the centre of our programme. What was becoming modern all about? What is it to be modern? In the intellectual sphere it seems to be a matter of faith in the ability of science to sweep away superstition and technology to make the material basis of a better life available to all – to liberate us from the caprices of nature. In politics it was large-scale organization of the State on the basis of national (linguistic) identity – a process of centralization and standardization which in the worst cases led to a glorification of the State as an end in itself. In economics it entailed a reaction according to which medieval rationality with its emphasis upon the priority of the common good (something essentially bound to the notions of common sense and common law in the Anglo-Saxon world) was replaced by a mechanistic notion of rationality as emerging from competing self-interests. This was accompanied by the development of a totally new industry, advertising, devoted to developing techniques for convincing us, in effect, that we are what we *possess*. So considered, the enterprise of becoming modern involved deeply monological and manipulative moments. It is impossible to turn back the clock here; what we must do is to obtain a critical perspective on all of this as it currently affects us. The great irony in all of this is that so much of this development was carried on in the name of notions like democracy, whose very form is dialogue in the character of public debate.

But what has all of this to do with the Dialogue Seminar? A great deal. The Seminar has raised many if not most of these questions. What is eminently clear is that there is at once considerably more ground to explore and a great interest on the part of both the public and those who have presented and discussed aspects of dialogue in continuing this crucial discussion. By trying to clarify the various senses of the concept – philosophical, literary, political, dramatic and spiritual – the Dialogue Seminar has demonstrated how that concept is among the most important points for a humanistic integration of the various spheres of cultural activity. It is abundantly clear from the Seminar that dialogue is not only a crucial perspective for discussions within the various spheres already mentioned but also equally crucial for a humanistic integration of the whole range of human enterprises. The Seminar has played an exciting role in revitalizing personalist thought within the context of that sort of social responsibility without which industrial democracy becomes a hollow cliché. It is an extraordinary achievement which demands due recognition.

Chapter 4

The Dialogue Seminar

Magnus Florin, Bo Göranzon and Pehr Sällström

The Dialogue Seminar is held on a regular basis at the Royal Dramatic Theatre, Stockholm, and publishes the quarterly magazine *Dialoger*. The Seminar approaches, directly and indirectly, various aspects of dialogue, applying a broad basis of philosophy, aesthetics and the history of ideas. Particular attention is given to the relationship between occupational knowledge and technology. The people behind the Dialogue Seminar are Magnus Florin, Bo Göranzon and Pehr Sällström, who exemplify here the concept of dialogue from sources which include Raphael, Plato, Shakespeare, Rousseau, Diderot, Offenbach and Goethe.

Introduction

The Dialogue Seminar has met regularly at the Royal Dramatic Theatre, Stockholm, since 1985. The Seminar is so named because it uses a broad basis of philosophy, aesthetics and the history of ideas in approaching, directly and indirectly, various aspects of dialogue. Particular attention is given to the relationship between occupational knowledge and technology. The Seminar has recently focused on Denis Diderot, leader of the French Encyclopedia project and author of dialogues such as *Paradox on the Actor* and *Rameau's Nephew*. One question the Seminar has considered is whether or not the knowledge to be found in the actor's craft may be seen as a model for all occupational knowledge.

The Seminar is arranged by the Royal Dramatic Theatre, the Swedish Center for Working Life and the Swedish Council for Planning and Coordination in Research. It publishes the quarterly magazine *Dialoger*, with issues devoted to themes such as dialogue and enlightenment, the value of work, computers and knowledge, tacit knowledge, artificial intelligence, Cordelia's silence, and paradox on the actor. What follows gives some illustration of the concept of dialogue as it has been considered at the Dialogue Seminar.

Towards a Philosophy of Dialogue

Raphael's fresco "School Athens" in the Vatican portrays numerous groups of people, young and old, engaged in lively conversation or listening intently. There is an awesome gulf between this scene and the picture of the individual "conversationalist" and his/her personal computer today. What is happening to our ability to develop and communicate thought, insights and knowledge via conversation? The concept of dialogue often crops up in cultural debate. "Dialogue" is as relevant in debates on education as it is for medicine, psychiatry, sociology and theology. But how seriously is it taken? Often the word "dialogue" is no more than a slogan, used carelessly, with no deeper meaning worth mentioning.

"Dialogue" as a concept is certainly not new. Nor is it particularly related to modern electronic means of communication and exchange of information. On the contrary, dialogue as a means of clarifying issues within a community of human beings, and as a basic component of their reality, has been the subject of pictorial as well as dramatic and literary works since antiquity, the most famous example perhaps being Plato's Socratic dialogues.

However, a philosophy of dialogue – i.e. attempts to elaborate on the phenomenon of dialogue itself as a basic component of human life and reality, something essential to human existence – belongs mainly to our own century. It concerns the deadlock between subjectivity and objectivity which was in evidence by the turn of the century, and the tension between unity and fragmentation of knowledge.

The question of a philosophy of dialogue has been touched on by most of the famous philosophers of our time – for example, Husserl, Merleau-Ponty, Heidegger, Gadamer, Sartre, Jaspers, Marcel and Guardini – and was at the very core of the philosophies of Martin Buber, Ferdinand Ebner and Ludwig Wittgenstein.

Nowadays, in everyday speech, the word "dialogue" is used more loosely than by those philosophers. It has become almost fashionable to speak of dialogue in discussions of any kind of communicative interaction between people, between man and machine or between interconnected systems in general. But then, considering the historical and philosophical perspectives, does this not mean that we are deliberately overlooking an important distinction, i.e. the distinction between "simple communication" (or "information transfer") and "authentic dialogue"? Not all conversations between two people are necessarily dialogues in a true sense. Any talk may, of course, be empty words.

The Dialogue Seminar at the Royal Dramatic Theatre was conceived as a practical means of presenting important so as to shed light on the subject from various sources.

Any attempt to clarify and elaborate any specific, more profound concept of dialogue would be invaluable as a basis for discussion and critical evaluation of the impact of modern information technology on various societal and cultural activities and traditions.

The Medium of Transformation

Dialogue is the medium of transformation in the theatre. Dialogue occurs where roles meet; it sets them in motion, leading to unexpected shifts. As it swings, thoughts, events and characters change form. Dialogue turns the scene into a place where firm positions and sharp contours cannot be maintained.

In the Dialogue Seminar, drama and theatre were constant points of reference. Their capacity for presenting human beings as incomplete creatures heightens our awareness of an essential aspect of the concept of dialogue. In dialogue differences can appear and be played off against one another, both within the individual and between people, and it sets all their various voices and contradictions in motion.

Often there is a clear ideological element in the way the term dialogue is used. It becomes linked with "understanding", "communality" and "honesty". The following, in various forms, is typical: "we must achieve a dialogue with one another if we are to reach a positive agreement". There is something unnervingly disciplinarian in these formulas; they are forcing us to express ourselves, to bring and be brought into the light.

In the Dialogue Seminar we were interested in defences against these demands for clear articulation. We studied dialogue in relation to language and life, which defies reduction to communicated content relating to forms of life and consciousness. We tried to show that there is always another side of life. This distinguishes ours from closed systems. Man cannot be described using the rules of formal logic.

Our developing technical culture in work and education often takes a reductionistic, rational view of language, knowledge and experience. In terms of philosophy and cognitive theory, it can be said to rest on a simplified I-versus-it model, viewing man as a Cartesian atom. When we speak of the concept of dialogue, it is to question that view. We focus instead on reciprocity, the mutual dependence from which man emerges and in which he lives, I/you or I/other relations are essential for us.

Plato's Dialogues

In one of Plato's earliest dialogues, *Euthyphro*, Socrates tries to characterize devotion. Euthyphro, a religious prophet, gives examples from his work. In this dialogue, Socrates pushes Euthyphro to formulate the rules defining an act of devotion, while Euthyphro claims to be able to judge what an act of devotion is – but he cannot explain the rules his judgement obeys. In Plato's view, experts (in this case a religious prophet) have consciously used rules, but have since forgotten them. The philosopher's task is to remember the principles that determine their actions.

It is generally assumed that Plato/Socrates devalued practical work in favour of the abstract intellect. This rests on the argument that people with practical skills cannot explain how they perform these tasks. The carpenter making a chair is unable to explain how he goes about it, but the philosopher can discuss the conceptual idea of the chair and its use, and is therefore superior to the carpenter who makes the chair (Plato, *The State*).

In *Gorgias*, Socrates casts suspicion on the art of oratory and argues against its being an "art"; rather Socrates sees it as a practical skill, the driving force and sole aim of which is a desire for recognition. But we would like to highlight one point of Gorgias' argument: Socrates denies that he takes a negative view of practical skills – he merely points to an indisputable fact, namely that practical skills can be used in the service of good as well as evil. What is missing is insight, the realization of what one is doing and why, and what purpose the action is supposed to serve. It is this intellectual dimension, "inner dialogue", that is necessary if a skill is to be called "art".

A doctor who understands how to practise the art of curing prescribes a treatment that may be unpleasant but will lead to lasting recovery. A bad doctor is one who takes only a short-term approach to the patient's desire to rid himself of all unpleasantness.

There are two levels here. On the one hand the relationship between language and action – to what extent can we describe our actions? – as highlighted in *Euthyphro*. The other perspective, the demand for insight and reflection, is a moral dimension which appears in *Gorgias*. How do these two levels relate to one another? Where do they contradict and cross over? This is what we must consider. Wittgenstein does so in his theory of knowledge which operates on both levels. "The unspeakable (what I regard as secret and am unable to express) may form the backdrop against which what I could say takes on meaning" (*Culture and Value*).

Shakespeare

In his lecture, *Dialogen hos Shakespeare* (*Shakespeare's Dialogue*), Leif Zern looks at the form of the rules Shakespeare thinks we should abandon. Order and disorder are two sides of the same system; together they serve renewal and fertility in a society threatened by death and sterility. Shakespeare is aware of the mechanisms that widen the gulf between language and people's experience. Crises occur when concepts become confused, when cracks appear in the very system of norms and agreements that make man capable of uniting around a homogeneous understanding (view) of reality. What Shakespeare describes is the crisis that blooms when this form of agreement ceases, when language and reality no longer coincide. It is motion itself, movement between two poles, transformation, that is one of the central elements of Zern's interpretation of Shakespeare.

What is essential is not what "is", but what "will be". The truth is never to be found at the point of departure. It grows in motion. It springs from meetings and passage – in ties that are constantly being undone and incorporated in new contexts. This motion cannot be frozen and translated into a formula.

Rousseau

Eva-Lena Dahl analysed the view of knowledge in Jean Jacques Rousseau's ideology, discussing, for example, the two levels (the linguistic and the moral) mentioned in connection with Plato's dialogues. In her interpretation, Rousseau's arguments indicate that he sees thought as a process in which man experiences reality as actual and moral at one and the same time. According to Rousseau, description and evaluation of reality are intimately related to the thought processes.

Rousseau says that if we divide knowledge into acquired and common, then common knowledge is infinitely greater than acquired knowledge. We have a shared, perhaps preconscious, knowledge, the scope and depth of which tends to be underestimated by the educated; rather, he says, they ignore it. Theoretical knowledge is not only enriched by experience – it creates chaos without it. For Rousseau the question is whether the concepts of scientific theory describe reality in such a way, whether they cannot be traced back to a reality that our senses can experience.

Diderot

Enthusiasm for technology – that which may be logically calculated – was the modernist manifesto in, for example, the French encyclopedia project during the Age of Enlightenment and in Vienna at the turn of the century. These periods saw the simultaneous emergence of interest in things that cannot be directly expressed, but which, given artistic form, become accessible to reflective thought. If we are to understand our most fundamental human needs, artistic expression must be taken seriously.

Denis Diderot, one of the leading figures of the Age of Enlightenment in France, gives his interpretation of the concept of professional competence in his dialogue *Le Neveu de Rameau*. It does not develop through methods and prescriptions: "He who needs rules will get nowhere." It is constant practice that develops and deepens expertise. Reflection becomes imperative: "I am forced to reflect. It is a sickness that must run its course."

Le Neveu de Rameau can be viewed as an inner dialogue on the conditions for creativity. Diderot distances himself from the two roles of dialogue. They are the Philosopher, who represents logical, calculable common sense, and Rameau, the vulgar Bohemian on the bottom rung of society, who has an affinity with the deeper layers of sensitivity in his personality. Diderot examines what maintains the links between these two different characters. Rameau attacks the Philosopher for retreating from complex reality into abstract personal isolation. The Philosopher criticizes Rameau for his excitement at pantomime pranks, and his inability to exercise any practical skill in his obsession. The agreement reached is that the discord is unbridgeable.

The mastery of *Le Neveu de Rameau* is apparent in the fact that Diderot does not take sides in the struggle between the senses and the intellect, but retains in this play complexity and contradiction at various levels in the individual. It may be possible to find a creative rhythm by maintaining the balance between the controlling common sense and complex, contradictory elements. Diderot wrote *Le Neveu de Rameau* intermittently between 1761 and 1774. In the same period, Rousseau wrote *Emile* (1762), and Voltaire *Candide* (1759). The overwhelming impression here is criticism of the Utopian aspect of the encyclopedia project, the merging of all forms of human knowledge in a logical calculation. Cracks were beginning to show in the façade. Minerva's owl was beginning to appear.

Offenbach

Dialogue requires a certain measure of scepticism: disagreement is not simply reconcilable with dialogue – it is one of its conditions. Dialogue involves opening oneself to criticism of one's own assumptions. There is an ever-present temptation to retreat into the dream world of monologue. Retreat into abstractions offers an escape from unpleasant reality, a kind of fantasy retreat from dialogue to monologue. When Allan Janik[1] uses Offenbach as an example to illustrate how the price of isolation is self-deception and dehumanization, it may seem bizarre, not to say absurd, because we tend to link Offenbach's work with the sickly sentimentality and general inertia of the Viennese operetta. Performance traditions must bear a large part of the blame for our inability to see the satire of his artistic production.

Dialogue in music was introduced at the Seminar by way of a fictional dialogue between "science" and "music", contrasting a scientific view of music as an acoustic phenomenon with a musician's appreciation of music as an essentially antonomous phenomenon, which emerges on a higher level of structural complexity than that described by the physicist. The essence of music can only be grasped by listening to music. We have a certain feel for music, which is also, according to the musicologist and philosopher Victor Zuckerkandl,[2] our sense of time: "There is hardly anything that can tell us more about time and temporality than can music . . . Music is temporal art in the special sense that in it time reveals itself to direct experience." Thus: "the truth of music, like that of mathematics, consists in this, that it serves us as a key to understanding the world we live in". So a dialogue between music and science is, in this very profound sense, fruitful and meaningful.

An element of dialogue in music itself can be found in the relation between the tune and words of a song: "Words that are sung are not empty. Something that remains silent in word merely spoken begins to flow, to vibrate; the words open and the singer opens to them. It is as though the tones infuse the word with a force that reveals a new layer of meaning in them, that breathes life into them . . . "

Words express a situation of "facing each other" whereas tones express togetherness. In the tones, things that are separated meet, and person and thing – the speaker and the spoken word – come into direct contact. The tone added to the word does not cancel out the word, but makes it penetrate to a greater depth, down to a layer where their separateness becomes togetherness.

Zuckerkandl says that: "The dimension disclosed by the tones can certainly be called 'inner life', but this is not the inner life of the subject as opposed to the object; it is not the inner world of the self but of the world, the inner life of things. This is precisely why the singer experiences inner life as something he shares with the world, not as something that sets him apart from it . . . Music prevents the world from being entirely transformed into language, from becoming nothing but object, and prevents man from being nothing but subject."

Knowledge Through Dialogue

Socrates' dialogues, as related by Plato, as well as Galileo's fictional conversation between Salviato, Sagredo and Simplicio, have not merely a pedagogical objective, but are also filled with a real search for knowledge. Achieving knowledge through reflective reasoning on concrete experience is what both are about.

The influence that Galileo's dialogues have had on the development of the ideas of physics cannot be underestimated. The thought experiment, physical reasoning and consideration, the support of mathematical models and play with mathematical concepts are still at the heart of the work of research laboratories.

The committed conversations between Nils Bohr, Einstein, Heisenberg and others in the 1930s, when quantum mechanics and the theory of relativity were revolutionizing physics, are still held in very special regard. Such dialogues belong to the most lively and creative periods in physics.

Knowledge and Familiarity

Only those who reflect on their experiences develop competence – ability to deal with new situations similar to those they have already experienced. An unreflecting, purely habitual action does not transcend what has once been learned. Knowledge requires inner reflection, a "dialogue with things". Martin Buber gets to the crux of the matter when he claims that, in order to know for example what "pain" is, we must ourselves actually "have" it, and then we become distanced from it at the same time, which may be a necessary stage in the creation of knowledge. But later we can reflect on our experience. This is how knowledge grows, through rhythmic exchanges between participation and distance, between action and reflection.

Natural Science

Natural science, too, requires an element of dialogue. Or rather two elements: it is partly a dialogue between researchers, the dialogue which validates the objectivity of the natural sciences, making them something that is not the creation of the individual researcher, but in a way occurs "between" them. As Goethe put it, the advancement of science is more the advancement of society, culture, time. It is also partly a dialogue between researcher and research object, nature. The poetic metaphor in which it has usually been presented sees natural research as a dialogue with nature. This is especially true of Goethe: "thus speaks nature to herself and to us through thousands of phenomena . . . "

The picture of nature as "respondent" to the researcher's questions may be felt to be playful anthropomorphosis, but is not without foundation, for the crucial element of all experimental research is precisely reference to other authorities, to things outside our control, the unpredictable – something we can only gain knowledge of through the results of the experiment, which to this extent is a dialogue situation. Nature's "answer" is something I receive.

This may be the principle that separates experimental natural research from purely speculative research. No physicist in his heart and soul imagines that we should be able to sit down and "think out" reality. There are things that can only be understood through "looking at how things behave". It is an element of pure factuality, not accessible in thought, only through observation, through touch, contact, making connections.

Even if the dialogues of physics are highly formalized, the dialogue is still concealed behind an arsenal of strange apparatus and methods. But it is not the apparatus, not measurements, that determine the content of the research – they function as instruments, notes whose value lies in there being an inaccessible "remainder", an element which the researcher cannot determine, which the instruments are there to eliminate, to remove barriers rather than build them. At bottom there is always present in the body of our natural scientific knowledge an acceptance of the existence of things we have not discovered, or been able to discover within ourselves – precisely what we have "found out" in the experiment.

Dialogue and Language

Can we say that the concept of dialogue, as refined in the Dialogue Seminar, is now ready for the Great Synthesis? On the contrary! This is the very point of the Seminar. We have gained a view of the scope of various significant elements. Conflicting aspects are what gives the concept of dialogue its vitality. Paradoxically, if we adopt that meaning which reinforces our preconceived opinions, "that in which we recognize ourselves", we enter another arena – that of monologue.

In trying to keep the threads together and work with the contradictions and complexities that lead into the various ways of thinking demonstrated in the Dialogue Seminar, it may be possible to top up "the genie in the lamp", a symbol of creativity. We realize that this is easier said than done, and that the conditions for shifting perspective are rather too complicated to allow us simply to change masks like a clown. The extent to which we are ready to enter this game is at the moment not a question of logical argument. The growth of knowledge, in all its various shades and forms, is a process that requires an inner life of its own, it own breathing rate. It can never be a uniform, linear progression. It cannot be built of prefabricated building blocks, one on top of another. Nor can it be fed with series of data like an electronic calculator. Dialogue is the concept that expresses the dynamics of knowledge.

The purpose of dialogue is to set knowledge in motion, to stop it fossilizing in empty forms.

Against this background, what are we to make of the relationship of dialogue to language? There is a contradiction in linking the concept of dialogue so self-evidently to conversation at the same time as dialogue, in its very essence, is wordless, belongs to the silence beyond all words . . . In order to solve this paradox, we require a deeper understanding of what language is and of man's relations to language.

Notes

1 In *Wittgenstein's Vienna*, Simon and Schuster, 1973.

2 This lecture was based on two books by Victor Zuckerkandl: *Sound and symbol* (1956), and *Man, the musician* (1973), Princeton University Press.

Chapter 5

The Essence of Dialogue

Pehr Sällström

Is there any sense in which a human can have a dialogue with a machine? In common usage dialogue means conversation, talk, discussion. However, the term is deliberately chosen here to signify a search for a certain quality in discourse, a quality not found in all conversations, some being nothing more than an exchange of empty words. A true dialogue does not persuade, delude or dumbfound another person, it is a process of finding something out together with another person. It has no pre-set goal, it has no end, and it is pure movement, movement which cannot be frozen and translated into a formula, a rule or a programme. Whether resulting in agreement or disagreement, dialogue helps to achieve clarity. Socrates used dialogue to demonstrate the falsity of the conviction that being able to state something is the same as possessing real knowledge. Dialogue is a means of gaining insight through inner reflection. "Intuition" places dialogue in a meaningful context, a "presence of mind" which gives it life and depth. Dialogue is not a particular behaviour or attitude; only something purely factual which, whether in the form of words, art or music, involves both parties in their total historical experience.

During the conference on *Culture, language and artificial intelligence* the concept of dialogue was touched upon every now and then, at the plenary sessions as well as in connection with the various topics of the workshops. Thus, the importance of dialogue in medical practice was pointed out – as well as its importance in education – as a means of breaking "the contract of error", to which Francis Bacon refers. A dialogical concept of language has been found essential in translating works of literature – in which case translation is regarded as a major factor of linguistic and cultural innovation. One of the workshops discussed the role of dialogue in attaining a critical perspective on the so-called modern and in revealing the anaesthetizing effect of clichés and unmasking the cultural counterfeiters who produce them. Celebrities such as Socrates, Pygmalion and Shakespeare were invoked to help understanding of the essence of dialogue, and several times the question was touched on as to whether there is any significant sense in which a human being can enter into a dialogue with a machine.

In ordinary usage, dialogue means approximately the same as "conversation", "talk" or "discussion". When we deliberately choose to use the word "dialogue" it is, however, to signify that we are hunting for a certain quality to be found in *some*, but certainly not *all*, conversations. Any conversation could be just an exchange of empty words.

Dialogue could also mean a written work in conversational *form*. There are a number of famous philosophical as well as dramatic works that have the form of dialogues. The point is, however, as is the case with Plato's dialogues, that not only are these written as dialogue, but the primary subject of the dialogues is – dialogue. Listening to Socrates we are taught the art of dialogue and we learn, if we are attentive, what dialogue *is*. And what we learn is that it is not enough to put intricate questions to people. A true dialogue does not aim at persuading the other one, nor deluding him, nor simply dumbfounding him. We enter into dialogue in order to find something out together. The dialogue has no pre-established goal. It builds up – and breaks into pieces again. This process has no end. Like music, like a melody, dialogue is pure movement.

What is essential is not what "is", but what "will be". The truth is never to be found at the point of departure. It grows in motion. It originates in ties that are constantly being undone and incorporated in new contexts. This motion cannot be frozen and translated into a formula, a rule or a programme.

We usually think that dialogue should promote mutual understanding and agreement, but it should be pointed out that it is equally important to establish *disagreement* by means of dialogue. How could you genuinely disagree about something if you have not made sure that you understand each other, i.e. convinced yourselves that you *do* speak about the same thing?

Dialogue is: to use language *against itself*; that is, against the petrifying effect of using formulas and phrases without bothering about all that good old rest which is silence.

Dialogue helps us to accept *paradoxes*. To be sure, there are semantic tricks to solve paradoxes – just by conjuring them out of existence – but these tricks, or so-called solutions, very often obscure, or even conceal, the *real* issue.

When Socrates asked people by what *maxims* they conducted themselves and came to their decisions, I do not think he expected to get an answer to that question. But nevertheless I am sure that he expected a result: the conversations aimed at making people *see* things. What he aimed at with uncompromising zeal was the falsity of the conviction that being able to *state* something is equivalent to having real knowledge. The basic concern for Socrates, however, was language *and* action. To what extent can we take refuge in linguistic conjuring tricks when, in moments of uncertainty, we want to do the right thing?

In dialogue, language is not used to lay down truths, but to guide one towards a better understanding. The words play their own joyful games, yet they mirror important glimpses – the hidden meaning of what is said, in the glittering play of words.

The essential thing about dialogue is this: it is a method of attaining insight; that is, of probing into the depth of a phenomenon – looking beyond the formal aspect of it.

To Socrates, dialogue is the *spoken word*, born out of the inspiration of the moment. Thus dialogue is unique, not possible to reproduce. The moment of dialogue is the eternal "now", and it all hinges on the *appropriateness* of what is said.

Nowadays, "the world of language" prevails over "the world of the senses". The discursive takes precedence over the intuitive. There is a widening gulf between the world picture we get through our common language, and our individual experiences. Only those who reflect on their experiences develop an ability to deal with new situations similar to, but not identical to, those they have already experienced. A purely habitual action does not transcend what has once been learned. Knowledge requires inner reflection, a dialogue with things.

A true dialogue is never only an exchange of words, separated from reality, as we apprehend it intuitively. Intuition places the dialogue within the framework, in relation to which what is said becomes meaningful. It is this "presence of mind" that gives any dialogue its life and depth, and makes it immediately understandable, in spite of formal imperfections.

Martin Buber, in *Zwiesprache*, states:

We may term this way of perception *being aware*. It by no means needs to be a man of whom I become aware. It can be an animal, a plant, a stone. No kind of appearance or event is fundamentally excluded from the series of the things through which from time to time something is said to me. The limits of the possibility of dialogue are the limits of awareness.

A dialogue need not be mediated by words. Looking at a picture you may find it pretty, skilfully made, well balanced in its composition of form and colour – but to *see* it is something quite different. To get into the depth of it – to make it come to life before your eyes – this is the mystery of artistic creation and re-creation: the dialogue that is suddenly established.

The same is true of a written dialogue; it may come to life when you hear it read or performed on stage, as if it were the first time that this particular string of words was ever uttered. Art thus helps us to penetrate behind the surface of things and establish dialogical relationships.

This applies to music too, of course. Dialogue and music spring from the same source. Victor Zuckerkandl, in his book *Man, the Musician*, relates the following episode:

Imagine a hillside in a warm country; it is morning and the sun is shining brightly. A young man is up in a pear tree, picking the fruit, and as he picks he sings. Why is he singing? I suppose most of you would say: Because it is a beautiful day, and it is good to be young on a beautiful day in a beautiful countryside, picking luscious pears. All this may be so, but there is another, deeper, more essential reason for song in this situation. Our young man might not sing as he picked if the day were not so fine or if trouble weighed on him, but if he sang at all as he picked pears, he would sing the same song – and a different song if it were grapes. The song he sings is the immemorial pear-picking song in his part of the world, a tune that musically makes fruit and picker one, that "brings" the pears to the picker's hands and consecrates his harvesting of them. It is as though the picker's hands did not reach out for the fruit but surrendered to it, as though the fruit, instead of resisting the hands, were meeting them halfway, dropping into them of its own accord. Instead of opposition, distinction, we have togetherness, unity.

Words divide, tones unite. Music prevents the world from being entirely transformed into language, from becoming nothing but object, and prevents man from being nothing but subject.

There is something truly *factual* about a dialogue. There are no *formal* criteria to determine whether a conversation is a true dialogue or not. But if there are no formal criteria, how can I *know* that a dialogical situation is a true dialogical event? The answer is: I cannot know it. The true dialogue has no unfailing external observances or distinctive features; it is not a particular behaviour or attitude, only something purely factual. It just takes place. And it involves both parties in their total historical existence.

We cannot give criteria, but as human beings we have a specific sense, attuned to the dialogical dimension of existence; in the same way that we have a sense for the beautiful, for moral values, or for the reality of the persons we are together with and the circumstances we meet with in life.

Section III:
Rational Language

Chapter 6

The Dream of an Exact Language

Stephen Toulmin

In the twentieth century there has been a debate on whether natural language is adapted to its human tasks or whether it has essential defects which make it unsuitable as a medium for expression and the communication of thought. Why did such questions arise? Russell et al. dreamed of a language which would serve as a mirror, reproducing and reflecting the eternal structure of Reality and Truth. Why was there this desire for an eternal language of permanent, universal meanings? The dream of an exact language, which goes back to Plato, was at its most powerful in seventeenth-century Europe, during the time of religious warfare and the need for religious toleration. A renewed dialogue was needed among theologians with contrasting views. Leibniz et al. believed there had to be a universal language to serve as an instrument of reason. The period from the Renaissance to the present time has also been one of great uncertainty in the religious, cosmological and social spheres – hence a further appeal for rationality in science and language. Today the problem is less one of religious toleration than of racial and cultural diversity. Today's project concerns the building of compatible transnational television and computer links. The obstacles, such as cultural conflicts and a lack of international understanding, are greater. Moreover, it must be borne in mind that it is one thing to perfect an instrument and quite another to ensure that it is put to just, virtuous or even rationally discriminating use. An exact language, rational method and a united science are the three dreams of rationalism. They are still dreams. Why? The move from science of matter and energy towards that of information means that the distinction between pure and applied science is blurring as theory and praxis merge. The increase in technical interventions in the natural world is giving rise to an increasingly uncertain world in which we are less confident in our ability to forecast or limit their effects.

When intellectual historians look back over the twentieth century, they will see it as the Century of Language: a time when, in all fields of art, thought, literature and science, people considered, or reconsidered, the place of language in human life, and the basis on which our reliance on language rests. A few earlier writers (e.g. Hamann around 1790) made tentative moves towards a "critique of communication" or *Sprachkritik*. But the subject attracted general attention only in the late nineteenth century, dominating discussion in a dozen fields, especially in Vienna. In those last years of Hapsburg rule, artists and scientists were like bicyclists: they pedalled with confidence just so long as no one asked how they did it; but once someone inquired how they avoided upsetting the machine, they lost their balance. The methods of representation and communication that had served well previously were all questioned: newer and more self-conscious techniques seemed to be needed, if one was to avoid the assumptions that were seemingly taken for granted in earlier language and literature, fine art and natural science. (Allan Janik and I explored that story long ago, so I need not pursue it further here.)

The ensuing critique of representation and language went through several phases, and brought to the surface one crucial issue, over which philosophers and psycholinguists have been deeply divided. To put this issue in the form of a question:

Are natural languages *in general* adapted to their human tasks, or do they have essential defects, which unfit them as media for the expression and communication of thoughts?

Concerning that question, there is a radical opposition between those who see natural languages as riddled with shortcomings and unsuitable as instruments of knowledge, and those who argue (like Wittgenstein) that "Ordinary language, just as it is, is *perfectly all right*."

In part, this opposition has been generational. The idea that our everyday means of expression, communication and representation are *radically* defective was a *fin de siècle* one. By the 1950s, it no longer carried conviction, and seemed quite out of date when Russell revived it in his late books on philosophy. Equally, the means of artistic, musical and intellectual expression that had defined the Main Road to the Future in the 1920s and 1930s (non-representational painting, twelve-tone music, the tensor calculus, etc.) lost their unique credentials in the cultural landslides of the 1960s. In the process, a dozen things that had been discredited in the 1920s (not least, the music of Anton Bruckner and Gustav Mahler) once again became high fashion.

By the late 1980s, the attack on natural languages launched by Gottlob Frege and Bertrand Russell at the turn of the century is by now a matter of historical curiosity. Looking back, it is no longer obvious what they saw wrong in natural language. Certainly, they did not want a practical refinement of specific sectors of language, in law, medicine or science. Such sectors of language are routinely improved in the day-to-day work of the professions; even colloquial speech takes on new features as the drive toward verbal compression and syntactical simplification has its effect. Such practical changes are neither radical nor general enough to demand a deep metaphysical or epistemological critique. Instead, they are usually localized in application and confined to professional usage, and so must be judged pragmatically.

The issue is not what the early twentieth-century philosophers *said*: we can read that for ourselves. It is what they *meant by* what they said: for, as Wittgenstein said, "What philosophers 'mean' is *always* right!" Frege and Russell both saw natural language as a fancy costume veiling from onlookers the true "logical forms" of statements; and this view kept some of its force in Russell's late writings. F.H. Bradley had denied that everyday concepts capture "Reality" with a capital R: all they can present to us is "Appearance". Though he claimed to have broken away from Bradley in 1903, the Russell of 1950 still called everyday language a "rough and ready" instrument, incapable of "Truth" with a capital T.

Both philosophers evidently dream of a language that serves as a *mirror*, reproducing and reflecting the eternal structure of Reality and Truth. Neither of them is happy to find that all everyday language works in *timely* ways, and lacks the *perfect timelessness* of "eternal objects". Yet why should anyone have expected language to work in eternal ways? Wasn't that always an unreasonable demand? About this, of course, an older story can be told in which Russell and Frege are not the primary characters. Plato's *Cratylus*, for example, asks if the "meanings" of our language cannot be freed of human convention and made clearly *right* and *lifelike*. Meanings existed *out in the world*, waiting for us to acknowledge them, and find a means to express them. (Fire *crackles*, water *rushes*, and "onomatopoiea" is only the crudest of these expressive techniques.) The dream of permanent, universal "meanings" whose immortal shadows flicker on the wall of Plato's cave has, thus, haunted the philosophy of language from the beginning.

Putting Frege and Russell in their context, then, we may ask:

Why did natural language appear so imperfect *around 1900*? What purposes did the Dream of an Exact Language then serve? And how was such "perfect exactness" to be achieved?

One initial warning – philosophical dreams are soap bubbles. Taken at their face value, they deceive us; but if handled roughly they disappear. Either way, latent meanings can be more revealing than surface sense, and a single dream can telescope several latent meanings. In dealing with such powerful dreams, we should step back and ask:

Why did this dream affect people when and where it did? What were they hoping or fearing at that time? So what was *at stake* for them, which found expression in the dream?

The dream of an exact language was most powerful in seventeenth-century Europe: it was shared by scientists and philosophers in many countries, not least from among the founders of the Royal Society in England. But, with good reason, we associate this dream especially with the name of Gottfried Wilhelm Freiherr von Leibniz: looking at Leibniz's case gives us historical clues to the *kinds* of underlying things that are at stake for all those thinkers who dream this particular dream.

Even while still a boy (Leibniz tells us) he conceived what he called a *characteristica universalis* – or "universal system of characters" – which would "express all our thoughts". Such a system, he declared,

will constitute a new language which can be written and spoken. This language will be very difficult to construct, but very easy to learn. It will be quickly accepted by everybody on account of its great utility and its surprising facility, and it will serve wonderfully in communication among various peoples.

Is Leibniz here anticipating Esperanto, Volapuk and other such artificial international languages? There is more to it. His new language will use mathematical symbolism, which will allow it to express *thoughts* "as definitely and exactly as arithmetic expresses *numbers* or geometrical analysis expresses *lines*." Such a universal language, Leibniz concluded, will not only have perspicuous meanings, so that people from different cultures *talk* together with shared understanding. In addition, it will embody and codify all valid modes of argument, so that different people *reason* together without fear of confusion or error; and this will make his language "the greatest instrument of reason".

Throughout his long and active career, Leibniz went on working on his project for a universal language, whose meaning and rationality were built in from the start. The resulting research took him off in a dozen directions – into Chinese ideograms, the infinitesimal calculus, and even into the divinatory technique of the *I Ching*. What led him to pursue the topic so assiduously? And why was the project to develop a perfectly exact language the issue of the hour for other seventeenth-century scientists, too? Both questions deserve serious historical answers.

Leibniz was never concerned with mathematics and metaphysics for their own sake alone: they were always, for him, a means to an end. He also had a lifelong theological mission, as an *ecumenist*, and people in his time did not find mathematics and theology distinct or separate, as they seem today. From 1600 on, indeed, all the countries of Europe faced the problem of devising ways in which a single nation could accommodate citizens of several religious beliefs. As Richard Ashcraft has shown, a central topic in all John Locke's writings is to work out the intellectual and political preconditions of religious toleration. But, for Leibniz, the issue was even more urgent. He was born in 1646, as the Thirty Years War was coming to an exhausted close with the Treaty of Westphalia. In the previous generation, prosperous cities were destroyed all across Germany; and some 30–40 per cent of the country's population were slaughtered to the greater glory of a Calvinist, Lutheran or Catholic God. So, from 1618 to 1648, Central Europe was the locus for a theologically rationalized brutality unparalleled even today in the Lebanon, Iraq and Iran.

It is no wonder, then, if Leibniz hoped to create practical conditions for a renewed dialogue among theologians from the different camps, and gave a lot of thought to the rational criteria relevant to that debate. With the ruined Germany of the 1650s on as its backdrop, there is thus a special *actualité* to Leibniz's dream of the *characteristica universalis*, which would be a means to "serve wonderfully in communication among various peoples". For some thirty years, therefore, Leibniz corresponded with colleagues on both sides of the theological gulf: he even exchanged letters with the French Catholic historian/bishop Bossuet, whom he was anxious to enlist as an ally in the work of reconciliation. But (it turned out) Bossuet was interested only in discovering on what terms Gottfried Wilhelm Leibniz, the heretic, might agree to save his soul by converting to Catholicism. So the exchange of letters aborted, and with it his last hope of an effective ecumenical conference.

If Leibniz had succeeded in persuading the rival theologians to talk together, what would they have discussed? The task he saw was to find shared elements in all the different bodies of doctrine, so as to define a system of indispensable beliefs, which believers from all the Churches could recognize as based on a minimum foundation of Sufficient Reason. In this project, his "universal language" was to serve not merely as the "instrument of Reason", but also as a means of healing the wounds in the body of Christian Europe. What *odium theologicum* had severed, during the first half of the seventeenth century, might be bound together again in the second half, with the help of the *characteristica universalis*.

It was a noble dream, but a dream nonetheless. For it rested on two assumptions that we now see were unfounded, and unrealizable:

1. That the "characters" of a perfect language can "express all our thoughts" without any need for conventional definitions, and so "constitute a new language that can be written and spoken" as easily as any natural language.
2. That, by substituting this new, artificial language for the natural languages of their own countries, the peoples of Europe might free themselves from the breakdowns of communication that fuelled the religious wars.

Unfortunately, there is no way to *equate*, as Leibniz hoped to do, private "thoughts" of people from different cultures, nations, *Lebensformen* or language communities. Nor is there any way to *guarantee* in advance, without some providential harmony, that different peoples spontaneously generate the same "thoughts" in the same situations. Constructing such a universal language was not only (as Leibniz had conceded) "difficult": it was downright impossible. For it assumed that the *Lebensformen* – and so the "thoughts" – of people in all cultures will be similar enough to yield identical "ideal languages" as their end products: i.e. it assumed *in advance* just what Leibniz's enterprise had originally been supposed to guarantee *as a final outcome*. Without prior agreement on "meanings", posterior intelligibility could not be guaranteed.

To sum up this historical point: a *rational method* of geometrical rigour, and a language in which to reason accordingly, were one strategy for transcending the Babel of doctrines around which religious conflict raged for much of the seventeenth century. But it was only one strategy among others. Such sixteenth-century humanists as Michael de Montaigne and Francis Bacon presented some real alternatives. A classical sceptic, Montaigne exhorted his readers to *live with* the kinds of ambiguity, uncertainty and plural beliefs that cultural anthropology nowadays familiarizes us with. An empiricist, Bacon discouraged people from asking for their beliefs to be "proved" with certainty, for *certainty* was a mere Idol: rather, they should explore the strengths and weaknesses of particular beliefs using experiential, not mathematical, methods. These undogmatic – not to say, *anti*-dogmatic – methods of enquiry appealed to the sixteenth-century heirs of Renaissance humanism. But from 1610 on the religious conflict was out of control, and Montaigne's urbane scepticism was no longer acceptable. By then, to adapt George Meredith's phrase, the people of Western Europe were "hot for certainty", and for the next thirty years their most urgent questions got only "dusty answers".

The *charm* of rationalism, which carried conviction with readers in the seventeenth century despite obvious objections, lay not only in the elegance of mathematical reasoning. Descartes and Leibniz lived in times of flux and turmoil. Religious diversity was the leading problem of their age. The emergence of nation states led to the "establishment" of national religions, and this bred the problem of religious toleration. The motto of conservative French Catholics was *un roi, une loi, une foi*: persecution of the Huguenots was a natural consequence, for how could loyal citizens of France reject the religion of "the French nation"? Conversely, in England, how were loyal Anglicans expected to tolerate "Papists" who planned to hand the country over to foreign control? The corrosive seventeenth-century rhetoric of "Popery" and "heresy" thus prefigured the equally destructive twentieth-century rhetoric of "Reds" and "Imperialists", threatening to break out again in a renewal of the earlier religious bloodshed.

Am I arguing that the rationalist impetus in seventeenth-century philosophy, which laid a groundwork for Leibniz's dream of an exact language, came from the ideological deadlock of the religious wars? This is part of the story, but not (I believe) the whole. The political foundation of European society was undermined at other times almost as deeply as it was in the years from 1610 on, when the confrontation of Protestants and Counter-Reformation Catholics fragmented the loyalties of Western Europeans. Yet seventeenth-century rationalism and foundationalism have only rarely been matched in the history of philosophy: and one of those times is the years on either side of the First World War. What more ought we to look for, then, to account for that historical similarity?

Our further factor is worth noticing. The flux and turmoil that led historians of early modern Europe from Roland Mousnier on to write of a "general seventeenth-century crisis" was grave enough. But it occurred just when the successors of Copernicus had called in question people's larger astronomical scheme. For many people at the time, the confluence of *uncertainties of different kinds* – religious, cosmological and social – was the last straw. Some of them even saw it as a mark of cosmic decay and expected God to plunge the world into the Apocalypse in (say) 1657. So serious-minded European intellectuals had a special reason for trying to reconstruct their world view on new and securer foundations. Thus, Descartes' philosophical project had a dual goal, with Galileo and Euclid as its joint totems. As a physical theory, his *Principia Philosophiae* was to decipher the code of material nature: as epistemology, meanwhile, his *Meditations* were a first step toward the parallel goal of re-establishing our grounds for certainty about the products of the human mind.

From 1690 right up to 1890, philosophers and natural scientists went ahead unthinkingly, confident that, between them, Newton's mechanics and Euclid's geometry were joint foundations of the order of nature and the order of mind. There might still be doubts about mental philosophy, but the mathematical foundations of *natural philosophy* had been laid with seeming certainty in 1687, and so they remained until the 1890s. The mathematical monopoly of Euclid's geometry had been challenged (it was true), with the Abbé Saccheri's failure to prove the indispensability of the axiom of parallels. But this point was generally treated as purely formal: the alternative formalisms of Lambert and Gauss, Riemann and Lobachevsky were seen as irrelevant to planetary astronomy, let alone physical cosmology. But, with the challenge to Newtonian physics posed by Maxwell's electromagnetism, and the resulting controversy about the luminiferous ether and absolute motion, the situation changed radically. The climax was a double blow: Max Planck's 1899 theory of "quantized" light absorption and emission was followed in 1905 by Albert Einstein's three classic papers about the special theory of relativity and the rest. Now, Newtonian mechanics too seemed to lose its unique intellectual standing and monopoly, and the cosmological framework of the accepted world view was once again called in question.

What does this have to do with the philosophical scene in the years just before or after the 1914–18 War? Frege, for his part, wrote little on physics or cosmology, but Russell recognized the interdependence of physics, logic and epistemology from the outset. He saw Einstein's work as a major challenge, and wrote popular books about the new ideas (e.g. his *ABC of Relativity*): after 1919, with the rise of the Vienna Circle, this relationship is obvious, and the name of Einstein keeps recurring in the positivist debate. So, Russell and Whitehead's *Principia Mathematica* became a founding document of the Unity of Science movement: inspired by Mach, the new epistemology tried to return to natural philosophy and theory of knowledge, the "objective certainty" they lost with Kant. The fortunes of epistemology and cosmology were once again historically linked, in the context of a debate about language; and, from then on, the subsequent story of twentieth-century philosophy – artifical languages and all – was launched on its familiar trajectory.

In the twentieth century, as in the seventeenth, the problem of language is thus the tip of an iceberg; and the dream of an exact language involves more than *intellectual* stakes. Today's problems are less matters of religious toleration than they are of racial and cultural diversity. What status can a Turkish *Gastarbeiter* achieve in the *Bundesrepublik Deutschland*? How can we reconcile a European "citizenship" with the fact of a dozen languages and several dozen cultures? So the project of transcending cultural misunderstanding and variety, with the help of instruments of "communication and reasoning among various peoples", is no less *actuel* for us today than it was for Leibniz in the 1670s.

As we enter the 1990s, we do not need to give up *Svenska* or English, *deutsche Sprache* or *langue française*, so as to adopt a *characteristica universalis* constructed on a mathematical model – particularly in our everyday life. In business as in air traffic control, Esperanto is dead: the only question is, "What could undermine the dominance of English?" Yet Leibniz's project is very much alive on another level, in the practical discussion of compatible television and computer links among different countries. Will PAL or SECAM be the international standard of television transmission? Will worldwide computer networks utilize an operating system designed by IBM, Toshiba or Machines Bull? (Leibniz was even right to see Chinese as a special challenge: ideograms pose notorious problems for designers of word processor software!). In practical terms, therefore, the people with best claim to be *legitimate heirs* of Leibniz's project are the computer and information engineers.

Still, the bright aims of Leibniz's programme face the same obstacles as before. International television and computer exchanges project across national boundaries, not just "universal ideas" and "error-free reasoning", but also cultural *conflicts* and international *mis*understandings. In 1677, the youthful Leibniz wrote in grandiose terms about his plan:

I dare say that this is the highest effort of the human mind; and, when the project is accomplished, it will simply be up to humans to be happy, since they will have an instrument that exalts the reason no less than the Telescope perfects our vision.

We resonate to a young man's ideals, but note also that his expression of those ideals is confused. Now, as 300 years ago, no technical system or procedure guarantees its own humane or rational use: it is one thing to *perfect* an instrument: it is another to make sure that it is *put to use* justly, virtuously or even in rationally discriminating ways.

So, the three dreams of rationalism turn out to have been aspects of a larger dream. The dream of an exact language, the dream of a rational method, and the dream of a unified science unite as one single project. Like Leibniz's exact language, the seventeenth-century scientific revolution was Janus faced. The new science was "mathematical and experimental"; but it was left unclear how the two leading features of the new method – its mathematical structure, and its basis in human experience – dovetailed together. This lack of clarity began as an oversight, but it soon became deliberate. The victory of rationalism made it seem that Pythagoras had been right: any scientific theory of mathematical power and elegance must have a practical application in human experience. As Galileo said, "The Book of Nature is written in mathematical symbols." Building up a scientific cosmology was a task of cryptanalysis: if philosophers used their new mathematical methods to decipher the Book of Nature, they could then *read off* the meanings of natural phenomena, as we today read (say) a text in Linear Minoan B.

The triumph of Newtonian physics was a vote in favour of theoretical cosmology, not for practical human dividends: the *ideas* of Newtonian theory were shaped by concern for their intellectual coherence with the accepted picture of God's Material Creation, as "obeying" Divine "laws". This view once again overlooked the message of sixteenth-century humanism. Francis Bacon's vision of a *humanly fruitful* science differed in both its spirit and its method from the mathematically structured vision of René Descartes and Isaac Newton, for whom science paid theological, rather than technical dividends; and it was only from the mid-nineteenth century on that practically minded scientists like Rudolph Virchow revived Francis Bacon's more humane vision of scientific technology.

During the three hundred years after 1660, then, the natural sciences did not march along a royal road defined by a universal rational method. Science advanced in a zig-zag manner, using alternately the rationalist procedures of Newtonian mathematics, and the empiricist methods of Baconian naturalism. So the growth of scientific thought was separated from a concern with its *practical fruits*. For a long time, people insisted on distinguishing the "pure" scientist's intellectual refinement of ideas, from the "applied" scientist's practical exploitation of their technical applications.

Under the Newtonian hegemony, Bacon's practical programme took a back seat. Many people found his concern with human good vulgar, even sinful. For them, it was enough that scientists discovered the laws governing natural phenomena, the better to glorify the God who had created nature: using the resulting understanding of natural laws for material welfare – to increase human comfort, and to reduce human pain – was secondary to the central spiritual goal of science. As late as January of 1939, John Desmond Bernal's book on *The Social Function of Science* woke reactions of horror in *bien pensants* British Newtonians, who dismissed it as an outrageous piece of Marxist political rhetoric. But, since the destruction of Hiroshima in 1945, the priorities of science have changed: these days, scientific research is planned and financed in ways that balance Isaac Newton's intellectual ideals against the technical aims of Francis Bacon. On the 25th anniversary of Bernal's book in January 1964, indeed, people noticed that the relations between science and government in Washington resembled those Bernal had called for even more closely than those in Moscow!

Whether we rely on the eighteenth-century sciences of matter, on the nineteenth-century sciences of energy, or on the twentieth-century sciences built on the idea of information, we face two experiential tasks: to exemplify the *abstract* theoretical ideas of science in the *concrete* world of actual experience, and use those *universal* calculations for the practical good of *particular* human beings. We are free to dream up all the mathematical theories we please, of communication and control, of deep grammar and brain function, neurophysiological holography and artificial intelligence. But, the further we move from the science of matter and energy toward that of information, the more we have to integrate *theoria* and *praxis*, and the more blurred becomes the distinction between pure and applied science.

By now, questions about exemplifying and utilizing the new ideas of science have to be addressed, even at the initial stage of conceiving of possible new theories. So, at this point, it is helpful to recall why the threefold dream of the rationalist philosophers proved a dream indeed. To coin some practical maxims – no formalism can interpret itself; no system can validate itself; no theory can exemplify itself; no language can decide on its own meanings. In the same way, for the same reason, no science can figure out which of the technologies it makes possible are of real value to human beings. When we face Baconian issues about the utilization of new knowledge for human good, we must set aside the seventeenth-century Cartesian ideal of intellectual exactitude, with its "idolization" of geometrical proof and certain theoretical knowledge, recall the human wisdom of sixteenth-century humanists, and try to recapture something of their practical modesty.

It is admirable to share Bacon's dreams for a *New Atlantis*, but we must be realistic about the practical obstacles to realizing that dream; and some of the most serious obstacles are *epistemological* ones. The larger the scale of our technical interventions in the natural world, the less confidently we can forecast or restrict their effects, and the more significant their *unintended* outcomes become. So all estimates of (say) the environmental impact of large-scale technological projects must be qualified by estimates of their intrinsic uncertainty; and, before taking any collective political decision about such a project, we need realistic calculations of unwanted but foreseeable side effects of its execution, so that our decision can claim to be arrived at with some measure of human wisdom. (Recall the sad story of the Aswan High Dam, which exemplified how the misplaced enthusiasm of engineers can override the hesitations of human scientists, only to generate an *engineering* disaster.)

These questions are especially weighty for the conference on which this volume is based, not least because the information sciences are having unforeseen effects on late twentieth-century social institutions. You may recall how Stevan Dedijer of Malmö wrote of "the subversion of historical materialism by science." Karl Marx and Friedrich Engels, for understandable reasons, saw material production as the base, or foundation, of society, and the world of ideas and fine arts as its superstructure. A century later, it is no longer clear how we are to tell the superstructure from the base, and the whole contrast is now problematic. Certainly, in telling the story of twentieth-century life and industry, we cannot refer to the ideas of (say) Norbert Wiener, Alan Turing or John von Neumann as mere "superstructure". The knowledge industry's output is not measured in tons of coal and iron ore dug from the ground, or megawatt hours of energy transmitted from one location to another. By now, the *material* products of industry depend on their foundation in the *mental* activities of human beings, far more than the other way around. In economically advanced countries, the key index of productivity is now less the sheer quantity of material goods they fabricate than the quality of their new ideas and values.

In the information age (it seems) our social institutions must adapt to needs defined by the technical capacity of, for example, our microprocessors. But the technical skills and devices made possible by intellectual work on (for example) computer software, silicon architecture and cryogenics call at the same time for institutional responses that rest on an understanding that goes far beyond technical ingenuity. In this, we live in a New Age. The intellectual imaginativeness of Isaac Newton is something that we nowadays take for granted; but, in criticizing the practical uses of our understanding, the humane wisdom of Francis Bacon is equally needed. The dreams of seventeenth-century philosophy – the infallible scientific method, the perfectly exact language, and the rest – will continue to fascinate us and to inspire powerful new theories. But the future will depend as much on our capacity to recapture the values of the sixteenth-century humanists, and to maintain the fragile balance between the refinement of practical skills and the human interests which they affect.

Chapter 7

Dialogue and Enlightenment

Horace Engdahl

Plato's dialogues found an influential interpreter in H.-G. Gadamer, who sees dialogue as a vehicle of truth, involving transformation. The utopian character of Gadamer's thought has been questioned by J. Habermas, who submits "true" dialogue with "noncoercive communication" which can be described as a democratic decision-making process on commonsense grounds leads to consensus rather than to truth and knowledge. However, when this modern Philosophy of Enlightenment is compared with the literary dialogues of Diderot, the encyclopaedist, we become aware of an enormous gap: here, dialogue is the opposite of consensus. An alternative tradition of dialogue is found in the Jewish tradition, with a contemporary exponent in Emmanuel Levinas, who describes the relationship of the "I" to the "Other".

The wittiest of all *romans à dialogue*, Diderot's *Le Neveu de Rameau*, written in the 1760s and 1770s, is set in a café. The dialogue is conducted between an "I" and a "He". The "I", according to the fiction, is the author himself, the philosopher Diderot. His partner to the dialogue is a gifted and eccentric wastrel, who free-loads his way around Paris, and is a relative of the famous composer Rameau.

The two men are each others' absolute opposites: the one an opportunist, utterly without principles, who ekes out a living by falsehood and flattery, the other an intellectual with Stoic learnings, a man of jealously defended integrity. The wastrel, however, is also an outstanding connoisseur of the manners and customs of the capital, a terrifyingly honest and sharp-sighted observer both of himself and of others. He bases his philosophy of life on the actual state of things; as the world functions, so he thinks: just as corruptly, and with the same affirmation of life. The other maintains an abstract ideal of virtue, but emerges, in all his honesty, as somewhat rigid and lacking in imagination, a solid, four-square theoretician who has not, perhaps, very much to say to live human beings. His ideas are admittedly true – nothing in the text allows them to be refuted intellectually – but what of their applicability? Let us characterize these two men by just one of their exchanges.

He: A strange vision indeed! Your happiness requires a certain romantic turn of mind which we do not possess, a soul of a particular type, a special taste. You decorate this bizarre

> learning with the name of virtue, you call it philosophy. But virtue and philosophy, are
> they for everyone? Whoever has them, has them; and may very well keep them. Just
> imagine if the whole universe were wise and philosophical; admit that it would be dull as
> the very devil. Look, long live philosophy! Long live the Wisdom of Solomon: drink good
> wines, stuff yourself with excellent food, roll around on pretty women, sleep on soft
> beds! . . . The rest is pure Vanity.

I: No! It would be better to lock yourself in your attic, drink water, dine on dry bread, and
       try to find yourself.

Studying the text with some attention, and knowing something of the personal background, one can establish fairly quickly that the "I" person (Diderot) is by no means the writer's self-evident representative in this book. He has donned, equally, the guise of the keen-sighted Rameau, borrowing a contemporary figure from the Bohemian world of Paris as mask. To be able to handle different sides of his thinking, he has dramatized them.

In other works he not only plays with different views, but also arranges collisions between different ways of approaching reality, for example in *Le Rêve de D'Alembert* between a scientific approach and that of the poetical visionary. The dominance of the dialogue form in his writings makes it clear that he regarded a dramatization of contradictions as "truer" than any uniform presentation of his conceptual world.

What, then, is a dialogue? An orthodox way of approaching this question is to be found, I think, in Hans-Georg Gadamer, a German philosopher who has emphasized more than others the dialogical principle in his writings, which has reintroduced the concept of dialogue in discussion of the humanities during the past twenty years.

A dialogue occupies a specific space in the language. This is Gadamer's initial premiss. It is not just any interaction. It has to be able to direct itself to a reality that lies outside each of the participants. In addition to the first ("I") and the second ("you"), there has to be a *third*, an issue around which the dialogue evolves, with a world in which this issue can arise. In other words the dialogue has a dimension of address (directed towards the "you") and a dimension of reference (directed towards the issue). For Gadamer, both are equally essential.

The centre of the dialogue is not either or any of the participants, it is the matter of which they speak. Dialogue also presupposes a measure of self-disregard. (This is one of Gadamer's pithier statements: "Language is essentially self-oblivion.") A dialogue that is aimed exclusively at some sort of mutual "understanding" has to be regarded, from this perspective, as double-headed narcissism. The natural genesis of the discussion should lie in the effort of the participants to clarify something that extends beyond their respective "I"s.

According to Gadamer, a dialogue consists of the laying bare of the essence of some matter by an interchange of questions and answers. It is to undergo an experience. It presupposes that each party's individual language, that with which he or she enters the dialogue, be modified in the course of the discussion. The dialogue creates a common linguistic state – or else it fails. Of the participants are thus demanded at the same time activity and passivity, that they affect the other party or parties, and allow themselves to be affected. "Understanding" in a dialogue, says Gadamer, does not entail self-promotion or the trumping through of one's own view, but involves a transformation into some common state, in which you are no longer what you were. What emerges from a true dialogue – since we can note that Gadamer is working here with a normative, perhaps Utopian concept – is a logos, which surpasses all the subjective opinions of the participants. Their opinions become subject to the truth of the matter. The dialogue to Gadamer is an element which makes the world appear in language. (The reader versed in philosophy will perceive how Heidegger's concept of language surfaces here in the theory of his disciple Gadamer.)

The necessary condition if such a rational centre is to emerge in the dialogue is thus that the participants be impelled into it by *a search for truth*. Truth in this context can be roughly translated as "experience of historical life". It is a question, as Gadamer explicitly states, of a knowledge that lies beyond the field of scientific control, a sort of existential knowledge of what it means to exist as a human being and participate in the experience encapsulated in literary and philosophical tradition. This is a pronouncedly humanistic theory. The knowledge of dialogue is not additive, but aims at a qualitative revolution in my understanding, which alters my "horizon". (All these concepts, of course, are problematical, but I must leave them as they stand.)

Gadamer sets further conditions for any true dialogue. It has to be conducted by responsible participants, who are concerned to be honest and treat the "you" as a fully valid party to the discussion. It presupposes both separation and a certain likeness and community of interests, which lend as it were a frame to the conflict in the debate. The situation excludes the exercise of power. The dialogue constitutes a dialectic process of question and answer. To pose a genuine question, one has to *want to know*, not just to see what the other will answer if I say this or that. An example of a false question is the pedagogic question. One has to leave something open, open up a direction of enquiry in which nothing is predetermined. This means that you have to be prepared to relinquish your initial premiss. You have to recognize the validity of what the responder has to say, not just regard it as a symptom or strategy, or adduce other causal arguments concerning it. It is thus a matter of a far-reaching trust. A tremendous *naïveté*, you may say. I will return to this matter below.

Let us now place ourselves outside Gadamer's linguistic theory and ontology and ask ourselves: "What is it that could make dialogue necessary as a vehicle of truth, and explain why the person who tries to express the truth in propositions will fail?". As I understand it, the answer lies in the structure of the speech-act. The word is always aimed at an encountering mind, and demands a productive complement on the part of the listener for its import to emerge. The dialogue is a synthesis of speaking and listening, not in alternating order but at one and the same moment. I have to listen to my words from a position that I presume to be that of the other. Every dialogue therefore bears the features of two twin internal dialogues. The distance between the speakers is modified by a probing identification. This is something that we have all experienced: a formulation that has been perfectly true and had produced the desired effect in one situation, with one type of listener, becomes if repeated word for word, false, and indeed mendacious, with another. Clear language is a matter of knowing whom you are addressing. But this clarity always has a limit; the other's real reaction and under-standing always remain essentially unknown to me, even if his replies can give me important clues. It is only he or she who can truly hear me, and breathe real life into the import of what I have said. Hence Derrida's formulation: "It is the ear of the other that signs [my text]." This is the kernel of the philosophy of dialogue: *Listening is more powerful than speech.*

"To understand", says Gadamer in an interview, "is to raise language to its true power of expression." He quotes Plato's *Phaidros*: the true, non-manipulative rhetoric is an art of formulation, which lends the utterances of the other greater acuity and force, which "listens forth" from the speech of the other that which he was incapable of saying. In Gadamer's case, we could have made the reference to Plato much earlier on. His entire theory – this is obvious, and he admits it willingly – is modelled on the dialogues of Plato.

Plato writes explicitly, in the seventh of the letters preserved under his name:

Only if the various principles – names, definitions, intimations and perceptions – are laborious-ly tested and rubbed one against the other in a reconciliatory tone, without ill will during the discussion, only then will insight and reason radiate forth in each case, and achieve what is for man the highest possible force.

This is the Dialogical Confession. No less interesting, however, is the con-tinuation of this locus:

There is therefore no question of any serious man writing down his thoughts on truly serious subjects, thereby exposing them to popular envy and confusion. From this, to put it briefly, you should draw the lesson that when you encounter written notes by a legislator concerning laws and other writings by another person, this is not to be taken as his most fully considered and serious opinion, always assuming him to be himself a man of weight, even if they occupy a place of honour in his own mind. If he undertakes, in deadly earnest, to pen such works, then admittedly not gods, but mortal men have "maddened his senses".

Plato, here, is setting up his well-known comparison between the spoken and the written language, to the infinite advantage of the former (precisely because oral speech can be incorporated in a dialogue of questions and answers). At the same time, he has left us a very considerable number of carefully devised writings, the content of which consists, to cap it all, of dialogues . . . With these words and actions he tosses us into an abyss of irony, from which 2000 years of interpretation and research have been unable to retrieve us.

Gadamer's concept of dialogical truth has been severely criticized for its latent cultural conservatism by German representatives of that country's critical philosophy. Above all Jürgen Habermas, himself markedly depen-dent upon Gadamer's thinking, has tried to revise the dialogical project in a way that would bring it more into line with the tradition of the Enlighten-ment. Habermas believes that extremely few discursive situations are free from elements of dominance and subordination. The power relationships of our society are far too uneven to permit, other than in fortunate and exceptional cases, a dialogue between parties whose rights are equal. Cen-tral to Habermas' view of "noncoercive communication" (which would be his term for "genuine" dialogue) is an idea of *consensus*. The dialogue, for him, is not so much a path to knowledge as a decision-making process: a road to democratic agreements, reached on common-sense grounds. It is assumed that the parties to his dialogues will consistently act in the discussion on purely rational grounds, avoiding all irrational influences.

The genuine dialogue situation, in Habermas' view, does not often exist; it can, however, be *set up*, namely by *criticizing* the power relationships that create a false and dictated "consensus".

The necessary conditions for Habermas' noncoercive communication are otherwise very much akin to those made by Gadamer regarding the dialogue. You must not regard the other party as pathological or dishonest, but have to treat him as a mature and thinking being, who, for example, is intentionally complying with certain norms. Both parties must be convinced that the other is endeavouring to speak the truth, and means what he or she is saying. We know, admittedly, that the reality seldom corresponds to this model, but – and here Habermas makes an interesting point – we nonetheless usually act in practice "counterfactually", as if it did. If we did not, in the discussion, tacitly assume an ideal dialogue situation, then it would be impossible to distinguish between false and true agreement, or indeed to ascribe any stable import to what the other says. Habermas states, in the language of Kantian philosophy, that the ideal discussive situation is a transcendental norm, which lays the foundation of linguistic meaning. In that it exists as an idea, we can fight for a true dialogue in which the language would not be an instrument by which to oppress others, and where no one could monopolize the last word, or invalidate the results of the discussion by reference to a higher authority.

Such a Utopian model as this could be realized in full only if neither of the parties exercised any societal power over the other, and the opportunities to practise such acts as "ordering", "allowing", "demanding an account of", etc., were distributed with absolute symmetry. Habermas' theory of the dialogue thus conceals the dream of an ideal form of life, without any ruling élite. It is all too simple to confute him by presenting, as does Niklas Luhmans, a portrait of the stallion debater. We see how dialogue in the Utopian sense, even if it is not presented by Habermas as a form of knowledge, is nonetheless indirectly or "transcendentally" necessary to all seeking after knowledge, since it presupposes true communication. The consensus-forming dialogue is, according to Habermas, the way in which the Enlightenment penetrates into our own society's confused fabric of rational motives and irrational myths.

If we compare this modern Philosophy of Enlightenment with the literary dialogues of the encyclopaedist Diderot, we become aware of an enormous gap. Nothing fits, neither the method nor the tone of voice. No consensus is aimed at in the discussion between Diderot and Rameau's nephew although they are speaking of fundamentally very serious matters: the nature of society, and of how a man should live. That they should end up under the umbrella of a common truth, their language having reached some special state that belongs to neither man personally – what a bizarre idea! They reach no agreement whatsoever, but they part as friends. Their discussion has achieved something different: a comprehensive illumination of their respective philosophies of life – and personalities. Any truth that may be launched by the novel as a whole has to be written in the plural. No firm contracts have been reached. When the story opens, the philosopher is sitting on a bench in the gardens of the Palais Royal, letting his fancies come and go. At the same time, with half an eye, he sees young men confusedly following one or the other of the seductive courtesans in the colonnades, only to be attracted shortly afterwards by another, and the similarity strikes him: "My thoughts are my trollops."

In Diderot's text a dialogue is conducted in fact not only between different views, but also between the senses. A considerable part of the text is devoted to the mimes that Rameau's nephew improvises at the café to reproduce his observations of the life of the Parisian upper classes, and to illustrate his position regarding music and opera. He is a brilliant imitator and quick-change artist, who needs no masks or props, but can evoke a theatre, indeed an entire opera house with its full repertoire by his voice and gestures. Diderot was one of those favouring the new type of ballet with a plot and action dance, the "pantomime ballet". In *Le Neveu de Rameau* he has created a "pantomime novel".

A complete dialogue, for Diderot, seems to go beyond any mere exchange of lines. It has to evoke the very life which the discussion is concerned to penetrate. The "subject matter" or "res", in Gadamer's terminology, has to appear vividly and tangibly before the participants. The dialogue becomes a theatre stage and eagerly discussing audience *in one*. Diderot's text give us an idea of the type of environment that gave rise to a new conception of man as radical as that of his Encyclopedia. By comparison, Habermas' Utopia of consensus seems thin and abstract, constrained by its demand for universality, even if it is always unfair to compare a social theory with a literary masterpiece. Or is it?

Diderot would have agreed with Habermas that reason is in its essence universal, that its truths are valid for all. Only how are they to be applied in everyday life? When reason is brought down to the level of the coffee tables and opera boxes, its oneness is dissolved into a variegated mass of perspectives that cannot with obvious certainty be demonstrated or rejected. Habermas, despite his modern and pragmatic posture, emerges as a seeker after light where Diderot looks for lighting, and the German thus seems the more metaphysical of the two.

We find a relationship in Diderot with the dialogical freedom cultivated by the humanists of the Renaissance. As the Russian historian of ideas Leonid Batkin has so convincingly suggested in his very attractive book on the Italian Renaissance, a great deal of Renaissance "contradictoriness" stems from the practice of defending all conceivable points of view to enrich the questions under discussion. Widely disparate positions were regarded as mutually dependent and equally necessary, in a way equally justified and therefore not final. Men's views are reflected against the background of a truth that cannot include any conclusions, since "what is" is inexhaustible. When the parties to a dialogue, with their eloquent pleas, enter battle on behalf of different systems or views, that which assumes the place of a synthesis in the text is often simply an illustration of thesis and anithesis, a variant that perhaps leads forward to other variants.

The discussions conducted in the written Renaissance dialogues recorded sometimes remind us in places of university disputations, but the technique of argument has acquired a new function. This is because the Renaissance had a way of achieving freedom of thought entirely different from our modern culture. It did not *reject* authorities, but *multiplied* them: perhaps a more efficient method, since it avoids establishing a rationalistic counter-dogma to destroy the old dogma. All authorities of the classical past were put into play during these patient discussions in cool gardens, and the tradition included everything from cynical materialism to religious mysticism, gathering its materials from East and West, pagan and Christian. By regarding *all* these sources as worthy of respect, the humanists gained an astounding freedom of intellectual action.

Speech is not uttered in a vacuum, but starts from a place and from the terms afforded by that place. In the context of the dialogue, we have reason to reflect on two essentially different places, which have given rise to two contradictory ways of using the language, namely the popular assembly and the banquet. Donald Broady, in an article in the publication *Skeptron*, has made a specific study of the royal stave, the sceptre (Greek *skeptron*), as an ancient symbol not only of the exercise of power but also of the right to speak and deliver a legitimate judgement. In the *Iliad* and the *Odyssey* the word sceptre occurs whenever some lord assumes his right to step forward among his peers and plead for a question of general importance. One of the most heavily charged scenes in the entire *Odyssey* is that in which Telemachos, at the urging of the goddess Athene, appears for the first time at the council on Ithaca and takes up the sceptre to complain at the importunate behaviour of the suitors. At that moment, in the eyes of his society, he becomes an adult, who can take up the struggle for his father's heritage. He now enjoys, for example, the right to bid his mother be silent. It was not everyone who could touch this "Speaker's mace". If anyone should utter who did not belong to the circle of trusted men, he could be beaten into silence with the sceptre, as occurs in several passages in Homer.

The rod, the mace or the sceptre symbolizes the authoritative word. We see its counterparts, in direct line of descent, in the "expert statements" of our own day. Our concepts of some formal competency that supposedly lends the words of certain people a superior weight, and the right to deprive the contributions of others any validity, stem directly from the sceptre. Broady demonstrates at length in his article how the European universities took over the symbolism of the sceptre, and the entire line of thought concerning the legitimate right to speak that is connected with it. The words uttered under the sceptre are essentially antidialogical.

However, our culture offers at least one further tradition of language – and it is there the dialogue arises. Its origin is the classical banquet of antiquity. An antique custom dictated an extensive freedom of speech at any noble gentleman's table. One had to tolerate both mockery and buffoonery from one's invited guests. At a banquet, free speech prevails (cf. the Greek *parrhesia*, which can mean both freedom of utterance and incautious speech). This custom is not unknown in our own latitudes, and traces of it are to be found in the old Nordic literature. The Swedish poet Tegnér caught up the idea afresh in "The Arrival of Frithiof to King Ring", in which he has the stranger, Frithiof, speak out defiantly to the King at table:

But the King smiled and said: "Audacious is thy speech,
Yet words fly free in Nordic royal halls.

The literature of classical antiquity contains some wild and satirical dialogues, above all those surviving under the name of Lucian, which deviate radically from the Platonic tradition. Bakhtin suggests that Lucian to some extent developed the freedom of expression that prevailed at banquets and the Saturnalia into a literary form. And, indeed, his dialogues portray in places some pretty swinish parties.

To some extent, the custom of speaking, as the Swedish phrase has it, "between goblet and wall" was subsequently transferred to other settings. In modern times, the same role has been taken over by the café (it was at the Café de la Régence, for example, that we found Diderot and Rameau). A streak of this anarchistic and disrespectful art of conversation leads to the sort of public debate conducted today. What makes a modern intellectual discussion so confusing is that it has acquired characteristics from *both* these fora and traditions. While some of those taking part enter the discussion, imaginary wine jug in hand, as mocking and bold critics of society, others angrily attempt to beat them down with an equally imaginary sceptre. The result can be fairly comical. The attentive reader of such contributions to the public debate should observe how the text is strewn with markers – name-droppings, concepts, turns of phrase – the purpose of which is to assert the writer's own superior authority, and to deprive his opponent of any right to function as a fully valid party to the discussion. For the bearers of the sceptre, the basic question in any exchange of opinion is who can *legitimately* take part in the dialogue. But the concept of formal competency of this kind is *per se* inimical to the nature of dialogue. It belongs, rather, to a guild system.

The home of dialogue is always by way of a protected area or preserve, from which violence, the exercise of power, the rights of officialdom, etc., must be kept away. Perhaps we can learn something from the way in which Renaissance dialogue used the disputative technique of the universities: this technique stemmed from the world of the sceptre, but it was transformed. No sophisticated dialogue, of course, can do without the type of knowledge achieved only by specialists; otherwise, it will remain at a very amateur level. It is necessary, in some way, to retain the expertise, while filtering off the role of the expert. Nice work, you may say, if you can get it, in view of the character of knowledge gathering, in our society, as an accumulation of symbolic capital and means of competition. But it was precisely what such men of the Enlightenment as Diderot and Rousseau succeeded in doing. Despite everything, some sort of accommodation between the two traditions is necessary. The sceptre provides the continuity, the stability, a possibility of learning, and something against which to rebel. And also the authority achieved in a free exercise of speech becomes, in the end, a sort of sceptre. Possibly, any living intellectual environment is of necessity a combination of the two principles.

As we have seen, dialogue can be regarded as a necessary condition for enlightenment, in whatever sense that term may be taken. But it contains, equally, the limits of enlightenment. To arrive at a more radical, less harmonizing perspective on the dialogue between "I" and "you", we have to go beyond the broadly speaking Platonic tradition that characterizes almost all Western philosophy. The alternative is offered by the Jewish tradition, one of the foremost contemporary exponents of which is Emmanuel Levinas.

Levinas was born in Kaunas, Lithuania, in 1905, but has been active for the greater part of his life in France. Beyond all doubt, his work has done much to reawaken the interest in ethics on the part of the French intelligentsia.

The relationship towards the "you" cannot, in Levinas' view, fall within the province of knowledge, because in the knowledge act the object is absorbed into the subject and the duality disappears. Nor can it be ecstasy, since in ecstasy the subject is absorbed into the object, and finds itself one with it. Both these alternatives thus end with the disappearance of the one or the other.

Light, clarity and capacity for thought return all experience to an element of recollection. Reason is alone. In this sense, knowledge never encounters in the world anything that is truly *other*. (This, says Levinas, is the measure of truth to be found in idealism.)

But in the experience of pain I am bound to something unknown, which cannot be translated into terms of light and knowledge, namely death. "That death is something unknown means that the relation with death can never take place in the light; that the subject stands in relation to something that does not come from himself. The relation to the other is a relation to mystery". Death is presaged by suffering, which is an experience of the subject's passivity. I cannot think away my suffering, I am subjected to it. In knowledge, on the other hand, all apparent passivity *vis-à-vis* the world is an activity, namely the taking of the world into possession through concept. (The reality of death is therefore the limit of idealism and, in translated terms, of the enlightened dialogue.)

Levinas, however, is concerned to demonstrate that there is also a relationship to "the other" in which the "I" can survive and escape destruction. This is the encounter with the other person. The latter is admittedly not unknown the way death is, but unknowable: "The relationship with the other is not an idyllic communion, not a sympathy through which we adopt his place, recognize him as like, but exterior to ourselves; the relation to the other is a relation to Mystery."

If one could own, grasp and conceptualize the other, it would not be an "other". These types of action are, in fact, expressions of power. The truly "other" is characterized by the fact that it lies beyond my power.

From Plato onwards, people have sought an ideal for society in the process of *unification*. The collective, the community, it is assumed, will devour the mutual alienness of its members. The group will stand shoulder to shoulder turned towards the sun of reason. Against this ideal, Levinas defends the face-to-face relationship.

The purely rational, issue-oriented dialogue is in his view rather a *monologue*. "The questions and answers which make up an 'exchange of ideas' could just as well be held within a *single* consciousness." (This, as we noted, was fundamentally the case with the discussion in *Le Neveu de Rameau*.)

The problem, namely, is that the human "I" stands outside the categories with which knowledge comprehends the world: variable/permanent, to be/ not to be, indeed the very idea of separative properties:

The self identifies itself regardless of any specific distinguishing property that could separate it from others, and in which it could recognize itself. The indiscernible special nature cannot be reduced to a difference in "content". So the relationship between one self and another self is not the bringing together of creatures in the sort of world we find in the conceptualization or synchronization that is achieved through knowledge.

The goal of dialogue is to achieve a relationship not to the formed "I" but to the formative, if we may be permitted to employ for a moment a Neo-Platonic terminology.

The human face evokes a nearness of a *different* kind from that which prevails in a synthesis combining phenomena in the world. It is tied, in Levinas' view, to a thinking that is older and more aware than knowledge or experience. "Fraternity, accusation, and my responsibility come before any contemporaneousness, any freedom in myself, out of an immemorial-non-representable-past, before any beginning to be found in myself, before any present."

The nature of the question is thus no longer, as in Gadamer, to *develop* thought. It is to *break up* thought, with a call, a shout, to the other. For Levinas, this leads us into a theology of a strongly ethical character. God is what appears in the faces of our fellow humans. But even if we avoid following him in this direction, Levinas' criticism has carried dialogue into an area that lies beyond intentionality in the phenomenological sense, beyond any allusion to a knowable "issue" in the discussion, in other words beyond enlightenment. Only the dimension of "address" remains. Nor does the exchange between "I" and "you", as conceived by Levinas, have anything to do with *consenъиз*. In a way, the encounter between "I" and "you" takes place beyond the language; it is perhaps drawn into language, but from a more primary region.

The words of the sceptre and of the banquet have both been largely reserved for men. The Greek tradition of dialogue consists of conversing *gentlemen*, who have plenty of time at their disposal. In this respect, the eighteenth-century Enlightenment hardly differs. In Levinas, the dialogue is expressly between man and woman.

His model for association with the other is love.

The discussion starts from the bottomlessness in the eyes of the other, but finds there, too, a reason to be silent and recognize its powerlessness. Over against each other stand two realities, on either side of a fold that can never be ironed out (it is constituted by the faces). But the glances of the two can cross the fold. Anyone concerned to penetrate more deeply into this dialogue beyond dialogue will find nothing of use in the philosophers, but he might well, for example, look up the central passage of the Swedish poet Gunnar Ekelöf's *Guide to the Underworld*:

Two glances between us,
                wondering
and in wonder, like two
        worlds, are of a love
too great to be consummated:
The moment of the dream, or
        the memory, without touching
without greeting, only with
        the glance – a bird!

The utterly inexperienceds'
            newborn experience
as great as that of the thoroughly
                    experienced.

Translated by Keith Bradfield

Chapter 8

Theatricality and Technology: Pygmalion and the Myth of the Intelligent Machine

Julian Hilton

Can machines think? The Cartesian test lays down that to be deemed intelligent the machine must be independent of the programmer, otherwise it is merely imitating. One way of considering the issue of the simulation of human behaviour is to look at the theatre. The theatre is both simulated and real because the actors have to convince the audience that they are real. The theatre has been exploring the representation and simulation of people's behaviour for thousands of years. AI could learn from it. In the theatre art is enabled by technology – by staging, sets, lighting, costumes, effects and so on. It is a complex aesthetic machine. The effectiveness of simulation therefore depends on the imagination of the audience. The same may apply to the knowledge-based machine. The story of Pygmalion and the myth of the intelligent machine highlights the discrepancy between surface mimicry and depth. The myth included ideals which Pygmalion mistakenly held about women. The later work, in which Higgins taught Eliza to speak like him and assumed that he had taught her to think like him too, illustrates the danger of divorcing words from meaningful context. The teaching of Eliza took place from a linguistic knowledge base. The implication for AI of not considering the context and environment within which knowledge gains meaning is that the knowledge engineering approach may fail to deal with the complexity of knowledge transfer.

Can machines think? No, said Descartes. Why not? Machines can give the appearance of thought in that they can be made to imitate man, but there is a fundamental difference between this power of imitation and real thought. This difference is best illustrated by analysing the relative capacities of speech of men and machines. Men can speak; even the most stupid of us can communicate vastly more effectively than other life forms. This power of speech is the outward manifestation of reason; and reason is what makes man. So, Descartes concludes, "We ought not to confound speech with the natural movements which indicate the passions and can be imitated by machines as well as manifested by animals".[1] Descartes' position is open to a number of serious challenges, not least in the way that it misinterprets the intelligence level of many animal communication systems. But in one respect his test is unassailably right: a machine must be capable of acts of reasoning and speech independent of the programmer before it can be deemed intelligent. All else falls under his criterion of imitation.

This test is hard-line and controversial; in her book, *Artificial Intelligence and Natural Man*, despite an avowed purpose in seeking to counteract "the dehumanizing influence of natural science",[2] Margaret Boden later tacitly admits that little of what she writes about would pass the Cartesian test: "Computer simulations in general attempt theoretical modeling of psychological function and structure, rather than ontological mimicry of mental reality, and it is in these terms alone that they should be assessed".[3] But even Professor Boden is bolder than many who count themselves specialists in artificial intelligence (AI), for whom AI is merely an extension of automated engineering.[4]

I have no answer to the question of whether machines will ever pass the Cartesian test, but I believe that there is a hitherto neglected area of enquiry for AI research which may bring us closer to an answer. This is the area of simulation of behaviour, or, more precisely, the area of theatre. Theatre is, to borrow Boden's phrase "ontological mimicry of mental reality". Aristotle, one of the first great systematic scientists, devoted a great deal of thought to attempting to codify what he regarded as the highest achievement of human intelligence, tragic poetry. Man's urge to create such poetry grew naturally, so he argued, from his urge to imitate, children's play (which so often involves role play) leading to theatrical plays: "Imitation is natural to man from childhood, one of his advantages over the lower animals being this, that he is the most imitative creature in the world, and learns by imitation."[5] (This propensity to imitate suggests that the imitative function Boden currently assigns AI may be the early part of a learning curve which will lead AI in due course to satisfying Descartes' standards.) Tragedy functions, according to Aristotle, as a complex system for simulating emotions, the purpose of which is to effect a catharsis in the audience, who leave the theatre cleansed.[6] For this to happen, the actors must persuade their audience that even though they are acting the emotions they generate are real.

So theatre rests from the outset on the paradox that it is simulated and yet real. When an actor plays Oedipus, he clearly is not the real Oedipus – if ever there was one. Yet, unless he convinces his audience that he feels as Oedipus felt, his performance is accounted a failure.

At the point at which an actor so identifies with his role that he collapses his own self into that of another, he has stopped acting and become simply mad. Theatre always depends on the maintenance of a critical distance between the actor and his role. Yet this distance must never be allowed to break the contract of probability between the actor and his audience – the contract that rests on the belief that theatre only functions if the actor can persuade the audience, and the audience signal to the actor, that they both believe that the events of which they are part could probably have happened, or happen.

This special nature of theatre has fascinated many scientists, including Bacon, Descartes and Diderot, so the suggestion which I now make that AI (as a science) needs to investigate theatre needs no particular defence. The possibility exists that the special nature of theatrical intelligence, which underpins the cultural success of theatre in society, will offer clues to the satisfactory replication of human reasoning and creativity in machines, or, alternatively, help demonstrate that such a possibility is unrealizable. It may also be that theatre offers us, by analogy, an intermediate test of intelligence, somewhere between Descartes' hard-line position, and the imitative position taken by Boden and many others.

There is another aspect to theatre which qualifies it for our attention: theatre is as much about technology as about art, the technology enabling the art. As such, it offers an integrated and integrative model of human intelligence of a kind fundamentally useful to AI.

The Theatre Machine

While theatre is an art form, it is an art form intrinsically enabled by technology. Viewed another way, theatre is a complex aesthetic machine, dedicated to the representation of the imaginable through performance. The performer and all the apparatus of staging – set, lighting, costumes, effects – are components of this machine, driven by the collective imagination. Since the industrial revolution, perhaps even since the beginnings of the new science in the seventeenth century, machines have, however, been associated in men's minds with dehumanization, with dark satanic mills, with the decline of human values. So theatre has rarely faced its own technological nature despite the fact that its mass appeal has rested as much on its technological as on its aesthetic genius, because it has wished to range itself on the side of civilized values in conflict with the world of enterprise and machines.

The purpose of this chapter is not to debate the relative merits of this attitude theatre has adopted towards itself, but rather to argue the case for seeing the experience of theatre as paradigmatic in the debate on the nature and value of AI. The affinity with science is great: both science and theatre can be broken down into pure and applied skills, the Jesuits for example, justifying the centrality of theatre in their curriculum for this very reason; rehearsal observation and empirical testing to the adoption of "least worst" hypotheses. Yet, for reasons it is not my purpose here to unravel, science and theatre have drifted further and further apart since the seventeenth century.

The challenge of AI may change this. In effect, AI is the attempt to replicate in machines the reasoning and imaginative powers of the human brain, which presupposes that we have some knowledge of what these powers are. In fact, science knows very little in this respect, while theatre, admittedly more tacitly than explicitly, has been exploring the problem of representing or simulating one person's behaviour by means of another for thousands of years. AI may learn a great deal from examining the theatre's extended investigation into the nature of human intelligence.

For Shakespeare and his contemporaries the metaphoric proposition that the world is a stage (*theatrum mundi*) hardly needed defending. It was clear all human action was played out on a great universal stage, and that men and women were actors in some great play. The Globe Theatre was the globe in microcosm, it was a cipher for representing all knowledge. Since the seventeenth century, theatre has lost confidence in its own centrality as mediating metaphor of reality as it has dissipated its energies in a fruitless debate between words and images as to their relative significance. It has also lost its power as a universal metaphor, embodying all knowledge in a single proposition: "All the world's a stage".

The way the microcosmic Globe Theatre functioned was a great space–time machine, driven by the energy of the imagination:

> Can this cock-pit hold
> The vasty fields of France? Or may we cram
> Within this wooden O the very casques
> That did affright the air at Agincourt?
> O pardon: since a crooked figure may
> Attest in little place a million,
> So let us, ciphers to this great account,
> On your imaginary forces work.

(*Henry V*, Prologue, 11–18)[7]

Not only can the space–time machine cram northern France into the cock-pit, it can also journey us around England and France in the course of a few lines. It does this through the agency of the fancy:

> Play with your fancies; and in them behold
> Upon the hempen tackle ship-boys climbing;
> Hear the shrill whistle which doth order give . . .
>   Still be kind
> And eke out our performance with your mind.

(*Henry V*, 3.0, 7–9, 34–35)

This summary by Shakespeare of how theatre works – technology mediated by the visual and oral imagination of the audience – helps pinpoint the role of the imagination in any representation of human intelligence, for without it, the boards of the Globe can never represent the great world stage. This single observation has profound implications for any attempt to create an intelligent machine, for however much knowledge is stored within the machine, it will be our imagination which determines our sense of its intelligence.

The nature of the theatrical imagination is itself central to the equation of the world with the stage for it rests, as Diderot recognized, on a central paradox, that the actor both was and was not the role he played. It was essential to the naturalistic effect of theatre that the actor represented his role with sufficient plausibility that the audience believed in it. Yet it was equally essential that a distance be maintained between actor and role that enabled the act of representation to be simultaneously one of analysis. I suggest that a similar paradox, perhaps even the same one, lies at the heart of the problem of machine intelligence. A machine intelligence is simultaneously a naturalistic representation of human intelligence and a representation of its meta-principles – principles no single intelligence can possess in entirety. (An expert system, for example, must feel like a single expert while embodying the knowledge of many experts.) As a result artificial intelligence is qualitatively different from human intelligence and may, therefore, be hard to define in terms intelligible to human intelligence (perhaps it will take an intelligent machine to recognize another intelligent machine).

The resolution of Diderot's paradox lies in the principle Keats identifies as the core of Shakespeare's art, "negative capability",[8] the capacity of a work of art to support many, even conflicting, meanings. There are as many ways of playing Julius Caesar as there are actors to play the role, and yet the role is always the same role. As Schiller expressed it, this very relationship between the specificity of the individual actor and the generic nature of his role is the basis of the aesthetic concept of "play" which he advances in his "Letters" *On the Aesthetic Education of Man*.[9] It is through the specific that the generic is created and legitimated.[10] These two positions identify for us further tests of the efficacy of the replication of human intelligence in machines. Firstly, the artificial intelligence must be capable of supporting conflicting interpretations of the same data; secondly, the specificity of its "mind" must be one criterion of its generic validity.

In the context of the Shakespearian view of the theatre as a space–time machine it is hardly surprising that one theme in theories of performance is that of the actor as intelligent machine. Practitioners in the theatre, such as Heinrich von Kleist, have advanced the theory that there is a fundamental and beneficial relationship between acting and animated puppetry, while the founders of modern scientific method, Bacon and Descartes, have expressed deep interest in the practice and metaphor of theatre. One of the purposes of the intelligent machine is to imitate actual human behaviour; another is to explore potential human behaviour. When we sit in Shakespeare's Globe, we are being asked to imagine what it would be like to travel in time and space – questions which, in a sense, create the aesthetic and imaginative preconditions for the technological realization of such travel.

We are also being asked to imagine something else, the possibility that it may be man, not God, who is the author as well as measure of all things. Such a claim was not original: Marlowe's *Dr Faustus* was about this issue. "Here, Faustus, try thy brains to gain a deity", says Faustus to himself in his opening speech.[11] The claim concerns theatre every bit as much as it concerns science. The playwright is a kind of god in that he writes words for imaginary people which then cause real people (actors) to bring those words, and those people, to life. In this sense he goes beyond actual into potential human experience. Technological research is also informed with this sense of the pursuit of the imaginable. If we can imagine flying to the moon, how can we actually do it? If we can imagine creating intelligent machines, how can we actually make them? One myth which addresses itself to these problems is that of Pygmalion and Galatea, the statue that comes to life. Under the influence of Freud and the psychoanalysis, it has been the Oedipal myth that has dominated much of our thinking this century. Now perhaps we are moving into the age of Pygmalion.

Pygmalion and the Perfect Machine

The myth of the intelligent machine perhaps enters culture in the story of Pygmalion and his statue. On the one hand, the story of a statue that comes to life seems to suggest that a technologist of genius can transcend the limitations of matter, turning stone to flesh; on the other, it expresses a basic truth about all art, that an artefact, once complete, achieves a life of its own. The terms of the myth are simple. Pygmalion, a sculptor of genius, is dissatisfied with all the women he encounters and sets out to make his own. He carves a woman in the image of Aphrodite and then begs the goddess to breathe life into his stone. She accedes and Galatea comes to life.

The affinities of this myth with the theatre are fundamental. A writer writes a script in which certain characters are created, in a sense in ideal form. Then, through the agency of actors, these characters come to life, in the process developing beyond what the original creator conceived for them.

The story is, like any good myth, much harder to interpret than to narrate. In terms of a Platonic theory of mimesis the statue is profoundly ambiguous. Within Plato's aesthetic, a statue, as with any work of art, is an imitation of an imitation of an ideal original. Since each imitative step is a degradation from the ideal, Pygmalion's statue cannot but be essentially flawed. Yet, this statue must be a special case, because it is not an imitation of a real woman but rather represents Pygmalion's ideal woman – the woman who has all the qualities real women lack – Aphrodite. The statue is beautiful because it imitates a divine ideal. The ambiguity is not, however, confined to the question of beauty and ideal form. Pygmalion presumably is seeking for a woman of ideal form character (content). What he creates is a woman of ideal form. His assumption, that beauty is a guarantee of sweetness of temper, is surely profoundly flawed, as indeed some versions of the myth indicate by making Galatea turn quickly into a typical woman, a shrew. Here the myth becomes something quite different. Pygmalion is a mysogynist at best, a hardline chauvinist at worst. His attitude to all women is reflected in his refusal of any of them, and his eventual disaffection with Galatea is not her fault at all, but his. In such terms, Pygmalion is the ultimate hate-object of all feminists.

From the perspective of AI research, the myth challenges us to think of the knowledge representation process in triangular terms – of expert, representational medium and expertise. Pygmalion, the expert, wishes to capture in stone, the medium of representation, the ideal woman, his expertise or idealized knowledge. His purpose is initially merely to record in stone this knowledge, but as his success in representation grows, so do his ambitions. Finally, he brings his knowledge base to life, only to discover that it was as flawed as any other. What is more, it is not his own hand, but that of a goddess, which effects the transformation from statue to woman. We are, in effect, in the same position as Shakespeare leaves us, that there has to be an agent of transformation to turn any mere representation into an active and independent creation. That agent is the imagination.

In the *Advancement of Learning*, Bacon, a committed Platonist, leaves us in no doubt that any positive interpretation of Pygmalion's ambition is inimical to Platonic notions of truth:

Here therefore, is the first distemper of learning, when men study words and not matter . . . It seems to me that Pygmalion's frenzy is a good emblem or portraiture of this vanity: for words are but the images of matter; and except they have life of reason and invention, to fall in love with them is all one as to fall in love with a picture.[12]

Pygmalion's frenzy is, however, crucial to the AI debate, for the risk of all AI research is that of mistaking the forms of intelligence for intelligence itself. Is the mere pursuit of AI a "frenzy", or can the danger Bacon points out be avoided? The answer may not perhaps be sought in science, but may lie in aesthetics. Bacon's objection to Pygmalion's behaviour is that he lavishes his affection on a representation with no original, a signifier with no signified. This is contrary to reason, or so argues Bacon. This may be so, but falling in love with pictures is a habit not confined to the stage or to fiction. Quite the opposite, it seems a basic tenet of powerful myths that they share with the Pygmalion story the property of being representations of actions and people who have no original, as Hamlet, Don Juan and Dr Faustus have no real-life models. In effect therefore, the successful creation of the ideal woman from stone undermines the mimetic theory of art. If they undermine mimetic aesthetics, do they also undermine mimetic theories of intelligence? For if they do, the representation of human intelligence in machines may require aesthetic as much as or even more than scientific skills.

Pygmalion, Knowledge Transfer and De-skilling

One influential aesthetic version of the Pygmalion myth is George Bernard Shaw's perhaps most popular play, *Pygmalion*, made even more popular by the musical *My Fair Lady*, which locates the myth within a feminist and a socialist context, both of great significance to the progress of AI.[13] It concerns a (natural) language expert, Professor Higgins, his colleague, Colonel Pickering and an object of experiment, Eliza Doolittle. Higgins bets Pickering that with his expert knowledge of language he can transform Eliza from cockney to duchess in six months (rapid knowledge transfer). He succeeds, to an extent that all London society is inflamed with Eliza's success.

The levels of the transformation are complex, engaging with Eliza's appearance, her manners, her speech and her thoughts. First, Eliza is made to look like a duchess, in which respect the original terms of the Pygmalion myth are observed. The ideal woman has to look beautiful. But Shaw's observation informed him that, especially in English society, class is determined less by appearance than by accent and linguistic practice, and Eliza's success is therefore significantly more dependent on her voice than her face. So secondly and thirdly, Eliza is made to move and sound like a duchess. Yet at this point, the wisdom of Bacon's warning against "frenzy" becomes opposite. Higgins may have made Eliza sound like a duchess but what she actually says (her thoughts) remain unchanged: she still thinks and swears like a cockney, but in perfect aristocratic tones. This is the danger of studying words divorced from meaning.

We may characterize this flaw in Higgins' knowledge transfer system as the flaw of virtual knowledge. Higgins assumes that if he teaches Eliza to speak like him she will also think like him. His system apparently functions perfectly; until, that is, it is required to display real intelligence, the generation of a solution to a problem unforeseen by the programmer. At this point, "system Eliza" crashes – she is ruffled, but has not been programmed to respond to being ruffled in a polite way; so she swears. Her learning is quite distinct from her understanding. In an expert such as Higgins, the knowledge that polite diction must equal polite semantics is obvious but tacit. In the expert system Eliza, no such tacit knowledge base is embedded. Eliza's failure is not linguistic but hermeneutic and sociological. At one level, Shaw has confirmed the old adage that it is not clothes that make the person but the inner mind – or tacit knowledge. Eliza betrays herself because her tacit knowledge system is totally different from that of Higgins. At another level, Shaw seems to be suggesting that any adequate practical definition of intelligence itself is not merely specific to a given culture, but specific even to small subsets of that culture. Cockney intelligence is not West End intelligence; male intelligence is not female intelligence.

This exacerbates still further the problem of knowledge transfer for it highlights the need for careful evaluation of what we might call the knowledge environment (all those factors conditioning tacit knowledge) in our study of knowledge transfer. It also returns us to another warning about knowledge transfer Bacon issues in the *Advancement of Learning*:

For as knowledges are now delivered, there is a kind of contract of error between the deliverer and the receiver. For he that delivereth knowledge, desireth to deliver it in such form as may best be believed, and not as may best be examined; and he that receiveth knowledge, desireth rather present satisfaction, than expectant inquiry; and so rather not to doubt, than not to err: glory making the author not to lay open his weakness, and sloth making the discipline not to know his strength.[14]

This "contract of error" indicates that, in Bacon's view at least, knowledge transfer is synonymous with error.

Higgins commits a system error of a second kind, equally relevant to AI, which is intrinsic to his own specialized memory system. He has perfected a use of sound recording onto discs which constitutes his linguistic knowledge base. He teaches Eliza from this knowledge base. The problem, however, is that the crucial part of the knowledge base was configured many years earlier and is now out of date. Eliza learns a static, and therefore archaic English: when she goes to take her place in society, linguistically it can already detect the difference between Queen Victoria's English and its own. Higgins' expert system crashes for a different reason, because it relies on a static knowledge base. Expertise is by implication always dynamic, a fact which contradicts any claim that an expert system will be able to solve a given task once and for all.

The third phase in Eliza's transformation comes when Eliza begins to discern what has happened, that she is capable of playing a duchess but is in fact no such thing. She first intuits this problem when she realizes that her new linguistic expertise has in fact de-skilled her in a different respect:

I sold flowers, I didn't sell myself. Now you've made a lady of me I'm not fit to sell anything else. I wish you'd left me where you found me.[15]

Will this be the fate of all users of expert systems, that they de-skill themselves? Eliza's response to this frightening possibility is to contemplate suicide. She runs away from Higgins, though, fortunately, straight into the arms of a nice young man, Freddie. This action leads to two challenges Shaw delivers back to his Pygmalion, Professor Higgins. The first is that despite the apparent success he has achieved in raising Eliza socially to such a level that she can marry Freddie as an equal, the economic reality is that she will support him in their married life, not vice versa. On one level, this is a perfect feminist riposte. On another, it is an indication of perhaps the most complex problem of all issues in knowledge transfer, that the recipient of knowledge, whether human or mechanical, may not do with the knowledge what the knowledge engineer envisages. As Shaw puts it: "Galatea never does quite like Pygmalion: his relation to her is too godlike to be agreeable".[16] In fact, Eliza goes back to her original trade, as a flower seller, and resists the de-skilling implications of her new expertise. It is now common knowledge that one of the problems expert systems face is that they tend to be rejected by experts. Is this merely luddite behaviour, or is it perhaps that Shaw is right – that the premise of an expert system is a god-like degree of knowledge, a feature which humans quite naturally find disagreeable?

Kleist and the Theatrical Perspective

The theatrical myth of the intelligent machine centres on the marionette and the marionette-like actor. The playwright Heinrich von Kleist explores this myth in a celebrated essay, "Über das Marionettentheater",[17] in which he argues that the combination of human operator and mechanical actant leads to a quality of dance unattainable by the human dancer. Kleist's theory focuses on the interaction (dialogue) of the puppeteer with the puppet. This interaction he describes as a "line (*Linie*)" along which the "soul of the dancer (*Seele des Tänzers*)"[18] moves. The geometric metaphor of the line is reinforced by an arithmetical analogy:

Vielmehr verhalten sich die Bewegungen seiner Finger zur Bewegung der daran befestigten Puppen ziemlich künstlich, etwa wie Zahlen zu ihren Logarithmen.[19]

The analogy with logarithms points to an underlying proposition in the essay that there is a meta-language of dramatic expression which functions to specific performances as logarithms function to real numbers. This relationship in turn establishes the preconditions for the dialogue between puppet and puppeteer through which communication with the audience takes place. Communication with an audience is therefore a function of communication between puppet and puppeteer.

The next step in Kleist's logic is to claim that through the meta-language of expression the mechanical representation of the dancer's soul can in fact transcend the limitations of any individual dancer:

er getraue sich zu behaupten, dass wenn ihm ein Mechanikus, nach den Forderungen, die er an ihn zu machen dächte, eine Marionette bauen wollte, er vermittelst derselben einen Tanz darstellen würde, den weder er, noch irgendeinen anderer geschickter Tänzer seiner Zeit . . . zu erreichen imstande wäre.[20]

The claim is analogous to Pygmalion's, that the statue he makes will be a woman superior to any the normal processes of nature can conceive. The claim is similar to that made for expert systems, that the elicitation of expert knowledge and its representation in mechanical form will in fact create a degree of expertise superior to that achievable by any human equivalent. Strikingly, what has emerged in expert systems as perhaps the central problem, discerning what it is experts actually know, is regarded here by

Kleist as merely circumstantial in the representational process. This process, again distinct from current philosophies of expert systems, proceeds on the assumption that the human expert will still be involved with the system once it is established.

Kleist's most problematic observation, however, lies in the suggestion that such involvement is at its most powerful and convincing when it is least conscious. The advantage the puppet has over the human is that because it has no individual consciousness it never indulges in "decoration", the addition to the aesthetic ideal of a personal, and superfluous, signature of individual style:

Denn Ziererei erscheint, wie Sie wissen, wenn sich die Seele (vis motrix) in irgendeinem andern Punkte befindet, als in dem Schwerpunkt der Bewegung.[21]

There is both a cultural and a physical aspect to this argument. In a cultural sense, Kleist is attacking one of the props of romanticism, the belief that intelligence and creativity are in some sense the product of a single, inspired mind rather than of a culture as a whole or a group within a culture. The attack is of great significance, for in our own time, we are still caught in a definition of creativity and intelligence that attributes the successful generation of new ideas and concepts to single thinkers. Kleist's implicit plea is for a recognition that what and how we think is a function of our behaviour, which is itself a social and cultural construct. In such terms, the way we approach machine intelligence could be radically affected, since it would permit a definition of machine intelligence to be contextual: a machine is intelligent if it is part of the creative environment of a creative group. If we were, as individual researchers, prepared to abandon the notion of ideas as personal property, we would by consequence enhance the possibility of generating intelligent machines.

In a physical sense, Kleist observes, rightly, that beauty and effectiveness in performance are functions of the overall physical state of the performer as reflected in their sense of balance, or centredness. This in turn leads to an equation of the physical state of centredness with the psychological or spiritual sense of being "centred", meaning a total concentration on the act of performance. Kleist sees such an equation, however, not as Schiller would, as a forward movement through the dialectic of form and content towards the imaginative free play of a transcendent, rule-free aesthetic, but rather as a falling back into that state of grace from which we fell:

"Mithin", sagte ich ein wenig zerstreut, "müsslen wir wieder von dem Baum der Erkenntnis essen, um in den Strand der Unschuld zurückzufallen?"
"Allerdings", antwortete er, "das ist das letzte Kapitel von der Geschichte der Welt".[22]

The consciousness to which we must "fall back" is one based on utter simplicity and economy of effort. This has profound implications for any definition of expertise, for it suggests that expertise at its most powerful is deeply embedded and unconscious, rather than declared and conscious knowledge. In practice, the mere process of knowledge elicitation from human intelligence, on which machine intelligence is of necessity based, violates this principle by attempting to make explicit that which cannot be articulated. The result is an inevitable degradation from human to machine intelligence, a degradation we experience in practice every time we use "intelligent" machinery. What this may imply is that robots are good at what they do purely because they are not intelligent enough to get bored or tired. If they were, they might malfunction.

Büchner: Testing the Intelligence of the Mechanical Human

Not the least of the many innovative insights of Georg Büchner, whose short creative life set the agenda for modern European theatre, was into the nature of machine intelligence. At the close of his comedy, *Leonce und Lena*, the nature of human identity is bound up with the identity and psychology of machines. Valerio, the valet and Pygmalion, brings in two androids. His speech is of such significance it merits full examination:

Valerio: Aber eigentlich wollte ich einer hohen und geehrten Gesellschaft verkünden, dass hiermit die zwei weltberühmten Automaten angekommen sind und dass ich vielleicht der dritte und merkwürdigste von beiden bin, wenn ich eigentlich selbst recht wüsste, wer ich wäre, worüber man übrigens sich nicht wundern dürfte, da ich selbst gar nicht von dem weiss, was ich rede, ja auch nicht einmal weiss, dass ich es nicht weiss, so dass es hoechst wahrscheinlich ist, dass man mich nur so reden lässt, und es eigentlich nichts als Walzen und Windschlaueche sind, die das alles sagen. *Mit schnarrendem Ton*, sehen Sie hier meine Herren und Damen, zwei Personen beiderlei Geschlechts, ein Männchen und ein Weibchen, einen Herrn und eine Dame. Nichts als Kunst und Mechanismus, nichts als Pappendeckel und Uhrfedern. Jede hat eine feine, feine Feder von Rubin unter dem Nagel der kleinen Zehe am rechten Fuss, man drückt ein klein wenig und die Mechanik laueft volle fümfzig Jahre. Diese Personen sind so vollkommen gearbeitet, dass man sie von andern Menschen gar nicht unterscheiden könnte, wenn man nicht wüsste, dass sie Pappdeckel sind; man könnte sie eigentlich zu Mitgliedern der menschlichen Gesellschaft machen.

(*Leonce und Lena*, III, 3)[23]

At one level, the speech is a comic rewriting of Hamlet's famous disquisition on the nature of man: what a piece of work is man – a clockwork masterpiece, or a tortured consciousness? Even were man consciousness, that proposition is so circumscribed with doubt that he can never be sure he is not in his human form merely the representation of the imagination of another form of consciousness altogether. This line, which Büchner pursues to its deliberate absurdity, is also curiously consoling in AI terms: for perhaps our worries about defining consciousness in machines needs to be contextualized by our inability to come up with any satisfactory definition of consciousness of any kind. Do we even need to know?

At another level, the speech pursues the analysis initiated by Kleist of the relationship between acting and mechanical behaviour. There is a sense that acting, which means speaking the lines of another, wearing the clothes of another, entering the consciousness of another, is akin to mechanical intelligence, the human body being merely a vehicle for the consciousness of another. The implication is significant: by analysing the process by which an actor assumes the consciousness of a role one may discover how a machine may be programmed to assume human intelligence. Büchner's analyses of this process of transformation of consciousness is perhaps the reverse of what one might expect a humanist to suggest: that the actor is the more

human the more he faces the machine within himself. And only by accepting the mechanical in himself can he assume the consciousness of another.
For AI this might mean that we shall be able to transfer our intelligence to a
machine at the point when we accept and understand the extent to which
our own intelligence is already mechanical.

The reason why Büchner may have thought this way lies in his other area
of skill in anatomy and physiology. Büchner will have studied and come to
admire the sheer brilliance of mechanical man, man the machine. And this,
for all his protestations of annoyance with Descartes, shows his debt to
Cartesian thought, on which in his brief life he spent a considerable amount
of time and about which he wrote at some length.[24]

Descartes and the Dissociation of Sensibility

In his *Discourse on Method*, Descartes addresses himself to the issue of man
the machine in positive terms: "Some persons will look upon this body as a
machine made by the hands of God, which is incomparably better arranged,
and adequate to movements more admirable than is any machine of human
invention".[25] In some respects, this is just how any performer sees his own
body, as a machine to be programmed by training and rehearsal to perform
tasks of great beauty and complexity. Such a perception may offer an
explanation as to the popularity of the performing arts in Western culture in
that they are widely, if intuitively, perceived to be in harmony with, rather
than in opposition to, a computer-based hi-tech culture. Until a machine can
choreograph like John Cranko or sing like Maria Callas, can it be thought of
as intelligent? The tests Descartes himself proposes are not dissimilar:

> But if there were machines bearing the image of our bodies, and capable of imitating our actions
> as far as it is morally possible, there would still remain two certain tests whereby to know that
> they were not therefore really men. Of these the first is that they could never use words or
> other signs arranged in such a manner as is competent to us in order to declare our thoughts to
> others . . . as men of the lowest grade of intellect can do. The second is, that although such
> machines might execute many things with equal or perhaps greater perfection than any of us,
> they would, without doubt, fail in certain others from which it could be discovered that they
> did not act from knowledge, but solely from the disposition of their organs.[26]

Yet there is a dimension to this problem which Descartes leaves unexplored
– one that theatre challenges us to consider. When an actor learns a role, in
a sense he has become the mechanical representation of another. He walks
and talks like someone else, someone who is not himself. In a strict sense,
his knowledge base of the person he represents is determined by his lines,
his part. But clearly this is far from being the true extent of his knowledge.

Below the surface of his words lies the subtext of the actor's role, a
potentially limitless body of tacit knowledge about what the character is like,
what he would do in certain situations, even though the explicit text does
not address itself to such situations or problems. When audiences witness
the performance of such roles, they experience a continuous paradox, that
the actor whom they are watching both is and is not the person he repre-

sents. He succeeds with his audience in as far as he convinces them that he is who he says he is. At a mechanical level, this means convincingly walking and talking like his character. But he also succeeds, as Brecht pointed out, when he does not collapse his own identity into that of his role's, but rather maintains an objectifying, defamiliarizing distance.[27]

The significance of this paradox is that it offers a model of how to resolve the problem of the "dissociation of sensibility" raised by T.S. Eliot in his reflections on post-Cartesian culture,[28] while at the same time offering a more sophisticated test than Descartes' as to the nature of machine intelligence. Eliot's theory traces back to the origins of modern science in the writings of Bacon and Descartes a fatal dissociation of sensibility in our culture, a divorce of *ratio* from *passio*, failure to resolve the dialectic of reason and emotion in faith. This cultural divorce is effected by the principle of systematic doubt embodied in Cartesian thought.

I have suggested in this essay that we might test the intelligence of a machine according to its ability to feel human to the user, to replicate the experience of dialogue with a human mind. But this argument needs qualification in the context of my arguments about theatre. We do not expect of actors that they so utterly identify with their roles that they surrender entirely to them. We accept an undeclared simultaneity of identity and distance. The same, by analogy, may be true of machine intelligence. We may be able to accept the spirit of our intelligence. We may be able to accept within the spirit of our aesthetic definition of performing intelligence that a machine both is and is not like human intelligence. In this way, the aspects of human intelligence defined as emotion and reason may not be in opposition on the same, dynamic, problem. To act a role intelligently I must be able to master the logical demands of the role and its feelings, and in rehearsal I will pursue feelings with a developed and logical technique. The foundation of this technique, as Brecht saw it, is observation, in itself the foundation of scientific method.[29] The test of its success, as Stanislavski saw it,[30] lies in the psychological credibility with which it is communicated. These perspectives equate in a single person, the performer, but halves of the knowledge transfer contract examined by Bacon. The performer seeks rhetorically to persuade his audience of the verity of his performance role while at the same time uses his intelligence constantly to observe and analyse whether the role stands up to his own scrutiny of it. If it does not, how can he plausibly present it to his audience?

The theory of a dissociation of sensibility in fact embodies two distinct fears for culture: on the one hand, a dehumanized and mechanical culture, premised entirely on reason, and logic threatens to fall off into the realms of Mr Spock in *Star Trek* ("too logical by half") or the excesses of Orwell's *Nineteen Eighty-four*. On the other, it threatens a dissociation of a different, hermeneutic, kind – that described by Bacon as a contract of error. The preoccupation with post-Cartesian mythology has been with the former problem, with such issues as whether machines can be intelligent or have souls or be compatible with humanist values. But in this essay I have examined a number of writers' attempts to explore, and perhaps explode, the myth of the intelligent machine by analysing not only the fear of the mechanical and robotic, but also the area covered by Bacon's phrase, the contract of error. On the face of it, the Pygmalion myth is about the vanity of human wishes in trying to achieve in a machine what is impossible in human beings – perfection.

But behind this problem lies another, the principle of the contract of error. It is in the very nature of Pygmalion's purpose in creating Galatea that he fail – fail not in the absolute sense of not being able to achieve anything remotely like human characteristics in his perfect machine, but in a relative sense. Pygmalion's failure is his own, and is intrinsic to the knowledge transfer process. Galatea cannot, by definition, become what Pygmalion expects; for the act of becoming human in itself is an act of distancing from any other human identity. Galatea's humanness is tested in the extent to which she throws off Pygmalion's intentions for her.

In a sense, the implications of this for machine intelligence are more profound than fears of a robotic culture. For it means that the real test of AI is whether or not the program is capable of devising a strategy for refusing the commands of the operator.

The Turing Test

How does such a definition match with Turing's test of machine intelligence? There are two aspects to Turing's presentation which immediately relate to this strategy of negation. First, the manner in which Turing himself thinks is transparent from the way he writes; secondly, the premise of the simulation game he proposes as a test of intelligence is negation.[31]

As he develops the terms of his simulation. Turing displays, even stylistically, that he is developing his idea as he writes. The approach is intuitive: "The ideal arrangement is to have a teleprinter communicating between two rooms. Alternatively the questions and answers can be repeated by an intermediary."[32] It is almost as if he is circling the problem, thinking out loud, waiting to find a crack in it that will offer a solution. Yet the intuition is empirically schooled; he presents a hypothesis – "the ideal solution" – but immediately negates it – "alternatively" – the subtext revealing that he has already thought up unstated objections to the supposed ideal. The game itself is about negation or deception: "It is A's object to cause C to make the wrong identification."[33] If a machine is to be able to replicate Turing's own method it must be capable of logical elision and deception. Both these properties involve negation; logical elision means the conscious suppression of intermediary working stages, something no machine can yet do, and deception means negating truth. It is hard enough trying to make a machine think, but consider trying to make a machine think untruthfully.

The strategy of negation continues: Turing accepts that an intelligent machine will not have to look like a human: "We do not wish to penalize the machine for its inability to shine in beauty competitions."[34] Possibly not, but if my argument about the power of the Pygmalion myth in our times holds, then this is, at a subconscious level perhaps, exactly the sort of absurd requirement we do make of an intelligent machine. The next negatory step is to exclude from the game all forms of simulated intelligence other than that within a digital computer.

This leads him to substitute the opening question "Can a machine think?" for another one: "Are there imaginable digital computers which would do well in the imitation game?"[35] The equation of "think" with "do well" is particularly interesting here, because for the first time the logic has taken a positive turn, thought being equated with success, and success not normally being seen in negative terms. There is, however, a negative side: "The original question 'Can machines think?' I believe to be too meaningless to deserve discussion."[36] Turing's conclusion here I dispute; but the point is not my disagreement, but rather that his thought, his intelligence, has worked primarily to negate the very question that started his thought process. He has therefore not only answered the question, but in turn challenged the hermeneutic basis of that question. This is what Galatea does in coming to both life and consciousness: she takes the terms of Pygmalion's creativity, refutes them and then challenges their very existence. We might express this in another way: a plausible test for the intelligence of a computer could be its power to negate the need for computers, including itself.

Turing's next move is to summarize and contest nine arguments against machine intelligence, the double negative strategy building the basis of a positive case. I do not propose to rehearse all his arguments, but one is of central concern – the question of consciousness. Turing quotes Jefferson's objection to the intelligence of machines: "Not until a machine can write a sonnet or compose a concerto because of thoughts and emotions felt, and not by the chance fall of symbols, could we agree that machine equals brain."[37] Turing dismisses this position as solipsistic. This may be so, but the Pygmalion and Galatea myth is also about solipsism and none the less tenacious for that. But the issue is not solipsism as such but rather whether there is a way of resolving Turing's weakly argued dismissal of Jefferson's objections while at the same time not insisting that a machine be potentially a Shakespeare before being declared intelligent (a test that would exclude almost the entire human race).

The way I suggest is in the theatrical model of a double, or simultaneous consciousness. That is, we can accept simultaneously that a machine both is and is not intelligent. We are capable of accepting that when we look at a computer we do not deny the possibility of intelligence because it does not have skin, while at the same time acknowledging that the intelligence it possesses is intrinsic to the role it performs rather than to itself. That is to say, the computer convinces itself of its intelligence as an actor convinces us of the intelligence of the role he plays, by doing it well within a designated context. When an actor is on stage he is representing another. When a computer we have programmed works for us, it is as if its mind were that of another. What both actor and computer will always rely on, however, is our imaginations, our intelligences, as audiences and users, to fill out the gaps in their own.

Why do I think Turing might accept this view? Because having examined all the arguments against machine intelligence, Turing admits "that I have no very convincing arguments of a positive nature to support my views".[38] This, rhetorically, is equivalent to the actor's admission of his own fictitiousness; he only exists because the audience is prepared to admit that the existence of his role is possible. Turing's paper only exists as long as the reader is prepared to entertain the possibility of machine intelligence, whatever the objections against. But given that possibility, the mind is remarkably fertile in enacting an equivalent reality.

In effect, therefore, my case is simply put. Turing at the end of his paper argues for beginning the quest for machine intelligence by trying to make a machine think first like a child before it thinks like an adult.[39] My suggestion is that we rather try to replicate "theatrical" intelligence in machines, the intelligence of role and context as a perhaps more promising line of enquiry.

This whole chapter is based on conjecture, but as Turing said: "Conjectures are of great importance since they suggest useful lines of research."[40]

Notes

1 Descartes, René (1912) *A discourse on method*, transl John Veitch. Everyman, London, p 46.

2 Boden, Margaret (1977) *Artificial intelligence and natural man*. Harvester, Hassocks, p 4.

3 Boden, *op cit*, p 55.

4 See, for example, the emphasis of such journals as *Artificial Intelligence*. On a general point of nomenclature, it may well be appropriate to count expert systems as non-intelligent in a Cartesian sense and term all such engineering applications expert systems.

5 Aristotle, "The Poetics". In: Ross WD (ed) *The Works of Aristotle translated into English*. Oxford, 1928, vol XI, p 1448a.

6 Aristotle, *op cit*, p 1449b.

7 Quotations from William Shakespeare, *Henry V*, Taylor G (ed). Oxford, 1982.

8 *The letters of John Keats*, Forman MB (ed). Oxford, 1931, vol I, p 77.

9 Schiller, Friedrich, "Über die ästhetische Erziehung des Menschen in einer Reihe von Briefen". In: *Gesammelte Werke in fünf Bänden*. Reinhold Netolitzky (ed), vol 5, pp 319–429. See especially: "Denn, um es endlish auf einmal herauszusagen, der Mensch spielt nur, wo er in voller Bedeutung des Worts Mensch ist, und er ist nur daganz Mench, wo er spielt". For Schiller there is a close interdependence of the concepts of play and machinery, the whole work being shot through with the metaphor of the state as a machine, threatening constantly to break down.

10 Schiller, *op cit*, p 427. "Das Schöne allein geniessen wir als Individum und als Gattung zugleich, d.h. als Repräsentanten der Gattung". See p 330 and other parts of p 427 for different aspects of the same theme.

11 From Marlowe, Christopher, "The tragical history of Dr Faustus". In: Ridley MR (ed) *Marlowe: plays and poems*. Everyman, London, 1955, p 122.

12 Bacon, Francis, *The advancement of learning and New Atlantis*. The World's Classics, London, 1951, p 30.

13 Shaw, George Bernard, *Pygmalion: a romance in five acts*, Laurence DH (ed). Penguin, London, 1986, *passim*.

14 Bacon, *op cit*, p 162.

15 *Pygmalion*, p 103.

16 *Pygmalion*, p 148.

17 Kleist, Heinrich von (1810) "Über das Marionettentheater". In *Heinrich von Kleist Sämtliche Werke Mit einer Einführung* von KF Reining, (Wiesbaden, nd), *passim*. The original was published in four sections in the *Berliner Abendblättern*, 12–15 December, 1810.

18 Kleist, *op cit*, p 982. The italicization is Kleist's own.

19 Kleist, p 982.

20 Kleist, p 982.

21 Kleist, p 983.

22 Kleist, p 987.

23 From Büchner, Georg *Sämtliche Werke und Briefe. Historisch-Kritische Ausgabe mit Kommentar*, Werner R Lehmann (ed). Hamburg, 1972, vol 1, p 131.

24 See Büchner, *op cit*, vol 2, pp 137–226. Büchner's disagreement with Descartes comes down to his objection to Descartes' reliance on God as the source of reason. "Gott ist es, der den Abgrund zwischen Denken und Erkennen, zwischen Subject und Objekt ausfüllt, er ist die Brücke zwischen dem *cogito ergo sum*, zwischen dem einsamen, irren, nur einem, dem Selbstbe-wusstseyn, gewissen Denken und der Aussenwelt. Der Versuch ist etwas naiv ausgefallen, aber man sieht doch, wie instinctartig schaff schon Cartesius das Grab der Philosophie abmass; sondebar ist er freilich wie er den lieben Gott als Leiter gebrauchte, um herauszukriechen." vol 2, p 153. On this basis, only the existence of God in a machine will make it intelligent.

25 Descartes, p 44.

26 Descartes, pp 44–45. See Turing's summary of "The argument from consciousness" in his paper *Computing machinery and intelligence*, see below, note 31.

27 The theme runs through Brecht's work, but see for example *Bertolt Brecht, Schriften zum Theater 3, 1933–1947*. Frankfurt, 1963, pp 155–205.

28 See Eliot TS, "The metaphysical poets". In: Kermode F (ed), *Selected prose of TS Eliot*. London, 1975, p 64.

29 On Brecht, *op cit*, pp 182–183. Brecht makes his own connection between theatre and science: "Die Wissenschaftler machen das seit langer Zeit", he comments in regard to the *V-Effekt*.

30 The theme is dominant in Stanislavski's work but see Constantin Stanislavski, *Creating a role*, transl Elizabeth Reynolds Hapgood. London, 1963, pp 83–84.

31 Turing, AM (1963) "Computing machinery and intelligence". In: Feigenbaum E and Feld-man J (eds) *Computers and thought*. New York, pp 11–35.

32 Turing, *op cit*, p 12.

33 Turing, p 11.

34 Turing, p 13.

35 Turing, p 19.

36 Turing, p 19.

37 Turing, p 22.

38 Turing, p 30.

39 Turing, p 32.

40 Turing, p 19.

Chapter 9

Humans and Automatons

Magnus Florin

I am an automation; my soul has been taken from me.

Georg Büchner

This comment on Julian Hilton's article discusses two of his examples: the writings of Georg Büchner, and Henrik von Kleist's *On Marionette Theatre*. While Hilton finds Büchner's parallel between people and automatons to be positive and constructive, Florin sees it as helpless and constrained. While Hilton sees in Kleist a connection between utopian dance and artificial intelligence, Florin focuses on the aspects of Kleist which do not permit a given conclusion or moral to be arrived at.

I should like to add certain commentaries to Julian Hilton's chapter, "Theatricality and Technology: Pygmalion and the Myth of the Intelligent Machine". I have been thinking in particular about a couple of the texts he raises, and since I have seen other things in them than he does, I feel concerned to try to record my own readings of these texts.

Julian Hilton's premiss is that we can study theatre and drama in order to acquire a view of fundamental questions that have consequences affecting our relationship to technology, knowledge and thought – and to AI. I am not concerned to argue against this premiss: aesthetic reflection includes questions of interpretation and representation, problems that also belong in the discussion of AI. I am also stimulated by the way in which he tests the question of understanding and knowledge in the new technology against the special *double awareness* involved in watching theatre (identification and distance).

Julian Hilton, however, goes further than I would dare in seeing parallels, consequences, and lessons to be learned when he discusses the issues of AI on the basis of certain selected texts: Bernard Shaw's *Pygmalion*, Heinrich von Kleist's *On Marionette Theatre*, and Georg Büchner's *Leonce and Lena*. His argument is inventive and often challenging; the same is true of the way in which he relates to the subject such thinkers as Shakespeare, Diderot, Schiller, Plato, Bacon, Descartes and Keats. The latter's locution "negative capability" is fruitful not only in aesthetics.

It is not my intention to comment upon his entire article; I will restrict myself to two of the examples from which he quotes, namely the texts of Büchner and Kleist.

Julian Hilton, who is an expert on Büchner and has published *Georg Büchner* (Macmillan, London, 1982), quotes the remarkable passage in *Leonce and Lena* where the servant Valerio, in the chanting voice of some market crier, presents the prince and princess as "those two world-famous automata", whom "it would be impossible to tell from ordinary people, if you didn't know that they are only papier-mâché". Valerio lists a whole succession of capabilities that these creatures are said to possess, for example that they "talk like gentlefolk", "get up at a specific time of day", "dine and retire to bed at regular hours" – they are also "educated, since the lady knows all the new opera arias, while the gentleman, as you see, wears cuffs".

Julian Hilton finds in this passage a parallelization between "mechanical intelligence" and "acting" (the saying of another's lines, dressing in another person's clothes, assuming the awareness of a role). He sees an implication in this: the more an actor opens himself to what is mechanical in him, the more human he becomes. And as an extension of this argument, Julian Hilton arrives at a further implication for AI – only when a person accepts and understands the extent to which his own intelligence is mechanical can he transfer his intelligence to machines. Julian Hilton thus reads something positive and constructive into Büchner's analogy, and considers it to be based in the fact that the author came to admire the mechanical aspect of man through his studies in anatomy and physiology.

Büchner, in his works, returns again and again to the motif of man as machine. This, indeed, is striking. But what, for him, are the characteristic attributes of this theme? I believe that such phenomena as mechanization, automation, masking, drama, games and dancing are for Büchner the signs of human existence in terms of ennui, impotence and emptiness. In his dramas *Woyzeck*, *The Death of Danton* and *Leonce and Lena*, his narrative *Lenz* and his published letters, life (society, humankind) appears as a determinated game, forced to repeat itself immutably and for ever. "I feel I see a frightening immutability in human nature, in people's relationships with each other, an implacable power of command granted to all and to none", writes Büchner in a letter to his fiancée Minna in March 1834. "The individual is just a fleck of foam on the wave, greatness a matter of pure chance, the dominion of thought a game with dolls, a vain wrestling with an iron law, to be aware of the highest that is possible, [but] to master it – impossible!"

The game that Büchner describes has nothing free or unrestricted about it; on the contrary, it presents the image of an existence that is helpless and constrained. When dance, song and spectacle appear, portrayed or alluded to, in Büchner's texts, they have a shadow of desperation and humiliation. In *Woyzeck*, Marie's dance with the drum major continues in Woyzeck's head – "Faster, faster! Just hear the fiddles and the pipes", he shouts, alone out in an open field – and after the murder he dances at the inn: "Faster now, faster, all of you!" By a stall in the market a child is dancing to the sound of a barrel organ and the song of an old man [woman], "On earth we have not long to stay, We know it all too well!"; after this a market busker appears, with a dressed-up monkey and a trained horse. The stage, the dance-floor, the playground – these, in Büchner, are the places of over-lordship and impotance. "We are marionettes, manipulated with threads by unknown powers", runs a passage in *The Death of Danton*, in which death by execution is simply "a little dance with a hempen noose around your neck". In April 1833 he writes in a letter to his family that what the princes have granted the people is nothing but "silly children's toys". In *Leonce and Lena*, the prince and heir to the throne Leonce urges his mistress Rosetta to dance, dance to pass the time. Rosetta dances alone, singing of how her feet would rather rest in the ground than move any more. Her dance is far from any Utopia, far from the visionary and absolute interpretation of dance that one can find, for example, in Friedrich Schiller, William Blake, Friedrich Nietz-sche or Paul Valéry.

The kingdom in which *Leonce and Lena* is set satirically reflects the society in which Büchner lived. Leonce embodies the young, romantic nobleman, with nothing to occupy him, and filled with theatrical agony at the meaninglessness of the world. The dance signifies for him, as for Schiller & Co., a mental state – but his dance-floor is empty, the steps of the dance have given way to a sad morning after. "My head is an abandoned ballroom, a few withered roses and torn streamers left on the floor, worn fiddles in a corner; the last couple have taken off their masks, and are looking with a deathly tired gaze into each others' eyes." The arena for unconfined being has changed shape, to become the haunt of a tedium which in *Leonce and Lena* is portrayed satirically, but without the accustomed protective distance of satire – and this tedium returns time and again in Büchner's texts as a fundamental condition of life in the shape of a binding spell, even in the most subjective wordings to be found in his letters. "Oh, this disgust, this terrible disgust", exclaims the eponymous character in *Lenz*, a hallucinatory portrayal of an episode, in the 1770s, in the life of the romantic poet Jacob Michael Reinhold Lenz. "How boring", yawns Danton, at the laborious prospect of getting out of bed. The whole gist of our feeble modern society's existence "is simply to avoid the most appalling accidie"; let it "go to hell", it can "just as well die out", writes Büchner in a letter. "Am I an idler? Am I without an occupation? How sad", says Leonce.

In his novel *Lucinde* (1799), Friedrich Schlegel praised idleness as the "breath of life of innocence and rapture". In Büchner, this atmosphere, so beloved of the romantics, has been thinned out. All that remains is the boredom, the tedium. And what does it hold? I would venture to claim that it is, in Büchner, a reflection of life's mechanization and automation. When, for example, Leonce, together with the court jester Valerio, spends his days lying on a bench and spitting on a stone 365 times, the meaninglessness of this activity corresponds directly to his predestined activity in the kingdom: he lives only to succeed his father. Love in this kingdom has for his part no other function than to secure the happy marriage between himself, Prince of the Kingdom of Popo, and Lena, Princess of the Kingdom of Pipi. It is in this light that Valerio demonstrates the young couple to the court as auto-mata, humanoid mechanical constructions. His demonstration constitutes an inauguration of Man as Mechanism. But the human being as subject, as an interpretive, perceptive, responsible, experiencing, thinking, dialogue-sustaining creature – that human being is absent, and barred entry. Do

Büchner's texts not shout aloud a complaint that what is human appears only as an irreparable lack?

It is true, as Julian Hilton notes on the subject of Kleist's *On Marionette Theatre*, that a puppet can be man's superior – as can AI. The perfect automata in *Leonce and Lena* have their relatives elsewhere in literature. I am thinking here of the humanoid mechanical doll that Tintomara, in Almqvist's *The Queen's Jewel*, is ordered to imitate. And in E.T.A. Hoffman's story *Der Sandmann*, the young Nathaniel falls in love with Professor Spalazani's daughter Olimpia – who subsequently proves to be a perfect automaton, with the ability to move, indeed dance, speak, play the piano, and sing; a whole repertoire of behaviour that in the life of society makes her impossible to distinguish from a living person. The terrible thing about Olimpia is not, as it is with Mary Shelley's monster, the fabricative but the imitative element. While Frankenstein's assembled being is a distorted body that has by chance acquired primitive feelings, Olimpia is a perfect creature without a soul. When Nathaniel, ignorant of the truth, dances with her, he finds that he – who had fancied himself as a dancer – is getting out of step with the mysteriously exact creature before him. A counterpart to this is to be found in H.C. Andersen's story *The Nightingale*, in which a real nightingale sings a duet with an artificial nightingale resembling it. Things didn't turn out well, Andersen records, "since the real nightingale sang in its own fashion, and the artificial bird worked by wheels". Since the artificial nightingale is immutably perfect and indefatigable, it wins the approval of the court and the Emperor, and the living bird flies for the time being off to the green forests.

The imitative capacity that characterizes Almqvist's "mannequine", Hoffman's Olimpia and Andersen's artificial bird is striking in the creatures presented by Valerio: they are "so perfectly constructed that it would be impossible to tell them from ordinary people, if you didn't know that they were only papier-mâché". However, the perfection of such automata in their construction and capacity seems to have one flaw: they lack any shortcomings. It is man's faults that make him human. He is uncertain, unintentional, mutable, interpretive, feeling his way. The automaton stands outside history and experience, cannot be influenced, is beyond the pace of time. At the end of his play, Büchner has Lena and Leonce point to their future in a sort of paradisiac state in which time has ceased to move: "We'll have all the clocks broken, forbid all calendars, and count the hours and months only by the chronology of the flowers, their blooming and giving fruit. And then we'll set up burning-mirrors around our entire kingdom so that it will never more be winter, and in summer we will be on a level of Ischia and Capri, and we can walk, all year round, among violets and roses, laurels and oranges." The French philosopher Emmanuel Levinas, in his book *Le Temps et l'Autre*, has described Plato's Republic as a world without time, a state in which people fail to encounter either history or their neighbour, neither the "other thing" nor the "other person". For Levinas such an absolute state is a sort of Utopia of horrors, an utterly monological society. Such a society is described by Büchner. "Ah me! Think if one might some time be someone else!", exclaims Leonce, and I do not think his author was laughing at him. Büchner lends shape to what is uniform and already concluded, and he also returns constantly in his text to the inexorable circle of time, and how it is locked in mechanical repetition. "Will the clock never stop?" is the question posed in *The Death of Danton*, in the face of this mechanism. And it receives no other answer than that given at the end of the play: "Everything is moving, the clocks tick, the church bells chime, the people throng in crowds, the water runs" – the automatic process continues. "I run almost as evenly as a Schwarzwald clock", writes Büchner in a letter. When August Strindberg, in his preface to *Miss Julie*, speaks of the "automaton" in terms of stopping, immobility and adjustment, he was polemizing against what he believed to be a false psychology of character in middle-class drama. His naturalism, he hoped, would better correspond to what people are actually like. Büchner's view is rather that the automatics and mechanics present a true picture of the way in which people live. He perceives this in himself. "They all turned their death masks towards me, their glassy eyes, waxy cheeks, and when the whole machinery was cranked into motion, the limbs began to twitch, the voice came rasping, and I heard the eternal barrel-organ tune waltzing around, and saw the little reels and needles jumping and twisting inside the sounding box – oh, how I cursed the whole concert, the barrel organ, the tune" (letter to his fiancée, March 1834).

We find in Büchner a strong desire to some day find a human face behind the stiff masks, a You in the throng. But no opening appears to present itself. In precisely the letter just quoted, the encounter with a You appears possible only in the form of a negation: "Your shadow hovers constantly before me, like the fleck of light you see when gazing into the sun."

In this situation, does art, or writing, become for Büchner a sanctuary beyond the range of constraint, a place where the promise of something different can be fulfilled?

We can seek the answer to such a question in what he has written. In a number of passages he violently attacks not only the mechanization of life but also that of artistic presentation. Lenz launches on a tirade against the so-called "Ideal" poets who claim to be portraying real people but create only "wooden puppets". Camille in *The Death of Danton* speaks scornfully of artists who carve out some marionette, who produce simple wooden copies. And in a letter Büchner writes that the "Ideal" poets never created anything but marionettes with sky-blue noses. What Büchner is demanding, instead of all this, is an art that portrays life as it is. Yet how far can this demand be fulfilled? *Lenz* contains an interesting passage in which the poet portrayed sees, out in the countryside, two girls sitting on a stone, the one plaiting the other's hair. Lenz reflects: "One would have wished to be a Medusa, so that one could have turned a group like this to stone, and gone and fetched other people to see." The Medusa, in classical mythology, is a monster whose gaze turns people to stone. When the poet Paul Celan was awarded the Büchner Prize in 1961, he spoke in his address of Büchner's aesthetic demands and drew attention precisely to this passage alluding to the Medusa. Is not this scene, Celan asked, with its desire for enchantment, a scene to be added to the others in Büchner's texts which take up the life-depriving force of art, its property of stepping out from life rather than point to it? "Just see what art can achieve!" declaims the busker in the market, of his dressed-up monkey.

And in the recurrent portrayals of the artist's wooden puppets and marionettes, Celan sees not a criticism of the art of others, but a deeper reflection on the subject of art as such. Art itself can be seen as imitative and false, with the connotation of its sister words artfulness and artificiality. Lenz's poetic fantasy is said compulsively to turn nature and people upside down, so that everything becomes "dreamlike, mechanical". What, Celan asks, is Büchner seeking, somewhere between mechanics and the abyss? Perhaps, he answers, an artless, art-free existence. If we take seriously Leonce's desire to be someone else, then it is with a view to an existence beyond the territory of the masks, the automata, the mechanics. In Büchner's works, however, it is impossible to find any indication of the places where such an existence might appear to us. Behind the illusion, the play-acting, there is Nothing. It is this Nothing that Valerio worries about finding beneath the series of masks. Woyzeck can find no firm ground; he stamps on it, listens, and breaks out: "Hollow, you hear? It's all hollow down there!" And for Leonce too, this Nothing is the last and absolute resort, the only thing to be found behind all the fabrication. "I dare hardly stretch out my hands, as in a confined cabinet of mirrors, for fear of banging into everything, so that all the beautiful images fall to the ground in small pieces, and I stand there eye to eye with the naked wall behind."

Let us now return to Julian Hilton's argument. He found in Georg Büchner a conception of the fundamentally mechanical in human life. He also found an implication in this, namely that in order to transfer knowledge to machines we should accept and realize that human intelligence (understanding, thought) is mechanical.

I agree that Büchner, in his works, associates man and his life with mechanics, and the properties of a machine. But I see no given implication in this, no insight that we could "inject" into any discussion of the problems and possibilities of AI. Büchner's attitude is far too radical, black, doubting, and insusceptible to reason for that. It offers no space for any human "artless" life between Nothing and mechanics. It is turned away from us. It forms a "via negativa".

Am I capable of making any point from this, my reading of Büchner? If so, it would primarily be that it is difficult to use a literary text instrumentally as an example: Büchner's own words resist any attempt to place them neatly in any argument.

The other text I have been thinking about among those quoted by Julian Hilton is Heinrich von Kleist's *On Marionette Theatre*. This is one of Kleist's most commented texts, but it has by no means been clarified.

A marionette is a wooden doll manipulated by a puppeteer who steers his dolls with his hand above their heads. Metaphorically, people or states are also manipulated by other people or states. Or, as in Bo Bergman's poem, by the lord of the halls of Heaven, who tugs at strings in their thousands to the human lives down there. But in Kleist's *On Marionette Theatre*, the "I" of the narration is confronted with one "Herr C" who assigns an entirely different meaning to the puppet on its string. Since my commentary demands some familiarity with the text, I will first present it, giving some quotations. It starts with the narrator speaking: "When, in the winter of 1801, I was staying in M, I happened to meet in a park one evening one Herr C. He had been employed for some time at the town's Opera House as *premier danseur*, and was much appreciated by the audience. I said that I was surprised at having seen him a number of times at a marionette theatre . . . Herr C told me that he greatly enjoyed the pantomime of these dolls, and he hinted that a dancer who was really concerned to advance in his art had a great deal to learn from them."

The text then records how Herr C explains the principle of the movements of the marionettes, and their handling. He says that the right play of lines can be achieved only if the puppeteer puts himself in the marionette's centre of gravity, which is to say if he himself dances. But at a further stage, Herr C believes, it is conceivable "that this last vestige of soul could be eliminated, so that the dance of the marionettes could be ascribed to the mechanical world". When the narrator expresses his surprise over the great attention Herr C pays to these wooden dolls, he receives the answer that it would be conceivable for "a mechanic" to be capable of producing a marionette that would surpass any living dancer. Using terms from algebra and geometry, Herr C describes the suprahuman world of the marionette: numbers and logarithms, lines and ellipses, hyperbolas and asymptotes, functions of the first and second degree. The ideal doll, according to Herr C, could achieve, thanks to the correct placing of its points of gravity, a perfect mobility, pliability and harmony. Such perfection, it emerges from his description, is beyond all human categories, since man, by reason of his constricting self-awareness, can never achieve the grace of the doll. Grace "appears in its purest form in the body that either possesses no self-awareness at all or else an infinite self-awareness, which is to say either in the marionette or in God".

The further import of Herr C's argument now emerges: the marionette, by its dance, recalls the pristine and innocent life of the earthly Paradise, before the Fall into constricting self-awareness. To man, however, such non-knowledge is irrevocably lost – he can only regain Paradise by a supreme degree of self-awareness, and the purely formal language of motion seen in the marionette suggests such a final step in man's development. Since "Paradise is sealed", says Herr C, we must "seek the earth over to see if it is perhaps possible to enter it from the back".

The "I" of the narrative lends Herr C his agreement, by adding a pregnant example of his own to Herr C's reference to the Tree of Knowledge. He describes how a young man of natural litheness and captivating charm completely lost his grace in the very moment that he began to observe it in himself, and tried to create it in himself: he became self-aware and therefore constricted, just as Adam and Eve were ashamed when they saw that they were naked. Herr C comes back at him with a further example: he had once encountered his absolute master in fencing, an art in which he was otherwise brilliant. His so superior opponent was no human being but a bear, who with a fixed gaze saw through his feints and parried his thrusts. Natural grace had revealed itself in the beast – and in this, Herr C believed, lay the connection to the marionette, the body without self-awareness, and to God, the infinitely self-aware. The text concludes with the following lines: "'When it comes down to it,' I said rather absently, 'we must eat once more from the Tree of Knowledge to fall back into innocence'. 'Exactly', replied Herr C, 'That is the final chapter in world history'."

We move in the romantic interpretation of dance as a Utopia, in which the highest forms of thought merge into pure movement, liberated from the weight of matter. We are close to Schiller's high aesthetic state in which knowledge has reached a second stage, beyond frustrating self-awareness, a world free and fair which he himself likened to a well-executed ballroom dance, in which complicated figures and steps are performed with the most elegant ease. But we are also moving within the dream of an exact and rational language, with logic and mathematics as the optimal forms of thought, and possible for man to achieve. Herr C's marionettes, with their purely formal movements, are related to Leibniz's calculus, Cartesian algebra, the calculating machines of Pascal and Charles Babbage, and the thinking machine of Alan Turing. There is a basis for Julian Hilton's linking together of Utopian dance and artificial intelligence. He goes even further and reads into Kleist a "moral" with consequences on the discussion of AI: the emphasis on the nature of supreme knowledge as a "fall" into the utmost simplicity, paradisiac innocence, hints that the highest knowledge, the expertise, should involve an ennobling reduction to simple rules in a minimum of systems, rather than increasingly complicated and unsurveyable rule systems.

Is such a reading of Kleist's text right? Are other interpretations possible that can also be of interest in the context of AI? Let us look at *On Marionette Theatre* a little more closely.

The final words delivered by Herr C (an affirmation of the conclusion that we must eat once again of the Tree of Knowledge in order to fall back into innocence, and his assertion that this will be the final chapter in world history) appears to be a consequence of the various steps of the preceding argument. Most interpreters of Kleist have found it to be a sort of aesthetic manifesto in the spirit of Kant and Schiller, in which the writer has achieved a balanced attitude that affords room for the true, the beautiful, and the exalted.

Such a position is in violent contrast to what Kleist wrote during his lifetime. His dramas, such as *Penthesilea*, are not edifying, and his narratives, such as *Michael Kohlhaas*, defy any clear interpretation. However, I do not wish to argue with the assistance of other texts than the one now in question.

To start with we can say that most interpreters of *On Marionette Theatre* have been far too hasty in identifying C's attitude with Kleist's own, and have thus far too lightly interpreted its moral as reflecting Schiller's or others' romantic and Utopian aesthetics. This is the view of literary critic Paul de Man, who in his essay "Aesthetic formalization in Kleist's *On Marionette Theatre*" has offered his own interpretation of Kleist's dialogue – and the text is very much a dialogue, even if it is related by a narrator in the "I" form, and not as an essay in which the author himself "argues" and "claims". Here, however, as in other literature, such a distinction must be maintained between the writer and the narrator/narration/characters in the narrative. Paul de Man finds in the dialogue a composite attitude, working at various different levels, towards the aesthetic theory and towards art and literature in general in their relations to human life. Like Paul Celan in the case of Georg Büchner's Medusa scene, Paul de Man notes the violence connected with art. He finds, in his reading, how the examples accompanying the dialogue all contain strong measures of brutality. Herr C makes a reference to "the mechanical legs that English artists have made for unfortunates who have lost their own", and claims that those fitted with such artificial limbs can move with "a grace that astonishes every thinking person". Does this strange example really argue for the thesis of the grace of marionettes? Does it not rather, asks Paul de Man, argue for mutilation for the sake of art? An act of assault takes place also in the example quoted by the narrative "I" of the young man who lost his grace due to his self-awareness. Having started, after a bath, to dry his feet, he noted the resemblance to a famous statue of a youth pulling a thorn from his foot. The young man thus himself becomes aware of the similarity. But what suddenly deprives him of grace is in fact by no means his self-awareness, but the fact that the narrative "I", who has also in fact seen the resemblance, rejects it and laughs aloud. Nor does the example of the fencing bear seem to correspond that well with the thesis pursued by Herr C. Let me quote from the relevant passage. Herr C tells us:

> He raised his right paw ready to strike. He stared me in the eyes – this was his fencing position . . . The bear executed a brief movement with his paw, and parried the thrust. I tried to deceive him by feints, but he never moved . . . The gravitas of the bear helped deprive me of my senses. Thrusts and feints were alternated and the sweat ran down me – but in vain! . . . Do you believe this story?

It is now time for the narrator/"I" to react to this remarkable tale:

> "Absolutely," I exclaimed cheerfully. "I should think it might happen to anyone, the way your tale seems so credible. In your own case, I find it even easier to believe."

While, in the case of the marionettes, it is their weightlessness and gracious, free movement that is underlined, the bear emerges as a heavy-limbed spoiler of the game, an immobile creature that ignores all the playful feints, is uniquely grave and serious, and puts an end to the play of swords.

Paul de Man draws our attention to the gap between Herr C's thesis of the marionette as the sign of a divine form of consciousness and the examples he lists in his argument. He further shows that their force as evidence is, to say the least, uncertain, by reason also of the contradictory nature and doubtful credibility. It does not immediately appear possible that people with false limbs are capable of calm, gracious movements such as will amaze any thinking person. There is something too prosaically ordinary, not to say comical, about the statue quoted of someone removing a thorn from his foot, and serving at the same time as an exalted example of grace. That the story of the bear also tends to the absurd is only emphasized by Herr C's question "Do you believe this story?" and the cheerful compliant response "Absolutely", which also continues "I should think it might happen to anyone", which is undeniably questionable.

The closing words telling us how we can achieve grace by recovering, via complete self-awareness, a paradisiacal grace appear, as we have said, to come as the consequence of a chain of evidence. But what is the "result" if the evidence is lame and the argumentation is dissolved into independent passages whose connection with each other is uncertain? And when the "I" of the narrative, confronted with Herr C's final point, is described as replying "rather absently", some scepticism would seem to be in place as to whether this is Kleist's history of maturity towards the attainment of a harmonic aesthetics.

On Marionette Theatre, which it has been claimed portrays the idea of an exalted free dance, beyond the weight and coercion of ordinary life, comes instead, in Paul de Man's reading, to present the picture of a mechanical dance, marked by death and mutilation. Paul de Man shows how Kleist's dialogue makes visible the suppressed obverse side of the aesthetics of ideals.

But Paul de Man does not stop at this point. He moves on, shifting his perspective. In his interpretation, he relates the mechanization and formalization that according to Herr C characterizes the dolls to the actual necessary condition for reading and writing. Paul de Man is a reader who lets the movements innate in the text appear, lifting up into the light the elements that have been placed in the shadow so that what is alleged can suddenly change shape; he captures the random and capricious oscillation of a text's movements, their manifold meanings at different levels, their luxuriant ability to make sense. He reads, attentively, in the field of tension between the path of the actual and the path of the expressed. He is very awake to the ambivalences and shifts that exist in that the formal side of the text, the signs, bears no absolute relation to the content. Above all, he has an ability to show how a text, at some point, begins to talk about itself, about the conditions necessary for its own existence.

The story of the bear that was said to be able to read its opponent's soul thus becomes, for Paul de Man, a scene describing the encounter between the writer and reader. The writer no longer has the power over what he has written. And the entire essay *On Marionette Theatre* becomes for Paul de Man a story of the hazards of reading and writing. When the Queen of the Amazons, in *Penthesilea*, has bitten to death her beloved Achilles, she is struck during her monologue by the heavily charged verse couplet "küssen/bissen"; she has confused kissing with biting. Paul de Man sees precisely such overlays and tensions between grammar and rhetoric, between the linguistic, material aspect of the sign and the semantic side of its content, as the basic source from which literature draws its energy. And in this sort of aesthetic formalization, he sees the true potential of reading and writing, divorced from any ideologizing and absolute aesthetic formalization of, for example, Schiller's type. The true, the beautiful and the eternal are words, not beautiful and eternal truths.

I like Paul de Man's interpretation – above all perhaps because it shows that Kleist's text is difficult to read, and invites further interpretations. Julian Hilton's interpretation also presents me with a challenge, but to some extent in another way – I notice how I object to his conclusion that the discussion in *On Marionette Theatre* leads to an insight that has consequences in the discussion of AI.

Is there, then, some "truer" lesson to be learned from reading Kleist's dialogue?

Not "truer" perhaps. But possibly a different view from the usual one relating to formalization and artificiality. The discussion on formalization usually excludes the thinking human being, the unique case, the leeway, the open and unexpected. What Paul de Man shows in his essay is that Kleist's text can be read as a live portrayal both in and of the art of writing and reading. And the movements of writing and reading occur precisely by virtue of the formalization that is included in language. If the art/the writing/

the sign (we recall here Büchner's example of the Medusa) has a fixative and eternally preservative capacity in relation to what is described/signified, then this capacity involves at the same time a linguistic energy that guarantees a tension betwen semantics and linguistics, between rhetoric and grammar. It is impossible to establish any symmetrical relationship between the written and the read.

How best can I conclude this commentary on Julian Hilton's readings of Büchner's *Leonce and Lena* and Kleist's *On Marionette Theatre*? Perhaps by omitting to offer, myself, any pregnant conclusion regarding the contents of these texts, and to what they are addressed.

But perhaps, also, by expressing one cautious "point": that if these texts in any sense possess *per se* an import, a knowledge, it is knowledge of another type than that of calculation, the Turing machine, and the expert systems: that the knowledge (reflection, interpretation, thought) that Büchner's and Kleist's texts set in motion is of a type that arises in a complicated and composite field of effects and repercussions between the written and the read, the signs and the signified, the interpreters and the interpreted; that this knowledge is far from the knowledge that can be portrayed in formal and logistic sets of rules. Julian Hilton would surely agree with such a "point"; nor is it in any strict polemical position to his own conclusions. My commentaries should rather be seen as a note in the margin, an attempt to reflect a little further from the premiss of readings that constitute a challenge.

Translated by Struan Robertson

Chapter 10

Turing's Paradox

Bo Göranzon

Two important articles by Alan Turing are discussed: *On Computable Numbers with an Application to the Entscheidungsproblem* (1936) and *Computing, Machinery and Intelligence* (1950). The second article demonstrates the conviction of the unlimited possibilities of the "universal machine" to imitate human intelligence. But, paradoxically, the first article points out the limitations of such machines. The distance between the ability of machines and the intelligence of humans is to be found throughout the development of computer technology.

The Turing Machine

In 1936 Alan M. Turing, the English mathematician, wrote an article which became a classic. This article, entitled *On Computable Numbers, with an Application to the Entscheidungsproblem*, contains the basic mathematical theory for computers.[1]

Is there a clearly defined method which will determine whether mathematical assertions are provable? David Hilbert called this "das Entscheidungsproblem".[2] The method needs to be a predictable mechanical process which may be applied independent of human judgement or choices. Gödel has demonstrated that mathematics can never be complete. There are always mathematical assertions of which it is impossible to determine the degree of truth.[3] The problem of decidability deals with this phenomenon.[4]

A well-researched biography of Alan Turing called *The Enigma of Intentions* by Andrew Hodges, the English mathematician, inspired Hugh Whitemore, the writer, to put the documentary material into the form of a play called *Breaking the Code*.[5] The theories of Alan M. Turing are presented with, among other things, ideas from Gödel's theorem and Hilbert's theories on the ability of mathematical models to reproduce. In *Breaking the Code*, Turing makes the following statement:

Gödel's theorem is the most beautiful thing I know. But the question of decidability was still unresolved. Hilbert had, as I said, thought that there should be a single clearly defined method for deciding whether or not mathematical assertions were provable. The decision problem he called it. "The Entscheidungsproblem". In my paper on computing numbers I showed that there can be no one method that will work for all questions. Solving mathematical problems requires an infinite supply of new ideas. It was, of course, a monumental task to prove such a thing . . . People had been talking about the possibility of a mechanical method, a method that could be applied mechanically to solving problems without any human intervention or ingenuity. Machine! – that was the crucial word. I conceived the idea of a machine, a Turing machine, that would be able to scan mathematical symbols – to read them if you like – to read a mathematical assertion and to arrive at the verdict of whether or not that assertion is provable . . . My idea worked . . . It was a machine of the imagination, like one of Einstein's thought experiments. Building it wasn't important; it's a perfectly clear idea, after all (and it has given me the opportunity to reword Hilbert's question like this: is there a machine of this kind – a Turing machine – which can test all mathematical assertions? And the answer is, of course, no, as is very easily demonstrated).[6]

From 1936 Turing's work was a contribution to the field of the mathematical theory of proof with theorems and symbols that were only accessible to experts in that special field. In the spring of 1947 Alan Turing met Norbert Weiner, the founder of cybernetics. They discussed the fundamental ideas of cybernetics.[7] At the beginning of the 1940s Norbert Weiner published an article which marked the starting point of cybernetics.[8] The article emphasizes that the principles of comparative analysis applied in examining the behaviour of humans can also be applied to machines. However, according to the authors, a functional study reveals major differences. Thus we need not ascribe to machines characteristics such as consciousness or motive, or intentions which are identical with the human constitution.[9] There is an important point to remember here. Cybernetics opened the door to the field of research known as artificial intelligence as it was developed in the 1950s.[10]

In his book *Materia, Machines, People*[11] Norbert Weiner developed the cultural aspects of his formal mathematical presentation of cybernetics. It aimed both to examine the possibilities of the machine in areas which had previously been regarded as purely human areas, and to warn of the hazards of selfish exploitation of these possibilities. One of the central themes of this book is language. In his research programme for the development of cybernetics Weiner places considerable emphasis on understanding what it is that characterizes human communication.[12]

Turing – The Paradox

In his work on the Entscheidungsproblem Turing introduced a view which was discussed forty years later by Hubert Dreyfus, the American philosopher, namely: *What Computers Can't Do*.[13] Dreyfus' book is a critique of the claim made in artificial intelligence research that it was possible to reproduce all forms of human knowledge.

The paradox is that Alan M. Turing also made this claim in an article entitled *Computing, Machinery and Intelligence*, published in 1950.[14] In this article, which was written in a popular vein and was polemic in tone, Turing advanced the theory that it was his conviction that computers should be able to imitate human behaviour perfectly and that this goal would be attained by the year 2000.[15]

One of Turing's fundamental themes is the computer as a universal machine, which Whitemore has explained as follows in the play *Breaking the Code*:

It's true computers are often used to do calculating because they calculate very quickly – but computer programs don't have anything to do with numbers. A colleague of mine has got our computer to hum tunes – it once sang "Jingle Bells". We've even got it to write love letters! Doing calculations, humming a tune, writing love letters. These are very different tasks, but they're all done by one machine – and that's an extremely important fact about computers. A computer is a universal machine and I have proved how it can perform any task that can be described in symbols. I would go further. It is my view that a computer can perform any task that the human brain can carry out. Any task. Now you might think from what I've said that a computer can only do what it's told to do. Well, it's true that we may start off like that – but it's only the start. (We can set the computer to modify its instructions in the course of the process.) A computer can be made to learn.[16]

Alan Turing's article served as a manifesto for a group of computer researchers in the field of artificial intelligence. Andrew Hodges, the English mathematician, makes the following comment on the paradox of Turing:

Given Turing's original interest in defeating materialism, perhaps it is surprising that he himself made little of his own discovery about this absolute limitation. On the contrary, his interest was more and more on exploring what a machine could do, not what it could not.[17]

Turing's Test

Turing sees a computer as a "book of rules". The most important part of the computer is the software. If one wants to make a machine imitate human behaviour in some complicated operation, one must ask the human how the operation is carried out and translate the replies into a computer program. "This is usually called programming", says Turing.[18] He maintains that it is impossible to create a set of rules which describes the way a person would behave in all conceivable circumstances. Turing introduces a distinction between the concepts of "rules of conduct" and "laws of behaviour". He uses the term "rules of conduct" to refer to rules such as "stop when you see a red light", rules which we can act upon and be aware of. He uses the term "laws of behaviour" to mean the natural laws of the human body, such as "if you pinch him he will scream". In Turing's opinion, uncovering this kind of "law of behaviour" is an important area of research which is a theoretical basis for automating human behaviour.[19] This is an epistemological attack made by John von Neumann in his classic article *A General and Logical Theory for Automatons*:

There is no doubt that every particular phase of every conceivable form of behaviour can be described "completely and unambiguously" in words. The description may be a long one, but it is always possible to make. To deny this would imply recognition of a form of logical mysticism which is undoubtedly foreign to most of us.[20]

The 1950 article presented a method of defining "intelligence" – the so-called Turing test. A person is placed in one room and a computer in another. Both are able to communicate with the outside world but only through the medium of typewritten texts. Another person is placed in a third room and, after questioning both these "intelligences", has to decide which of them is human. Turing maintained that if the interrogator fails in his task then intelligence must be ascribed to the computer.[21]

A Difference in the Use of Computers among Different Occupational Cultures?

David Bolton develops the implications of Turing's approach in his book *Turing's Man: Western Culture in the Computer Age:*

By promising (or threatening) to replace man, the computer is giving us a new definition of man, as an "information processor", and of nature, as "information to be processed".[22]

Here, parallels are drawn between the way information is processed by the brain and the computer. The human brain has always been likened to the technology of the time. The brain has been described as a telephone network, as a telegraph and, today, as a computer. What else can it be? John Searle, the American philosopher, criticizes the choice of these metaphors in an article which discusses the epistemological foundations of "cognitivism".[23]

The basis of cognitivism is that a study of computers will teach us something about the processes by which humans solve problems.[24] The "behaviouristic trick" is to define intelligence in terms of behaviour. The ability to imitate a specific piece of behaviour is said to be "intelligence".[25]

It is this intellectual position which Joseph Weizenbaum attempts to tackle in his now classic ELIZA computer program which was intended to be a pedagogical example. He wanted to increase awareness of the limitations of computers by developing software which simulates a psychotherapist's questions and responses.[26] For Weizenbaum, the reaction was totally unexpected. The psychoanalysts who were directly affected by this application were enthusiastic. They now saw the possibility of acquiring an instrument which would shorten the waiting times for patients in psychiatric care:

If the ELIZA method proves beneficial, then it would provide a therapeutic tool which could be made widely available to mental hospitals and psychiatric centres suffering a shortage of therapists. A computer system could deal with several hundred patients an hour.
  A human therapist can be viewed as an information processor and decision maker with a set of decision rules which are closely linked to short-range and long-range goals. He is guided in these decisions by rough empiric rules telling him what is appropriate to say and not to say in certain contexts.[27]

Weizenbaum's application demonstrates that the Turing test is not satisfactory. We can be misled. This gave Weizenbaum an insight into a fundamental problem: human beings are liable to ascribe to new technology, in this case a diagnostic programme in the field of medical care, more intelligence than it has. We lose our distance. We fail to realize what the limitations are. This is a feature of the emergence of technological culture.

In a previous example on computer-aided activity in the valuation of forests, attention was drawn to the risk that computer technology can force the emergence of the precise determination of concepts and a quantification which can "kill off" qualitative aspects. The administrators, the forestry technicians, put priority on the human dialogue with the buyers and sellers of forests rather than on the possibilities of a sophisticated "dialogue" with the developed computer system.[28]

How can we understand the background to the different views these two professional categories have of computers in their work?

Disagreement on the Significance of Concepts

It is an incontrovertible fact that a systems engineer with no experience of a particular professional field lives in a different world of concepts from a person who has professional knowledge in that field.

In an example taken from a construction company which I shall describe briefly here there is disagreement on the importance of understanding a computer system.[29] Two of the actors involved, the systems engineer and the heating and air-conditioning design engineer in a construction company, live in different conceptual worlds. The systems engineer finds it difficult to produce a reliable specification. He feels he has given clear definitions of selected terms and that a few days' training in systems technology would make it easier for other designers to express their professional knowledge. Let us listen to what the systems engineer has to say:

Years of experience have developed and modified the work methods applied in the field of heating, water and sanitation engineering to suit the capacity of the human brain, and these methods are, moreover, strongly individualized. This means that the systems engineer has to listen to the views of a number of design engineers and then try to form an opinion of the methods to be applied when the superior memory and calculating capacity of computers become available.

Now there is a phase in this development which is both intensive and is a potential conflict area, that is to say the phase which is intended to convince experienced design engineers that they have to reconsider their methodology, to coordinate and adapt it to the new aids which are to be made available to them. At the same time the systems engineer is forced to question the design engineers' knowledge of what lies behind the computers which they use.

With the benefit of hindsight, I can now say that it would have been well worth investing in a few days' training in systems technology for the heating, water and sanitation design engineers who would be involved in data collection. Not to turn them into systems engineers but solely to give them a better view of the relative importance of various aspects of the systems engineers' work.[30]

The systems engineer tries to elicit information from the design engineers. He interprets the design engineers' inability to describe their work processes as an attempt to withhold important information. This is an example of *Turing's Man* in practical work:

In my efforts to chart the work methods used, I was able to observe that many design engineers who wished to appear to be professionally knowledgeable did not even know how an elementary single pipe system worked. However, professional pride prevented these gentlemen from admitting their ignorance; instead, as soon as I tried to elicit a response they began to make demagogic statements on the relativity of everything. I have often met this phenomenon when professional pride has been set at risk, and I should therefore like to recommend that all systems engineers give some thought to the approach to adopt on such occasions. Should I continue to press my victim for information which he probably does not possess, or should I accept his vaguely formulated responses and try to find the answers to my questions somewhere else? Or should I force him to admit his ignorance and then ask him to find the correct answers?[31]

A design engineer with 35 years' experience says that if the computer system is static it will become a cul-de-sac. The system must be a dynamic one, capable of dealing with new ways of solving problems. At the same time he emphasizes the importance of concentrating mainly on a discussion of the methods of evaluation, the computation principles which are built into the software. One idea at the systems development phase was to provide heating, water and sanitation design engineers with further training in a more sophisticated theory for calculations in this field as a preparatory step to the introduction of more sophisticated software.

Technology with a capital T emphasizes logic. It may run counter to everyday technology which emphasizes degrees of freedom. The link between everyday technology and technology with a capital T must be dynamic, not static. This is a crucial factor.[32]

The systems engineer in a building company had no professional knowledge in the field of heating, water and sanitation. He was a technician with the task of implementing administrative rationalization. The systems engineer was working on the basis of parallels between the information-processing capacity and the calculating capacity of the brain and a computer. His evident ignorance of the professional knowledge possessed by design engineers forces a confrontation which has serious consequences for the company as a whole. This is an example of a meeting between two quite separate perceptions of language. The position of the systems engineer coincides with an objective view of language – a dream of the exact language. The systems engineer has no professional knowledge in this particular field of engineering. An examination of the problem of fundamental conflicts rooted in different perceptions of language can help us bypass cliches such as "we have to agree on a common language".[33]

Notes

1 Turing, AM (1937) On computable numbers, with an application to the Entscheidungsproblem, *Proc London Mat Soc* (2), 42:230–265.

2 Gödel, Kurt (1986) *Collected works*, vol 1, publications 1929–1936. Oxford University Press, p 136.

3 Karlqvist, Anders (1984) Om Skapande Improvisation – några reflektioner utifrån matematikens perspektiv. In: Per Sällström (ed) *Funderingar kring VETENSKAP & MUSIK*. Royal Academy of Music series no. 44, Stockholm, p 14.

4 The author Göran Printz-Påhlson gave a penetrating portrayal in his poem "Turingmaskin", published in *Säg Minns Du Skeppet Refanaut?* Bonniers, 1984, p 96.

5 Whitemore, Hugh (1988) *Enigmakoden*. Royal Dramatic Theatre, Stockholm (translated into Swedish by Per-Erik Wahlund), p 26ff. The play is based on *Alan Turing, the enigma of intelligence*, by Alan Hodges, Counterpoint, Unwin Paperbacks, 1983, and is published in English as *Breaking the Code* by Hugh Whitemore, Amber Lane Press, 1987. A Swedish radio programme on Alan Turing was broadcast in the series "Vetandets värld" on Programme 1 on 19 July 1988. It was called "Jag vill bygga en hjärna", (I want to build a brain), and presented the ideas contained in the Andrew Hodges biography of Alan Turing.

6 As above, p 26f. Translator's note: The parts of the quote in brackets do not appear in the English text of the play; they are translated from the Swedish version.

7 Wiener, Norbert (1961) *Cybernetics, or control and communication in the animal and machine*, 2nd edn. MIT Press/Wiley, p 23.

8 Rosenbluth, Arthur, Wiener, Norbert and Bigelow, Julien (1943) Behaviour, purpose and teleology. *Philosophy of Science* 10:18–24. The interest is focused on a characteristic of theology or, in other words, "appropriate behaviour". This requires the term behaviour to be classified. In this classification "theological" is used as synonymous with "intention controlled through negative feedback". This means that a given goal gradually influences a course of events, with the aim of achieving the goal.

9 As above, pp 18–24.

10 John McCarthy coined the phrase "Artificial Intelligence" as a heading for the first research seminar at Dartmouth College, USA, in 1956. Those present included Marvin Minsky, Allan Newell and Herbert Simon. See Pratt, Vernon *Thinking machines: the evolution of artificial intelligence*. Basil Blackwell, Oxford, pp 203, 215. See also Bolton, David (1984) *Turing's man: Western culture in the computer age*. Duckworth, London, p 193.

11 Wiener, Norbert (1952) *Materia, Maskiner, Människor*. Cybernetiken och Samhället, Forum.

12 Early in his research programme Wiener established contacts with the prominent social anthropologists Margaret Meade and Gregory Bateson. See Wiener (1961) p 18.

13 Dreyfus, Hubert L (1979) *What computers can't do: the limits of artificial intelligence*. Harper Colophon Books.

14 Turing AM (1960) *Can a machine think?* Published in Swedish in *Sigma* vol 6, Forum.

15 Bolton (1984) p 12.

16 Whitemore (1988) p 56. Compare the following quote: "We may hope that finally machines will compete with humans in all purely intellectual areas. But which areas is it best to start with? That too is hard to determine. Many people think that some very abstract activity, such as playing chess, would be the best. It may also be asserted that the best thing would be to equip the machine with the best possible sensory organs and then teach it to understand and speak English. This would be the normal teaching process for children. One could point at objects and ask the machine to name them etc. I do not know which is the best solution, but one should attempt them both." From Turing (1960) *Can a machine think?* Forum, p 227.

17 Hodges, Andrew (1987) Turing's conception of intelligence. In: Gregory RL, Marstrand PK (eds) *Creative intelligences*. Francis Pinter, London, p 84. The English philosopher AJ Ayer discusses this paradox of Turing's in the preface to Bolton (1984) p XI. The most remarkable thing in this context is, however, Kurt Gödel's refutation of Alan Turing's article, *Can a machine think?* Gödel: "Expressing opposition to Turing's mechanistic view of mind", Gödel (1986) p 25.

18 Turing (1960) Forum, p 2207f.

19 In his article, Turing refers to Charles Babbage when he says that the idea of computers is an old one. Charles Babbage, professor of mathematics at Cambridge from 1828 to 1893, planned such a machine, the so-called analytical engine, but it was never completed. Even though Babbage had understood the basic principles, at the time his design did not look particularly attractive. Turing also says that Babbage's analytical engine, being exclusively mechanical in its working, helps us shake off the common prejudice of placing great importance on the fact that modern calculating machines are electrical, as is the human nervous system. As Babbage's machine was not electric, and as, seen logically, all computers are equivalent, we realize that whether we use electricity or not can have no theoretical significance. In the nervous system, chemical phenomena are at least as important as electrical phenomena. David Bolton writes: "The artificial intelligence specialist is not interested in imitating the whole man. The very reason he regards intelligence (rational 'problem solving') as fundamental is that such intelligence corresponds to the new and compelling qualities of electronic technology. Today, as before, technology determines what part of the man will be imitated." Bolton (1984) p 213.

20 Neumann, John von En allmän och logisk teori för automater. In: *Sigma* vol 6: 2194.

21 Descartes formulated a robust version of Turing's test, which we discussed in the previous chapter. The Cartesian test looks like this: before it can be judged to be intelligent, a machine must be capable of language actions and sensible actions independent of the programmer. Descartes arrived at a completely different conclusion from Turing. The difference between a

human and an animal – machine is that because he has a language a human is able to develop his thinking and the way he formulates concepts.

22 Bolton (1984) p 13.

23 Searle, John (1988) Kognitivism och datormetaforer. In: *Dialoger*, no. 778, Artificial stupidity.

24 Buttimer, Anne (1983) *Creativity and context*, Lund's Studies in Geography, Human geography no. 50. Royal University of Lund, Department of Geography, p 17.

25 Sällström, Pehr (1987) Editorial comments in *Dialoger* magazine, no. 5, Artificiell intelligens, p 4.

26 Weizenbaum, Josef (1967) *Computer power and human reason: from judgement to calculation.* Freeman, San Francisco.

27 As above, p 181.

28 Buttimer (1983) pp 14–15. See also the editorial comments in *Dialoger* no. 1, Dialogens väsen, and Denett, Daniel (1984) The role of the computer metaphor in understanding the mind. In: Pagel HR (ed) *Computer culture: the scientific, intellectual and social impact of the computer. Annals of the New York Academy of Sciences* 426: 274. The crossing of boundaries in this way was noted by Aristotle who, in *Ethica Nichomachea*, states that a sign of an educated person is that he only attempts to achieve the degree of precision in each subject that the nature of the subject permits. Using more exact terms than the subject permits may lead to a false description of reality. This theme is also discussed in Degerblad, Jan-Eric (1988) Planering och yrkeskultur. Council for Building Research, and in Göranzon, Bo (1985) Bildning vid systemutveckling. En förståelse av den mänskliga dialogens karaktär. In: Ahlin J (ed) *Konsekvenser för industri – och arbetsmiljöplanering av ny informationsteknolovi, Projektrapport 3.* Department of Architecture, Stockholm Institute of Technology, pp 101–120. This essay is a comment on *Systems development: a presentation of four different views.* Development Programme for New Technology, Work Organization and Work Environment, Work Environment Fund, 1984. See also Göranzon, Bo (1991) *The Practical Intellect*, Unesco, Paris, and Springer-Verlag, London.

29 It may be of interest to introduce a distinction between two main categories of computer applications. One group comprises software for simple calculations of the type previously done by manual calculation, while the other group comprises software intended for problems for which there were no manual calculation methods or which are too lengthy and cumbersome when done by these methods. Thus the two groups aim at either a quantitative improvement of the competence of an occupational group, or a qualitative improvement of the competence of an occupational group. Folke Peterson, professor of heating, water and sanitation technology at the Stockholm Institute of Technology, who introduced this distinction, now says that the use of software to improve qualitative competence requires: the staff to have a high degree of professional knowledge (in the case of heating, water and sanitation technology, they must have a good engineering qualification); and the ability to analyse the results of the calculations. Peterson puts particular emphasis on the second of these two factors. Without profound knowledge of the physical processes that underlie the software (the models), and the ability to analyse the calculations, they will give virtually none of the information it is possible to get. In addition to a thorough knowledge of heating, water and sanitation technology, the technicians of the future in this field will have to have a strong aptitude for analysis. The main use of the computer is to perform complex technical calculations.

30 This quote is from Göranzon Bo (ed) (1983) *Datautvecklingens Filosofi. Tyst kunskap och ny teknik*, Carlssons, p 46.

31 As above, p 48.

32 As above, p 48.

33 See, for example, Janik, Allan (1988) Reflexioner över teknologi, konflikter, medborgarskap och mod. In: *Dialoger* no. 7–8, p 44.

Translated by Struan Robertson

Section IV:
Dialogue and Translation

Parody and Double-Voiced Discourse: On the Language Philosophy of Mikhail Bakhtin

Lars Kleberg

In his studies of literature and the philosophy of language Mikhail Bakhtin sees parody not as a criticism of an original but a "dialogical" dimension in literature closely related to intertextuality. The parody is not seen as a "form"; it is a function – a relation between one text and another. All language is related to other language and the deeper consequences of Bakhtin's thinking bring one face to face with the impossibility of monological, monolithical approaches to literature and other human expression – to all forms of culture. Man is characterized by ambivalence, dialogue and multiplicity.

What is a parody? How do we recognize one? Let us listen to a voice of authority, *The Oxford Dictionary* (second edition, 1989):

A composition in prose or verse in which the characteristic turns of thought and phrase in an author or class of authors are imitated in such a way as to make them appear ridiculous, especially by applying them to ludicrously inappropriate subjects; an imitation of a work more or less closely modelled on the original, but so turned as to produce a ridiculous effect.

Classical examples of parody in accordance with this definition can be found, for example, in Dwight Macdonald's anthology *Parodies* (London: Faber & Faber 1960). Let us take a closer look at the following fragment:

Sunday is the dullest day, treating
Laughter as a profane sound, mixing
Worship and despair, killing
New thought with dead forms.
Weekdays give us hope, tempering
Work with reviving play, promising
A future life within this one.
Thirst overtook us, conjured up by Budweisserbrau
On a neon sign: we counted our dollar bills.
Then out into the night air, into Maloney's Bar,
And drank whiskey, and yarned by the hour.
Das Herz ist gestorben, swell dame, echt Bronx.[1]

For the intended readers of this parody, there could be no doubt that the target of the parody is the introduction to T.S. Eliot's *The Waste Land*:

April is the cruellest month, breeding
Lilacs out of the dead land, mixing

Memory and desire, stirring
Dull roots with spring rain.
Winter kept us warm, covering
Earth in forgetful snow, feeding
A little life with dry tubers.
Summer surprised us, coming over the Starnbergsee
With a shower of rain; we stopped in the colonnade,
And went on in sunlight, into the Hofgarten,
And drank coffee, and talked for an hour.
Bin gar keine Russin, stamm' aus Litauen, echt deutsch.[2]

The text by "Myra Buttle" fits exactly into the traditional definition of parody as a ridiculing imitation of the style of a work, through which the latter's content is being degraded.

At the same time, there is something awkward about this definition of parody. There are formal criteria that allow us to recognize a poem in iambic pentameter, a tragedy or a short story. An advanced computer would probably be able to classify texts in accordance with these criteria and perhaps even generate such texts if it had a sufficiently detailed set of rules. *But how do we recognize a parody?* It cannot be described independently or classified as part of a group of similar texts, i.e. a genre. That is, it would of course be possible to classify *Sweeney in Articulo* as a poem, in which case it would fall into precisely the same category as *The Waste Land*. This would, however, mean that the very quality we are attempting to delineate, the quality of parody, would be lost. In this descriptive system, the parody is an elusive shadow or a kind of "double" stalking a text or class of texts with which it overlaps and yet from which it is distinguished. Without its prototype *The Waste Land*, *Sweeney in Articulo* ceases to be a parody. Thus when we read it as a parody, i.e. in a meaningful way, we are reading not one text, but two simultaneously.

Parody is therefore not a form, but rather a relation between one text and another; it is a *function*. It was thus described by the Russian formalists in the 1920s with critics like Viktor Shklovsky and Yuri Tynyanov at the fore. They paid a great deal of attention to the parody as a literary phenomenon indicative of a crisis, symptomatic of the breakdown of an established formal system, style or school. They studied parody as the lever in the process by which a new stylistic development wrests the power from an old one. Take, for example, the battle of the romanticists against the classicists. In the parodies of the young romantics the forms of classicism were "laid bare", shown to be clichés, and forced to abandon their hold on the centre of the literary canon and retreat toward the peripheries (where they were, incidentally, soon joined by the clichés of the romantics, when they were, in turn, attacked by the next generation). The formalists drew attention to the function of the parody in the perpetual war being waged between old and new. Yet while the formalists did make the parody visible, they also reduced it to the rank of saboteur or private in the perpetual battle between old and new, centre and periphery.

Parody has a very different status in the philosophy of literature and language developed by Mikhail Bakhtin, a contemporary and fellow countryman of the formalists. To Bakhtin, the fact that *when we read a text we are actually dealing with two or more texts* is not a quality peculiar to the parody, making it unique, or an elusive shadow or saboteur. Just the opposite.

Mikhail Bakhtin is generally considered the main source of inspiration for contemporary research on intertextuality which, greatly oversimplified, considers a work of literature not as one fixed point but as the juncture of various contexts. Bakhtin spoke not of intertextuality, but of "dialogue" and "dialogicity".

For Bakhtin, as for Martin Buber, with whose work he was very familiar, dialogue is a basic philosophical concept, in fact the fundamental concept. In an essay on intertextuality and the concept of dialogue as it is used by Buber and Bakhtin, the Swedish critic Mona Vincent writes:

> How do they use dialogue in their theories of linguistic utterances?
>
> They see language as the bearer of the experience of the subject and the relation between an interpreting subject, and the world of phenomena is maintained. All reality is interpreted reality. The subject endows the world with meaning while simultaneously being the source and origin of all meaning. The units that structure a literary text are semantic units, in which every utterance is *directed* and *intentionally determined*.[3]

I will now attempt to exemplify Bakhtin's view of language and then indicate the ways in which this view leads to a conception of parody as central to literature and even to culture in the wider sense of the term.

In his *Problems of Dostoevsky's Poetics*, Bakhtin gives a very simple example, consisting of two sentences:

> *"Life is good"* and *"Life is good"*

From the point of view of logic or grammar, these sentences are identical. But if we assume that they are uttered by two different subjects, then we are dealing with two different utterances: "Life is *good*" and "Life *is* good". To a logician or grammarian, the sentence is identical with itself. But to a philosopher or linguist who considers every utterance to be directed and intentionally determined, as Mona Vincent says, these are two different utterances in a dialogical relationship (provided they are uttered at the same place and time). The second is a response to the first, a confirmation, a query, or an ironic pique – depending on the intention underlying the two utterances. In intentional space there is no repetition.

In order to become dialogical, according to Bakhtin, the logical and semantic relationships pertaining in a given sentence "must be embodied, that is, they must enter another sphere of existence",[4] become a dynamic utterance giving expression to the position of its author. Bakhtin goes on to state that there may be a dialogical relationship not only between utterances, but also permeating any given utterance or even individual word "the moment two voices meet there, in a microdialogue".[5]

For an actor, of course, this is no news. Actors work continually with words inhabited by various, often contradictory, intentions. On the other hand, it has taken nearly fifty years for literary theory and linguistics to realize the consequences of Bakhtin's concept of dialogue, presented in his book on Dostoevsky in 1929. Yes, for literary theory *and* linguistics. Bakhtin's concept of dialogue is in no way limited to the smallest building blocks of language:

> dialogic relationships are also possible between language styles, social dialects, and so forth, insofar as they are perceived as semantic positions, as language world views of a sort, that is, as something no longer strictly within the realm of linguistic investigation.[6]

In his book on Dostoevsky, Bakhtin applies his theory of "dialogicity" to literature, particularly the novel. Bakhtin asserts that in a novel there are actually no monological, univocal words or utterances. Every utterance is full of intentions: the words are "inhabited", they can hold other words, they are words *about* words. Particularly important forms of intentional or dialogical language are stylization, imitation of foreign styles, and polemical stylization or parody.

Thus, in Bakhtin, a parody is not a particular kind of literary work, but rather a mode in which the dialogical receives special emphasis. An individual word, a phrase, an utterance, a character, a course of events or a whole work may be guided by parodic intention. Later, in the context of his 1930s study *Discourse in the Novel*, in which the ideas from his Dostoevsky book are further pursued, Bakhtin says:

> Except in those cases where it is grossly apparent, the presence of parody is in general very difficult to identify (that is, difficult to identify precisely in literary prose, where it rarely is gross), without knowing the background of alien discourse against which it is projected, that is, without knowing its second context. In world literature there are probably many works whose parodic nature we do not even suspect. In world literature in general there are probably very few words that are uttered unconditionally, purely single-voiced.[7]

Bakhtin deals with the tradition of the parodic novel beginning with Apuleius via Cervantes and Rabelais, Sterne and Diderot, Gogol and Dostoevsky, through to Thomas Mann in several contexts. In his book on Rabelais, written in the 1930s but not published until 1965, he relates the parodic novel to the popular carnival culture.

Bakhtin's book on Rabelais is a remarkable work, written in the midst of the terrors of Stalinism as a celebration of laughter, the anarchy of the popular festival, fun and games and blasphemy: creative chaos. It contained a tremendous challenge to the monolithic, instinct-denying, totalitarian culture of Stalinism:

> True ambivalence and universal laughter does not deny seriousness but purifies and completes it. Laughter purifies from dogmatism, from the intolerant and the petrified; it liberates from fanaticism and pedantry, from fear and intimidation, from didacticism, naiveté and illusion, from the single meaning, the single level, from sentimentality. Laughter does not permit seriousness to atrophy and to be torn away from the one being, forever incomplete. It restores this ambivalent wholeness.[8]

But above all, Bakhtin's book on Rabelais is a work with a revolutionary theoretical value of its own. Not only because it places the works of Rabelais into a tradition and a context of cultural history, showing the "dialogical" nature that permeates individual words, phrases and images, but also and primarily because it reconstructs the ambivalent nature of the carnival in a way that has affected almost every work on popular culture written in the last decade, in both east and west.

Let it suffice to cite one element of the Bakhtinian reconstruction: the ambivalent nature of the carnivalesque culture. The fopperies of the carnival, its grotesque practical jokes, its role-switching, are a celebration of death and chaos that permits the reincarnation of life and cosmos. The ultimate aim of the profanation of all that is sacred is to maintain the distinction between the sacred and the profane, rather than to do away with it. A culture requires this dynamism, the double modality. A culture which is incapable of blasphemy is equally incapable of sanctity.

In his book, Bakhtin shows that it is from this cultural ambivalence, this double-voicedness, that the parodic novel has gleaned its nourishment, from the ancient Greeks to modern times. Actually, Bakhtin does not deal with twentieth-century literature, either in this book or elsewhere. There are several explanations. The most obvious is that if Bakhtin had gone into the literature of the twentieth century he would have had to deal explicitly, and not only implicitly as he does, with Soviet literature and the exceptionally monolithic and monological cultural model of socialist realism. It must be kept in mind that although authors like Mikhail Bulgakov were Bakhtin's contemporaries, Bulgakov's *The Master and Margarita*, like Bakhtin's book on Rabelais, was not published until twenty-five years after it was written.

Many of Bakhtin's followers have, however, dealt with contemporary literature. One example is Bertel Pedersen, whose *Parodiens teori*[9] (*The Theory of Parody*, carnivalesquely subtitled *Teoriens parodi*, *The Parody of Theory*), anyone with an interest in the subject at hand has good reason to examine. It is a work well deserving of translation for a wider audience.

Pedersen pursues intertextuality, showing how nearly every great contemporary work of literature, including Joyce's *Ulysses*, Mann's *Doctor Faustus*, and Eliot's *The Waste Land*, not to mention the theatre of the absurd or the works of Borges, Nabokov and Gombrowicz, are examples of parody in the extended sense of the term in which Bakhtin uses it. According to Pedersen, the mode of parody *is* the mode of modern literature, indeed of modern times. And from behind this literature and this way of reading it, Nietzsche, with his huge moustache, can be seen hovering with an awesome, bellowing laugh.

The reader of Pedersen's book may be tempted to wonder whether there is any great work of contemporary literature, art, theatre or music that is *not* parodic. It is evident that we have come a long way from the dictionary definition of parody as a ridiculing imitation of a work by contrast between high style and low contents. Instead, parody has become an ambivalent mode, in which high and low are indissoluably united in dialogue, in which we cannot have one without the other, and the only sure thing is that tragedy and comedy are two sides of the same coin. The question that gains increasing importance, then, is the question of context, of which perspective we adopt.

Leszek Kolakowski, the Polish philosopher, has written a fable that may be read as a comment on the critical situation which arises when anything and everything may be a parody.[10] He tells us that in the country of Lailonia there once lived a man named Ajio who discovered one day that he was growing hunchbacked:

The hump, in the meantime, continued to grow, and it grew with increasing speed. The various parts of the body which branched out of it were forming themselves more clearly and beginning to take on definite shapes. . . . Hardly had there been time to look around before the hump became a fully developed human figure. And this figure was simply a second Ajio, as like the first as two peas in a pod. Apart from the fact that it was joined to the first Ajio's back, they were identical. It also began at once to talk.[11]

Yet this was not the worst of it. While the first Ajio was a quiet man of integrity, his double was a cruel man who showered criticisms and curses on everyone. And even worse: he claimed to be the real Ajio, and shouted at the gentle Ajio, crying: "Just look at that – the hump wants to be human!... Excise that hump before I burst with rage."

The physicians, who had long puzzled over the problem, had now made up a hump powder which, if taken three times daily, would get rid of humps in a matter of days. As the real, good Ajio wept silently, his malevolent double got hold of the hump powder. The medicine did work, and soon there was only one Ajio. Only Ajio's young son could see that what was left was not his father but the cruel hump.

But the worst was yet to come. Cruel Ajio began to terrorize the inhabitants of the town, accusing them of being hunchbacks or at least of being humps, who had managed to do away with their human beings. He, Ajio, was the only human being left. What happened then? Well, the people of the town took to the hump powder, and in the wink of an eye they began to become hunchbacked.

and by the time people had realized this, it was too late. Everyone had gown doppelgänger-humps, which, as in the case of Ajio, immediately began to insist, screaming loudly, that they were the real people and the things on their backs mere humps.[12]

These humps were just as cruel, insolent and prone to yelling as Ajio. In the end they declared that they had had enough of being hunchbacked and did away with their human doubles by taking the hump powder.

This was how there came to be, in Lailonia, a town of humps where there was not a single human being. The only one who refused was Ajio's little son. He left town dreaming that he would return one day and give the humps what they deserved. But, the story ends, he was full of grief.

Now isn't that an awful story? Doubles are upsetting, but doubles with no originals are really far worse.

Let's return to the parody. Let us, in fact, return to the very word "parody". It is, of course, a Greek word, as is *dialogue*, that double word. *Para* denotes alongside, and *ode* denotes song: Song alongside, sidesong; on its own it does not exist. It is the slave in the triumphal chariot, the fool in the funeral train.

As we have seen, the Russian formalists thought of parody as a crisis phenomenon, signalling the fact that a style or genre was being pushed out of the centre of literary action. We often encounter the idea that parody is generally a late-occurring phenomenon, a mode that builds on the loss of innocence. A parody comes into being when it is no longer possible to be serious; in some people's opinion it is even a phenomenon of decadence.

Marx writes in *The Eighteenth Brumaire of Louis Bonaparte* that Hegel's comment that all events in world history occur, so to speak, twice, required the following detailed explanation: "the first time as tragedy, the second time as farce". We might also say: "the first time as tragedy, the second time as parody". Milan Kundera seems to be an author virtually possessed with this thought. All his protagonists are driven by the idea of revenging a tragedy in their lives. Yet they always fail. The joke they would like to play on history always backfires on them; the tragedy is repeated as a farce. The gods or God has abandoned them.

This, according to Kundera, is also how the parodic novel arose, a tradition in which he is deeply rooted and of which he considers himself the ultimate defender. For Kundera the contemporary parodic novel begins with Cervantes' Don Quixote, in which the crusade from the courtly tradition is "repeated as a farce" under the silent sky of the new age:

> As God slowly departed from the seat whence he had controlled the universe and its order of values, told good from evil, and given a sense to each thing, then Don Quixote came out of his mansion and was no longer able to recognize the world. In the absence of the supreme arbiter, the world suddenly acquired a fearsome ambiguity. The single divine truth decomposed into myriad relative truths shared among men. Thus was born the world of the Modern Era, and with it the novel – the image and model of that world – sprang to life.[13]

Kundera celebrates the novel but is still longing to see a new beginning. Not only his protagonists, but he himself appears to be battling with the dream of being able to vanquish history. But the tragedy just keeps repeating itself as a farce. And when the farce repeats itself, the vacuum appears, a gaping abyss. The other side of that coin is nostalgia, the dream of the return of the pastoral state of innocence.

In actual fact, though, the farce is just as old as the tragedy. At the theatre in Athens, a satyric drama was performed after the three tragedies. The parody is not an effort to reconcile man with the loss of the sacrosanct, not solace for the death of the gods, but rather a prerequisite for solemnity. Shakespeare does not "mix" the comic and the tragic. The comic and the tragic were both there from the beginning, as two sides of the same coin, as the two aspects of dialogue.

Mikhail Bakhtin shows that every culture, every language presupposes this double modality, the ability to translate the comic into the tragic and vice versa. In this perspective parody is neither a marginal phenomenon, nor a late one. Parody is the retention of the double modality, the modality which cannot be translated into an unambiguous language in which "life is good" and "life is good" mean one and the same thing.

Notes

1 "Myra Buttle" (1960) *Sweeney in Articulo*. In: Macdonald D (ed) *Parodies*. Faber & Faber, London, pp 219–220.

· 2 Eliot TS, *Collected Poems 1909–1935*. Faber & Faber, London, 1951, p 61.

3 Olsson, Anders and Vincent, Mona (1984) "Intertextualitet – möte mellan texter". *Bonniers litterära magasin* no. 4.

4 Bakhtin, Mikhail (1984) *Problems of Dostoevsky's poetics*, ed and transl Caryl Emerson. University of Minnesota Press, Minneapolis, p 184.

5 *ibid*.

6 *ibid*.

7 Bakhtin MM (1981) *The dialogical imagination. Four essays*, Holquist, Michael (ed), transl Caryl Emerson and Michael Holquist. University of Texas Press, Austin, p 374. (The translation has been slightly amended here – L.K.)

8 Bakhtin, Mikhail (1984) *Rabelais and his world*, transl Hélène Iswolsky. Indiana University Press, Bloomington, p 123.

9 Pedersen, Bertel (1976) *Parodiens teori*. Berlingske, Copenhagen.

10 Kolakowski, Leszek (1989) *Tales from the kingdom of Lailonia and the key to heaven*. University of Chicago Press, Chicago.

11 *Op cit*, p 19.

12 *Op cit*, p 17.

13 Kundera, Milan (1984) "The novel and europe". *New York Review of Books*, 19 July, p 15.

Translated by Häkan Lövgren

Chapter 12

Notes on Metrical and Deictical Problems in Shakespeare Translation

Clas Zilliacus

Taking examples from Shakespeare's *The Taming of the Shrew*, *As You Like It* and *Hamlet*, Clas Zilliacus gives practical evidence of the degree of difficulty in a translation into Swedish which can claim to be similar to the source. Both syntactic and metrical problems are involved, added to which is the difference between Swedish and English blank verse. The deictical function (referral, indication, reference) is dealt with separately. How, for example, should the difference between "you" and "thou" be treated in a translation to a language which does not have corresponding forms? This may be a very important issue in a translation. Hamlet first says "you" to Horatio but he dies saying "thou". This kind of difference in language may be used with powerful dramatic effect.

The topic of this chapter is the pursuit of equivalence in Shakespeare translation. I propose to look at a few concrete problems involving metrics and deictics respectively, my point being that in theatre translation no element is small enough to be of no consequence for the pragmatics of the stage. All of them involve decision-making; at least they will emerge as having done so. And even if one tries to scrap the concept of equivalence for the less emphatic one of adequacy, the pursuit remains.

My field of choice is Shakespeare in Swedish, but I trust that the problem areas which I shall be focusing on are common to most Germanic languages. These are all basically amenable to blank verse: they are ready, if not uniformly willing, to play by the rules of that particular game. It seems to me that the recent upsurge of new Swedish translations – caused, I think, by box-office considerations and directors' vanity as much as by an acute demand for actable versions – has brought a kind of normalization pressure to bear on Shakespeare: iambic pentameters should be very recognizably just that, an even five-foot measure. That is how a translator documents his proficency. The result is that Swedish Shakespeare invariably sounds like early Shakespeare.

There are, however, licences, subject to laws. Jiří Levý, in his theory of literary translation, pairs off three basic opposites.[1] One is syntactical (end-stopped as opposed to run-on), two are metrical (iambic versus dactylic line beginnings, and masculine versus feminine endings). Beyond these confines of alternatives, translators find that no recognition of their professional skill is forthcoming, even if the original material may have been much craggier. But within the set of legitimate options all six are considered to be freely available.

The main difference between English and Swedish blank verse lies in the latter's frequent hypercatalectic, hendecasyllabic, weak-stress endings. There are various reasons for these supernumeraries. Swedish prosody calls for them: trochaic verbs and verb forms abound; the definite article is suffixed to the noun. Feminine verse endings were more reminiscent of the Alexandrine traditionally used in Swedish; hence it was easy to consider them more mellifluous than decasyllabics, which were perceived as curt and chopped-off.

Translators into Swedish, then, seem to have regarded the choice between masculine and feminine endings as a non-distinctive issue. It often is. At times it does matter, and not just because a consistent use of the latter might make a play 10 per cent longer but rather because it may end up having built a cumulative effect. In that case the resonance of the lines will counteract or deflate what the lines were constructed to convey.

I shall pick an instance from *The Taming of the Shrew* (I, ii). It is a passage which exposes the technical terms of masculine and feminine as something rather more than that. Bianca's suitors have addressed the question of what a vixen Katherina is. Petruchio counters with a very macho exposition of what he has been up to in his days. It is an enumeration of feats devised to persuade, verbally and phonically, by sheer force. Petruchio's purpose is no other than to woo the shrew:

Why came I hither but to that intent?
Think you a little din can daunt mine ears?
Have I not in my time heard lions roar?
Have I not heard the sea, puff'd up with winds,
Rage like an angry boar chafed with sweat?
Have I not heard great ordnance in the field,
And heaven's artillery thunder in the skies?
Have I not in a pitched battle heard
Loud 'larums, neighing steeds, and trumpets' clang?
And do you tell me of a woman's tongue,
That gives not half so great a blow to hear
As will a chestnut in a farmer's fire?
Tush, tush, fear boys with bugs!

Petruchio's tirade runs for thirteen lines, and its medium is a palpable part of its message. The lines all have emphatic endings; he whips them into place, as he will Katherina. A glance at the corpus of Swedish translations indicates that they dilute at least one third or even half of the lines by feminine endings. Unstressed syllables in the wrong place, particularly if they are consistently applied, produce an elegiac cadence. They eat away the rhetoric, and proceed by gnawing at semantic content. (Male and other chauvinisms are curiously alike in this respect. Kornei Chukovsky, the Russian advocate of translation as a high art, found one of his keys to Kipling in an emphasis on jingoistic masculine line endings.)[2]

This is to say that, in the last analysis, adequacy in verse translation for the theatre cannot be achieved by checking the sum total of solutions. It has to be got at in each specific case if it is to be found where needed. The repertoire of "legitimate" solutions in blank verse translation is not an abstract set. All solutions have to be made *in situ*; there is no line, whether verse or prose, that is not to be carried by a voice, uttered. That goes for the strictly metrical pair of opposites, masculine versus double endings; it applies in equal measure to the syntactical pair of end-stopped versus run-on lines.

Shakespeare is commonly credited with having broken the confines of the line unit: he expanded the set of acceptable strategies to the point where non-enjambement came to be recognized as a solution on a par with the run-on line. Both are of the game; both are audible, as devices or minus-devices. There is a celebrated passage in *As You Like It* (II, vii) which is, by a daringly duplex manoeuvre, an instance of both. I have, for purposes of clarity, slashed Jaques' tirade on the ages of man into acts, as he has.

All the world's a stage,
And all the men and women merely players.
They have their exits and their entrances,
And one man in his time plays many parts,
His acts being seven ages. / At first the infant,
Mewling and puking in his nurse's arms. /
Then, the whining school-boy with his satchel
And shining morning face, creeping like snail
Unwillingly to school. / And then the lover,
Sighing like furnace, with a woeful ballad
Made to his mistress' eyebrow. / Then, a soldier,
Full of strange oaths, and bearded like the pard,
Jealous in honour, sudden, and quick in quarrel,
Seeking the bubble reputation
Even in the cannon's mouth. / And then, the justice,
In fair round belly, with good capon lin'd,
With eyes severe, and beard of formal cut,
Full of wise saws, and modern instances,
And so he plays his part. / The sixth age shifts
Into the lean and slipper'd pantaloon,
With spectacles on nose, and pouch on side,
His youthful hose well sav'd, a world too wide
For his shrunk shank, and his big manly voice,
Turning again toward childish treble, pipes
And whistles in his sound. / Last scene of all,
That ends this strange eventful history,
Is second childishness and mere oblivion,
Sans teeth, sans eyes, sans taste, sans everything.

There is very little in this speech that insists on syntactical completion when the line is up. The dynamics of it are found elsewhere, in the movement from one line to the next. There are seven acts, i.e. six cuts, and they cue each other as filmically as Shakespeare's scene changes generally do. Only one act, the first, ends where a line ends, in the infant's "nurse's arms". All the others begin within lines.

Shakespeare translators as a rule are sensitive to enjambement but this kind of end-stopping in mid-line, a kind of monological stichomythia, seems easier to overlook. The most recent Swedish translation of *As You Like It*, for instance, portions out the last four ages in end-stopped chunks, and the flow of acts is weakened in the process. The overall end-stoppedness of the lines in Jaques' tirade provides for a shift of focus to the in-stoppedness of the ages they depict. Much like my previous example of hypercatalectics in *The Taming of the Shrew*, this is no merely formal matter. Life, according to

Jaques, is over and done with before we know it. Our ages cue each other at a rapid pace. Life is no pompous procession; it is a relay race.

Deictics, with the present surge of interest in the pragmatics of verbal interaction on stage, is a very active field of research. I wish to take a quick look at a narrow sector of it, viz. the use of the second person singular, with specific reference to *Hamlet*. I shall use my example as a case for doggedly verbatim translation. The idea is not even mine: it has been put to the test by Benno Besson, the Swiss-born director, in translations commissioned for his German, French, Swedish, and Finnish productions of the play. (I was involved in the making of the Swedish version; hence my loyalty.)

A great deal of printer's ink has been spilt on the difference between *you* and *thou* in Elizabethan English. Most of it has been spilt in English, which goes to show that the feeling for this extinct distinction has gone numb. E.A. Abbott, providing the bard with a grammar in 1869, tried to make clear what *thou* stood for: it was "the pronoun of (1) affection towards friends, (2) good-humoured superiority to servants, and (3) contempt or anger to strangers. It had, however, already fallen somewhat into disuse, and, being regarded as archaic, was naturally adopted (4) in the higher poetic style and in the language of solemn prayer."[3] After a wealth of examples, many of which give instances of pronoun shifts in mid-speech, Abbott concludes: "In almost all cases where *thou* and *you* appear at first sight indiscriminately used, further considerations show some change of thought, or some influence of euphony sufficient to account for the change of pronoun." Shakespeare's usage in fact indicates that these wordlets are much more than mere stand-ins for nouns. They are deictic markers that alter the dynamics of the discourse. They recharge the relationships between the *dramatis personae*, and in so doing become part of the action.

How is the *you/thou* problem to be tackled in translation? In Swedish the distinction is extant. Swedish pragmatics, however, knows few of the nuances discussed by Abbott, and certainly does not know how to mix the two, or how to exchange one for the other profitably: vacillation creates anomy, unease. One option would be to decide once and for all upon the pronominal level on which a certain character confronts another, and to consider that what is lost in the process is dispensable. This is the usual way Swedish translators go about it. There seems to be a fairly strong preference for *du*. This solution tends to inform court dramas such as *Hamlet* with a kind of homely intimacy that forestalls any sense of things capital, such as heads, being at issue. Another possibility would be to take care of the source-text nuance by other, indirect means; but the verse rarely parts with the syllables necessary for such detours. Alternatively, one could decide that *you* is *ni* and *thou* is *du*, literally and intransigently. This has been the solution opted for in the translation made for Besson's *Hamlet*. I venture to suggest that it has proved its viability on the stage, even if it does look confusing on the page.

The Elizabethan manner of oscillating between *you* and *thou* is, among other things, a way of keeping uncertainty alive. The characters enter into relations with each other which are unstable; their status may be revoked, altered, up- or downgraded. Characters are built by being manoeuvred into relations; thus they are, in part, constituted by the deictics they use, or are made objects of.

I may be overstretching my point but I seem to have noticed when reading Swedish versions of *Hamlet* that the text and what takes place in it is lulled into a false sense of security by making these pronominal deictics unequivocal instead of using the gamut. I seem, moreover, to espy greater dangers ahead. By affixing an unvarying mode of address – e.g., opting for *du* when Hamlet talks to Horatio; this is the regular Swedish solution – the relationship freezes into a *donné*; the dialectics are lost. Horatio becomes "friend to Hamlet", as he is usually characterized in the list of *dramatis personae*. There can be little doubt that Horatio is, has become, friend to Hamlet when the play is over. But this is no established fact when the two first meet. The building of this friendship, the whys and wherefores and the context of its coming about, are an integral part of what happens in *Hamlet*. It is conveyed on many levels, one of them being deictics. Hamlet first says *you* to Horatio but he dies saying *thou*. The change to *thou* in this case is an audible, one might say dramatic, non-occurrence of *you*. But it is audible only if the pronominal pair has been taken over into the target text.

Notes

1 Levý, Jiří (1969) *Die literarische Übersetzung: Theorie einer Kunstgattung*, transl Walter Schamschula. Athenäum, Frankfurt, p 258ff.

2 Leighton, Lauren G. (transl and ed) (1984) "The translator's introduction". In: *The art of translation: Kornei Chukovsky's "A High Art"*. University of Tennessee Press, Knoxville, p xxii.

3 Abbott EA (1929) *A Shakespearian grammar*. Macmillan, London, p 153f.

Quotations from plays follow The Arden Shakespeare.

Chapter 13

The Translator's Knowledge

Susan Bassnett

Translation studies have emerged as a new discipline in the last 20 years. What is becoming increasingly obvious – and what Bassnett argues for – is the degree to which the work of a translator involves criteria that transcend the purely linguistic. One example given here is the translation of knitting patterns from Danish into English, which involve highly complex translation problems because the conventions that operate between English and Danish knitters are so different. A text belongs to its culture, its language, and its world and is changed when transferred to another culture and another language. Thus the task of the translator is to create a text in a target culture which in its context fulfils a similar function to that of the original. There can be no ideal "equivalence" between words and phrases in different languages, between text and translation. Translating is a highly skilled and highly creative activity.

The past twenty years have seen the development of the new discipline of translation studies, involving the systematic study of both the diachronic and synchronic processes of translation. Of course there had been a substantial amount of previous work involving translation, particularly from within linguistics, but the whole vast field of literary translation especially had been dominated by two equally unproductive discursive modes: the highly individualistic statements of translators, often overly defensive or highly critical of other colleagues' work, and the kind of value judgement criticism that assessed translations in terms of vague qualities such as the capturing of an undefined "essence", "spirit" or "quality" and the ability of the translator to be "faithful" to those indefinites.

By focusing on the processes of translation, it becomes possible to avoid both the pseudo-metaphysical discourse of the "essence" of a text and the simplistic value judgement, and enables us to look more closely at what goes on during the various stages of what is in fact a series of highly complex shifts between cultures. The late James Holmes has described the levels of reading involved in the translation process, showing how the translator/reader abstracts a mental concept or map of the whole which will be:

a conglomerate of highly disparate bits of information. In the first place, as a map of a linguistic artefact, it will contain information, at a variety of ranks, regarding features of the text in its relation to the linguistic continuum within which (or violating the rules of which) it is formulated, that is, contextual information. Secondly, as a map of a literary artefact, it will contain information, at a variety of ranks, regarding features of the text in its relation to the literary continuum within which (or rebelling against which) it is formulated, that is, interlingual information. And third, as a map of a socio-cultural artefact, it will contain information, at a variety of ranks, regarding features of the text in relation to the socio-cultural continuum within which (or transcending which) it is formulated, that is, situational information.[1]

Translation, therefore, is not a mystical process, nor does it take place in a vacuum, and despite its pedagogical use in foreign language learning, "faithfulness" to a so-called original is not really quantifiable. A text, as Holmes points out, is a socio-cultural artefact, and the translation of that text is a different socio-cultural artefact within the new (target) culture. Moreover, the more precise the function of the text in the source language, the greater the "freedom" of the translator will be (and it is very significant that the terminology associated with translation should be so loaded and so heavily moralistic, even continuing in the present age of deconstruction!)

As I have argued elsewhere, a translator operates criteria that transcend the purely linguistic, and the process that goes on in translation is one of decoding and recoding across language boundaries.[2] At times, that process may involve much more than the replacement of lexical and grammatical items between languages, and may even involve discarding the basic linguistic elements of the source language text in order to effect a functionally valid translation. We can find examples of this process in the simplest form of public instruction notices; intercontinental European trains carry instructions that state DO NOT LEAN OUT OF THE WINDOW; NE PAS SE PENCHER AU DEHORS; È VIETATO SPORGERSI, where no attempt is made to translate the linguistic items and instead the emphasis is on rendering a functionally correct instruction in each language. Some of the hilarity than can be occasioned by defective translation of instructions is always caused by the literal rendering of phrases in one language without regard for the shift in expression in the target culture.

Recently, working on a project that involved the translation of knitting patterns from Danish into English in order to create a new market for a new brand of yarn, I encountered a set of highly complex translation problems that involved much more than linguistic transfer. For a start, different conventions operate between English and Danish knitters, both in pattern layout and in actual knitting technique. Secondly, although the British knitting market has extended enormously over the past decade and pattern making has become much more adventurous, there is a solid core of home knitters who remain loyal to traditional layouts and techniques, and this was precisely the market that the new Danish yarn manufacturers wanted to reach. Traditionally, this group tend not to knit on circular needles, for example, yet most of the Danish patterns carried instructions for this type of knitting. The British group tend to knit sleeves from bottom to top; most of the Danish patterns laid out sleeve instructions as knitted from top to bottom, picking up stitches on the main body of the garment. Most importantly, the British group require fully calculated instructions, so that if decreasing for a neck opening, for example, a British pattern will give instructions such as:

Pattern x sts. and leave on a spare needle for right front neck pattern x sts. and leave on a st. holder, pattern to end and work on these last x sts. for left front neck.

This is quite unequivocal; the knitter counts her stitches according to the size of garment she is knitting, and the pattern is calculated mathematically to conform to correct size. The Danish pattern, on the other hand, gives far fewer instructions:

Nu sættes de midterste x m. på en nål og hver skulder strikkes færdig for sig.

The principal difference between the Danish knitter (and this is true of most Continental European knitters also) and the British knitter lies in the pattern layout, for whilst the Danes are used to fairly minimal instructions and to a spatially conceived pattern, the average British knitter is used to very precisely calculated numerical instructions. Although some of the younger, more adventurous British knitters are prepared to experiment with the spatially designed pattern, the traditional knitter still opts for the numerical system. A translator is therefore faced with what effectively is a re-modelling of the pattern, not only to accord with the conventions of the target culture knitter in terms of layout, but also to accord with the actual knitting technique, which is different. Clearly, in this case the translator's knowledge must extend far beyond the printed text and include an awareness of the spatial and physical dimensions of the task.

If we turn to a literary text, we find that the problems are remarkably similar, for once again the question of the original function of the text arises, and the underlying question is not so much whether the text *per se* is translatable but whether the function fulfilled by that text is translatable. Frequently, there is a gap between text and function in the target culture. So, for example, if a text originally devised as a spoken epic is translated and set down in print in another language, then a double shift has taken place: there has been a straightforward movement across language boundaries of a verbal text, but there has also been a much more significant transition from the oral to the written. In the case of much early germanic epic, the effect of this shift is to alter radically the status of the text, so that a popular oral form becomes a high status written text, read only by an elite intellectual group. The text may be translatable, but the function of that text is not, and as a result the text loses its power and authority.

The task of the translator is to create a text in the target culture that works, ideally (and there is a great deal of idealism in the art of translation, with translators constantly aspiring towards some imaginary perfect goal) a text that fulfils a similar function to that of the original, even though this may well not be feasible. The vexed term "equivalence", which was taken for so long to mean some kind of absolute sameness, an unfortunate relic of the days when it was confidently believed that language could be neatly fitted into a dictionary and more than one language into a bilingual dictionary, is now used with much more circumspection, and the search for sameness between texts is recognized as impossible. Iurii Lotman has taken up Mukařovský's view that a literary text has both an autonomous and a communicative character,[3] and has pointed out that the signs of a text are in a dialectical relationship with signs and structures outside the text. In consequence, a translator must bear in mind both the autonomous and communicative aspects of a text, which effectively destroys any notion that the translator may be able to create the "same" text in the target culture.

The translation of poetry created in a language and culture that is totally unlike the target culture provides a good example of some of the shifts that take place in the translation process. If we take the famous Chinese poem "Meditation in Autumn", by the thirteenth-century poet Ma Zhiyuan and consider some English versions, interesting light is shed on the translation processes. A transliteration of the poem reads:

k'u-t'eng lao-shu hun-ya
hsiao-ch'iao liu-shui jen-chia
ku-tao hsi-feng shou-ma
hsi-yang hsi hsia
tuan-ch'ang-jen tsai t'ien-ya

The poem is structured according to fixed conventions of rhyme and syllable patterns, with a fourth line that is two syllables shorter than the others. A word-for-word English version, that of necessity ignores any formal patterning, gives:

Withered/vine/old/tree/evening/crow
Small/bridge/running/stream/people's home
Ancient/road/west/wind/lean/horse
Evening/sun/westward/goes down
heart-broken/man/at/heaven's edge

The word-for-word translation effectively provides a blueprint for a poem in English, since it gives a series of evocative words strung together to give images of loss and ending. Using this blueprint, three English versions offer:

(A) Dry vine, tree, evening crow:
    Lone hut, quick stream, small bridge,
    Old road, west wind, lean horse.
    Sunset suggests
    To this old man his fate.

(B) Withered wines hanging on old branches,
    Returning crows croaking at dusk,
    A few houses hidden past a narrow bridge,
    And below the bridge a quiet creek running.
    Down a worn path, in the west wind,
    A lean horse comes plodding.
    The sun dips down in the west
    And the loversick traveller is still at the end of the world.

(C) The crow still sits in the tree at evening
    But the old vine has withered.
    Down by the cottage a small bridge
    Crosses the swift flowing stream.

    The west wind blows down the ancient road,
    Where the poor horse once trod.
    The evening sun sinks in the west
    Like a broken hearted man at heaven's edge.[4]

To summarize briefly, these three versions use completely different poetic conventions. Version A attempts to utilize the Chinese convention, and although the rhyme is lost there is an attempt at syllable coherence and the shortened fourth line. Version B relies on the established eighteenth-century convention of evening poems, and there are strong echoes of Gray's "Elegy Written in a Country Churchyard" in the language of this piece. It is considerably padded, and the man, who is described as "old" in Version A, is here a "lovesick traveller". The formal structure of this piece is quite random, and there is no attempt either to invent a new form or to utilize existing forms, unlike Version C which uses the four-line stanza, though in this case without rhyme.

What these versions show is that in each case the translator has used a "literal" translation as a starting point and has then gone on to expand the original in different ways to create different effects. All three claim to be translations of the same poem, and yet all three are quite different because in each case the translator has established a different set of priorities and used a different poetic model.

A comparison of translated texts, even when presented as cursorily as above, exposes a fundamental problem for the translator – the impossibility of determining what is the invariant core of the text. Various hypotheses have been advanced, but either the content material of a text is taken to be the invariant (and in the case of the Chinese poem and its English versions even a simplistic content analysis does not reveal sameness but rather highlights variations) or we have to follow Anton Popovič's thesis that the invariant core is represented by constant semantic elements in a text whose existence can be proved by experimental semantic condensation, i.e. that the invariant is that which exists in common between all existing translations and the original work.[5]

It seems to me to be far more useful to move away from speculation about any possible invariant core and to focus instead on the question of text function. If we do this, then any assessment of the English version of a Chinese poem will be made on the basis of the effectiveness of that text as a piece of poetry in English, given that the conventions of the original cannot be reproduced in a language which has an alphabet and verbal forms as opposed to a character language. The crucial knowledge for the translator is therefore an acquaintance with English poetics, and this effectively means that ability to create a target language poem is more important than detailed knowledge of the source language. And lest this be seen as a heretical view, we can recall Ezra Pound, when taken to task for his "incorrect" translation of the Roman poet Propertius, who said bluntly:

No, I have not done a translation of Propertius. That fool in Chicago took the HOMAGE for a translation despite the mention of Wordsworth and the parodied line from Yeats. (As if, had one wanted to pretend to more Latin than one knew, it wouldn't have been perfectly easy to correct one's divergencies from a Bohn crib. Price 5 shillings.)[6]

My own work as a translator has varied widely and ranged across different genres, which led me originally to reflect on whether translation theory could be trans-generic or whether different types of text necessitated different translation strategies and hence different theories of the text. The constant line, however, in all forms of translation work returns us to the fundamental question of what the source text is doing and whether it is possible for the target text to do something similar. I remain convinced that the more precise the function of a text or unit of text is, the less the translator will be bound to follow its linguistic structures. We do not translate idioms literally; we translate what those idioms signify, just as we translate the function of the instruction manual and not the manual itself. Literary texts, though ostensibly more complex, can be translated following similar principles. Hence, if a story is comic in the source language, it follows that the notion of comicity is a fundamental element in the translation. At the same time, it must be recognized that the notion of what is or is not comic may well vary considerably from one culture to another, and here the task of the translator is a delicate one, for he/she needs to understand the function of the comic in both cultures and substitute where necessary.

It is also important that what is not comic in the source text should not be inadvertently made comic in the target text. When translating Luigi Pirandello's play, *Trovarsi* for BBC radio in 1986 with David Hirst, we had the greatest problems with the young male protagonist, a dashing young sailor who sweeps the heroine off her feet but who ultimately is unable to cope with her need to continue her career as a world-famous actress. The young man is described in the play as half-Swedish, and is called Elj Nielsen, an Italian version of a Swedish name. Therefore he is an outsider in the play, a native speaker who is also a foreigner, and just to complicate matters further the character has strong textual links with Ellida Wangel, for *Trovarsi* was heavily influenced by Ibsen's *The Lady from the Sea*. Translating Elj's dialogue into English proved very difficult, because his language seemed completely artificial and we were constantly in danger of making him sound like a parody of a man about town from the 1920s, a somewhat silly P.G. Wodehouse character. At the same time, we could not give him too many contemporary expressions, since we needed to retain the periodization of the piece, nor could we coarsen his language in an attempt to make him more "masculine", because of the high-class status of the characters (Elj has been brought up by his uncle, the Count). In short, the problem was one involving linguistic markers of class and gender, which varied hugely between Italian and English, with the added problems of translating a text written fifty years earlier and one that showed the influence of another playwright from another culture and yet another time. All this besides the question of the man's character and role in the drama and the problem of creating a text that could be spoken by actors for radio.

Andre Lefevere has coined the term "refractions" to show the way in which texts interconnect and bounce off one another across cultures,[7] thereby exposing the fallacy that translation is a simple process of linguistic transfer. Lefevere also claims that:

Translation is one of the most obvious forms of image making, of manipulation that we have . . . It is responsible to a large extent for the image of a work, a writer, a culture . . . It introduces innovations into a literature. It is the main medium through which one literature influences another . . . Translation can tell us a lot about the power of images and the ways in which images are made, about the ways in which authority manipulates images and employs experts to sanction that manipulation and to justify the trust of an audience.[8]

There is always an ideological dimension to translation. It does not happen in a vacuum, and the translator is always engaged in a relationship of power with the source text and with the target culture. The knowledge that a translator requires in order to translate extends outwards far beyond the linguistic, indeed at times transcends the linguistic altogether. Perhaps, as awareness of the complexities of translation gradually becomes more widespread, the status of the translator will rise accordingly, and translation will finally be recognized not as some secondary activity that can be carried out by anyone with a minimal acquaintance with more than one language, but as a highly skilled and highly creative activity.

Notes

1 Holmes, James (ed) (1970) Forms of verse translation and the translation of verse form. In: *The nature of translation: essays on the theory and practice of literary translation*. Mouton, The Hague.

2 Bassnett-McGuire, Susan (1980) *Translation studies*. Methuen, London.

3 See Fokkema DW (1976) Continuity and change in Russian formalism, Czech structuralism and Soviet semiotics. *PTL* I(1): 153–196. Also Ann Shukman (1976) The canonization of the real: Iurii Lotman's theory of literature and analysis of poetry. *PTL* I (2):317–339.

4 I am grateful to my students, Mu GuoHao, now of Shanghai International Studies University, and Lynn Long, University of Warwick, for providing me with these examples.

5 Popovič, Anton (1976) *Dictionary for the analysis of literary translation*. Department of Comparative Literature, University of Alberta, Canada.

6 Ezra Pound, quoted in JP Sullivan (1961) The poet as Translator – Ezra Pound and Sextus Propertius. *The Kenyon Review*, XXIII (3):462–482.

7 Lefevere Andre (1985) Why waste our time on rewrites? In: Hermans T (ed) *The manipulation of literature*. Croom Helm, London, pp 215–241.

8 Lefevere, Andre (1988) Translation history: mirror upon mirror mirror'd, Plenary Lecture at *Beyond translation*, conference held at University of Warwick, July.

Section V:
Art and Knowledge

Chapter 14

Information Technology

Henrik Sinding-Larsen

The development of information technology is approached here through the concept of "externalization". Computer programming is seen as a step in the human history of externalization which can only be compared with the invention of speech and writing. But what happens to human knowledge when it is externalized as computer programs? Sinding-Larsen uses the development of the system of musical notation as a comparison. He finds complex relationships between the notation system and the music, as he does between computer technology and humankind's knowledge. As musical notation transformed music, computer technology transforms our knowledge.

Introduction

In order to understand what role computers are playing in the evolution of our society, we must investigate how computerization is a special case of more general trends in the history of information technologies. Musical notation is a system for representing musical knowledge and hence an information technology. The mutual evolution (co-evolution) of notation and music is used as a source of comparison with the present computerization of knowledge.

I have found the concept "externalization" useful for an understanding of the history of information technologies. *Externalization is used to denote a process whereby an implicit structure of events becomes explicit and gets an external form that can act both as a model of and a model for other events*. For instance, all live music has a structure but, in an oral tradition, this structure has no external existence outside the actual performance. What musical notation does is to give external reality to some (not all!) aspects of music. This act of externalization has consequences for the further development of music and organization of musicians. Similar processes are valid for writing and spoken language, and also for computer programs and thought processes. The concept of externalization, therefore, characterizes a process of change in a society's management of knowledge.

Three major inventions mark the human history of externalization: speech, writing, and computer programming.

The reason why computers are considered that fundamental is their ability to simulate and thereby represent natural and mental *processes* that formerly could not be "expressed". Common to semiotic systems before the computer is that they can only describe the *static structure* of a process. A recipe, for instance, is static and contains no "motion" until someone uses kitchen utensils and lets the structure of the recipe guide the process of cooking. Similarly, a novel is the static structure of a story which is set in motion and brought to life through the process of reading. On the other hand, computer programs store descriptions of structures which can guide physical processes directly by means of computers. *Running programs are processes that represent processes*. This makes the computer an entirely new *tool of description*. Therefore, to make historical comparisons, we must look to other periods when new systems for representing knowledge appeared. Musical notation may provide such an example. At the end of the article we will look at the computerization of language as humankind's most ambitious attempt at externalization.

Fields of Complexity

Many textbooks present the history of music as a development from simplicity to complexity. In certain respects this is quite correct, but as a general conclusion it is mistaken. Rather, it is a question of *replacing one kind of complexity with another*, or replacing complexity in one dimension (or domain) with complexity in another. For example, improvisation results in a kind of musical complexity that disappeared from orchestral performances as the orchestras increased to ever larger dimensions. Presented with a score with the complexity of *The Rite of Spring* it would only lead to disorder if each musician should add or disregard notes in accordance with his/her own mood. The performance as a totality may become extremely complex even though the task of each musician may be simple. Classically trained musicians of outstanding quality may often react as helpless amateurs in front of a demand for improvisation.

There seem to be some general trends in the development of semiotic systems for description and prescription of human activity. Each elementary symbol in early musical notation was more composite and complex, i.e. contained more information than each note in modern systems. As a semiotic system develops, the elementary contrasts tend to be simplified in ways that make them more suitable for combination into more complex statements. If the symbols are simple and context independent on an elementary level, then they can more easily be combined to produce complexity on a composite level. The syntactic (grammatical or combinatorial) aspects of the semiotic system will accordingly increase in importance.

I think this is valid in most or all processes of externalization since the same tendency can be observed in a whole range of fields: the letters of the phonemic alphabet can be combined to form more numerous and more complex words than the signs in a pictographic system. Each industrial worker building a moon rocket can learn and accomplish his job more easily than a traditional carpenter building a house. The ultimate simplicity of the electronic binary code has produced an unforeseen complexity of computer applications. The modern complexity seems to appear at more *composite levels* than the "primitive" complexity, but this does not mean that its total complexity is greater.

The other day I received a leaflet that showed how experts in artificial intelligence do not share my view of the evolution of knowledge. It was an invitation to participate at the 2nd International Symposium on Commercial Expert Systems in Banking and Insurance. The chairman, Professor John Campbell from University College (London), introduces the conference theme with these words:

> Knowledge is the key to success. Knowledge is growing exponentially. Ninety per cent of mankind's knowledge has been produced over the past 30 years.

If we define knowledge as the ability to survive in a sustainable way in a natural environment then I think we would be closer to the truth if we stated that 90% of mankind's knowledge has been lost over the past 30 years. But if we add some more of the above-cited text we also see more of the context within which his statement make sense:

> The right knowledge at the right time is crucial for the competitiveness in today's global market ... Today already a number of systems automate expert reasoning for business advantage. For their future successful application, however, a better view on knowledge management and engineering is necessary.

It is my hope that the historical reflection put forward in this article will make it more difficult to put forward statements about the progress of knowledge in such a categorical way as in the citations above.

Musical Notation as the Creator of "False Notes"

Scales with a great variety of (and varying!) intervals are found in many orally transmitted musical traditions. A scale with twelve identical steps is only found in the Western classical tradition. The traditional way of tuning fixed-pitch instruments became inadequate when both instruments and compositions, to an increasing degree, were made for polyphony. The tuning had to be standardized to exploit the full range of tonalities made possible by notation. This was especially important for keyboard instruments. A major work of Bach (*Das wohltemperierte Klavier*) is dedicated explicitly to the exploration of harmonic transformations made possible by the new tempered tuning of his keyboard instruments. A simplification (standardization), at the level of the elementary pitch intervals, was the basis for an increased complexity at the more composite harmonic level. This standardization of scale was unnecessary in earlier periods because the music was concentrated on a few closely related tonalities (keys). If one attempted to use non-standard intervals within the "new" polyphonic music the result would sound dissonant or "false".[1]

Through the prestige power of bourgeois music, the equalized twelve-step scale was gradually adopted as *the standard for all music*, making some of the tones regarded as correctly pitched in traditional scale systems "false notes". Standard scale and complex harmonies became a hallmark of bourgeois music appreciation. The system of notation was mentally coupled to this particular scale. All notes that could not be placed within this system were considered false. This will be illustrated by an example from an encounter between classical and folk music. The story, as well as the other references to Norwegian folk music, are based on my thesis on the cultural history of Norwegian folk music (Sinding-Larsen 1983).

A "Millimetre" from the Tradition

Some time in the 1880s, the country musician Olav Brenno played the folk instrument *langeleik* for tourists at a hotel in the Norwegian mountains. The old Norwegian *langeleik* is a stringed instrument in the dulcimer family. The pitch of each tone in the *langeleik*'s scale is determined by the position of its frets. The principle is basically the same as for the guitar, with one important difference: the intervals of the scale on a *langeleik* are not necessarily standardized as they are on the guitar.

After the performance, a member of the audience walked up to the musician and praised the music. However, the tourist, referring to his position as an organist, insisted that two of the tones of the *langeleik* were "false". He offered to correct this by moving the relevant frets a few millimetres. Olav Brenno agreed to this, without knowing how miserable the outcome would be. The classically tuned scale imposed by the organist was incompatible with Brenno's conception of, and way of, remembering his tunes. When he tried to play on his "correct" instrument, he did not recognize the tunes and "lost track". In the end, he gave up playing the *langeleik*.

Several decades later after the turn of the century, when Brenno had become an old man, he was contacted by young scholars in folk music who realized the cultural value of the old scales. They helped him move the frets back again to their original positions. They also gave him back some of his self-confidence by redefining the "false" notes as a valuable cultural trait. Brenno resumed his *langeleik* playing and many of the tunes came back to his memory after almost a generation in oblivion. The dominance of the standardized scale was, in this case, absolute because it was imbedded in the sound-producing instrument.

The "imperialism" of the standardized scale is more subtle but obvious enough in a text written in 1850 by the Norwegian musicologist L.M. Lindemann. The citation is taken from an introduction to a collection of folk songs that Lindemann himself had collected and transcribed. Observe to what extent the notation of the music is intimately linked to the standardized scale:

The problem of transcribing the melodies does not only consist in the lack of distinction and clarity in the old people's way of singing. Far worse is the fact that one repeatedly is presented with notes that are *a quarter of a step higher or lower pitched than the appropriate ones*; i.e., notes that are placed exactly in between our half-note steps. It is the task of the collector to determine to which note, the higher or the lower they belong . . . By frankly confronting the old people with the two alternatives the singer can be *guided to a choice of his own* as to which tone to be considered as the right one. [Cited in Dal 1956, p. 182, my emphasis]

In this case it is obvious how the musical notation, as a tool of description, strongly influences its object of description. Lindemann did not recognize this as an inadequacy of the tool, but rather as a "deficiency" of the reality to be described.

Knowledge Engineers and Elusive Answers

It is possible to draw some parallels between the collecting of folk music and knowledge engineering. The important task in both cases is the preservation of oral and unformalized knowledge by means of formal tools of description. While the ethnomusicologist uses musical notation as a tool for the description of music, the knowledge engineer uses various programming languages as tools for the description of professional experts' skill and knowledge.[2]

Knowledge engineers commonly complain of vague and elusive answers from experts whose knowledge does not easily lend itself to precise description. Because their job is to make running programs, they will have to use tools of formalization to confront the experts with the possible programming alternatives. The experts will be *guided to a choice of their own* as to which knowledge to consider as the right one.

Once the knowledge is embedded in an expert system we may encounter the same kind of problems as the old *langeleik* player. The computerized form of the knowledge may be incompatible with a pre-computer way of thinking. The knowledge that "sounds false" will slowly be forgotten or actively suppressed.

As in the case with the notation and the piano, the expert systems and the knowledge acquisition tools may set the standard for all knowledge, not only what is subject to computerization.

The Tape-Recorder: A Perfect Tool of Description?

With the above-mentioned problems in mind, it should be obvious that tape-recorders have some great advantages for the preservation of music when compared with written musical notation. For instance, taped music renders all the subtleties of traditional scales that are eliminated in the abstractions of written music. But the problem of preserving the knowledge of music-making is by no means eliminated by this technique.

Norwegian folk musicians have always placed great value on a correct transmission of the tunes of their tradition. The registration of folk music by means of music textbooks and, to an even greater extent, by means of cassette tape-recorders has contributed to the idea that a correct transmission from one generation to the next is equal to detailed copying of the old forms. But music as living aesthetic expression is not something that it is possible to *copy* in every detail. To some extent it must always be *re-created* at each single performance, and its success as music will never solely depend on an accurate transmission of every tone. The detailed and truthful rendering of *a single musical performance* does not show how intonation and improvisation are related to changing public reactions and performance situations.

In a certain sense, learning orally transmitted music from tape will preserve the tradition in a better way than learning from simplified and formalized written music. But the descriptive (and prescriptive) power of a tape-recording is so great that an exact copying will leave even less room than written notes for giving the music a personal flavour. What has happened in some extreme cases among Norwegian folk musicians is that fanatic guardians of the tradition detect and arrest any deviation from well-known taped forms. Their corrections are particularly effective when these guardians act as judges in the annual contest of traditional fiddlers.

Lately this kind of traditionalism has been criticized. A growing number of young Norwegian folk musicians argue that the very idea of a detailed registration and copying of *music as sound structure* is incompatible with the intention of preserving music as a living tradition of *music-making*. Improvisation, change and spontaneous response to each unique audience have always been important in folk music. The mastering of these aspects is the result of second-order learning, above the morphology (first order) of a single tune (Bateson 1973, pp. 250–280). *These aspects cannot be fully described with the actual tools of musical notation or registration.* Perhaps they never will. This is knowledge that is rooted in a very complex interpersonal level.

Improvisation, intervals outside the standardized scale, and other characteristic traits of Norwegian folk music not captured by musical notation have been gradually disappearing since the beginning of this century. There have been two basically opposite strategies to counteract this development. The scientific folkloristic strategy is to refine and improve the tools of description to avoid losing information in the act of description. The other more paradoxical strategy, followed by some young folk musicians, has been to *delete information* from written tunes that are considered too detailed. In this way, the written music once more *increases its dependence on an oral learning context*; the score as description becomes so coarse-grained that it is worthless as a prescription unless the musician considers the performance situation and the oral tradition. Learning the tunes directly from old performers with a minimal use of any descriptions or recordings is, by some fiddlers, considered the only real way of perpetuating the tradition. In their opinion, the concept of tradition should not be attached directly to the music at a describable morphological level but to the traditional conditions for learning and performance.

This story has relevance for the current situation where previously human-dependent knowledge becomes externally available through knowledge-based systems. Many expert systems are made and marketed with the idea of making expert knowledge more cheaply available to students. This is achieved as computers decrease the dependence on human experts as an expensive oral learning context. Explicitly or implicitly, it is assumed that this is a way of preserving knowledge traditions currently maintained by living experts. But it is an open question what kind of maintenance the computers enhance since computer-based descriptions can never capture more than some aspects of the total knowledge. And it is an equally open question whether more refined tools of description will make the situation better.

The Norwegian folk musicians realized that it was not the "bad" descriptions that were the most threatening to the living tradition but the "good" ones. A good description generally means a context-free description, which means the folk musicians as a social group (the context) lose control over their music tradition.

Gregorian Chants and the Reconstruction of Authenticity

At the Benedictine Abbey of St Pierre at Solesmes in France, monks have been working for more than a hundred years on the restoration of the old Gregorian chants. Their situation is, in many respects, similar to that of the young Norwegian fiddlers. In the opinion of the Solesmes monks, the old chants have been "killed" by a too sophisticated and precise system of notation. Their strategy is twofold; on the one hand they re-edit facsimiles of the oldest Gregorian manuscripts, and on the other hand they develop an oral practice around these rudimentary manuscripts. A thousand years after these chants were written down with the first systems of musical notation, we see a systematic work of reconstruction of lost qualities of pre-notational plainsong. The Medician edition of the chants (1614) was considered to be the most oppressive and standardizing one, and the monks of Solesmes laboured to recover from this papal act of description several centuries after it was imposed. The music had been trapped in its own system of preservation.

In an earlier version of the present chapter, the story of the Solesmes monks ended at about this point. However, I met a French musicologist, Marcel Perez, who made me reconsider my view of the project of Solesmes where he himself had been a pupil. Perez was doing research on the role of improvisation within Gregorian chant, when he found new evidence that it was formerly in widespread use. Primarily, it was an oral praxis, but early manuscripts contained many symbols indicating when the singer should elaborate or improvise and when he should follow the written music. The system of notation implied some kind of alternation where the initiative and control moved back and forth between the singer's imagination and the prescriptions of the score. This was eliminated in later and more precise systems. But the skills of improvisation survived as an oral tradition within certain schools until the nineteenth century.

The monks of Solesmes dismissed this practice as unauthentic and insisted on the study of the earliest notation as the sole way to the "true" Gregorian chant. Because the early notes contained less information, we could say that their strategy increased the music's dependence on an oral tradition. However, all their studies of the oldest and most "correct" manuscripts made them more obsessed with notation than ever before. The result of this quest for authenticity was that the little that remained of the still living traditions of improvisation disappeared completely. Instead they founded and promoted an entirely "new oral tradition" based on the "oldest written tradition". As the justification for authenticity is based entirely on notation, there should be no surprise that the resulting music is rather rigid and without improvisation.

Externalization and Progress

When humans make tools for describing human activities, they will always involve themselves in a coevolutionary process. An improvement of the tools for *description* of a certain domain will, in general, also be the starting point for new design and *prescription* which will change the domain originally to be described.

Tools of description (languages, semiotic systems) are one basis for externalization of knowledge; the storage and processing of knowledge independent of the individual human mind. Since the dawn of civilization, human knowledge has always been perpetuated and developed by an interplay between internalized and externalized representations of knowledge. Oral tradition is the typical case of internalized knowledge while writing is the most widespread tool for externalization. The balance between the two kinds seems to be important for creativity and flexibility.

Looking at the history of culture, we see a general trend where tools of description become increasingly more precise and comprehensive. This is generally considered as a positive development. However, as demonstrated by the examples in this article, we also find cases where people consider precise descriptions negatively. The above-mentioned Norwegian fiddlers, and to a certain extent the monks of Solesmes, seem to perceive the externalized versus internalized representation (or dependence versus independence of an oral tradition) *as a choice.*

In my opinion, the tendency to think of precise descriptions as something inherently good or, at least, as an inevitable result of science expanding in accordance with some kind of destiny or natural law, is too strong. With the advent of the computer, and in particular, with the development of artificial intelligence and knowledge engineering, we should become increasingly conscious of our possibilities to choose in this domain. Many essentially oral knowledge traditions stand at the threshold of an era of description comparable to that of music in the Middle Ages, but the current tools of description are far more refined and powerful.

Computer technology has made possible dynamic descriptions of processes through simulation. The range of possible tools of descriptions will widen as science makes progress in the understanding and description of fundamental properties of communication, perception and reasoning. The descriptive power of the computer may be reducing the role of human language itself from the principal *tool of description* to the principal *object of description*. Principles of advanced computation have already become meta-knowledge and meta-language in many domains.

Most critiques of artificial intelligence have concentrated on the limitations of computers. Typically, one of the most famous books criticizing artificial intelligence is entitled *What Computers Can't Do* (Dreyfus 1979). I think it is time to realize that we are caught in a situation with a twofold threat (and twofold possibilities). If the computer's power of description is too poor then we loose subtleties and details. It the tool of description is "too good", we may lose in orally based improvisation and flexibility, and that will, in the long run, be more serious.

Flexibility and improvisation are not only aesthetic concerns. Every knowledge tradition needs living sources for its renewal. History can teach us how the long-term processes shaping culture are the expression of a balance between two regimes; one characterized by notation, explicit knowledge, fixation and standardization, the other by oral tradition, tacit knowledge, openness and improvisation. Our choice is of course not one side or the other but achieving a viable balance between the two.

Some Remarks on the Externalization of Language and the Evolution of Culture

The ambition of the theory of externalization is to be able to conceptualize seemingly independent historical processes in a common framework. The evolution of musical notation, writing, computer programming and many other processes have something in common that the concept of externalization can help us to grasp. (We could even say that the concept of externalization helps us to externalize the phenomenon of externalization.)

In a sense human language is a premiss underlying all of the other forms of externalization. But personally I think it is more fruitful to look at what we usually call language as just one kind of externalization, although a very basic one. The history of language then becomes an aspect of the general history of externalization.

It we look at the three main periods in this perspective the second step, writing, externalized the ephemeral structure of the first step, speech. That prepared the ground for an unprecedented accumulation of knowledge. But it also had an important influence on spoken language itself.

Languages of illiterate people have in general no concepts for the characterization of linguistic entities like verb, noun, grammar, etc. Some tribes don't even have a concept corresponding to our word "language". Language is something they use, not something they talk about. The externalized quality of writing made it possible to inspect and analyse sentences in ways inaccessible to oral cultures (Goody 1977). In a most important sense, it was writing that made language, as a conceptual entity, emerge from speech. But traditional writing was just able to externalize the end-product of our linguistic activity, namely the *structure* of speech (i.e. fixed sequences of sounds and words). By means of computers we are able to make an externalization of several of the linguistic *processes* producing speech, e.g. simple syntax and semantics. This externalization creates new possibilities for reflection upon the phenomenon of language as well as providing new conditions for the linguistic practice. To program a computer is to be able to think and express ideas in programming languages. Thus it is reasonable to say that computer programming (and to some extent every use of computers) is a kind of linguistic activity. To a greater extent than ever before language has become a question of conscious choice, we can evaluate the properties of one language against another. Through programming, and particularly through the construction of programming languages, language has become an object of construction and invention.

We may compare this process of externalization with the case of music notation. In the first phase of externalization the development of a tool of description is used to describe a domain existing independently of the new tool: notation of chants in oral tradition; computer simulation of natural language. In the second phase of externalization we see a coevolution of the tool of description and the domain to be described. Spoken language has already been heavily influenced by externalization through writing. And it is beyond doubt that computer-simulated language will influence our way of speaking as well as writing. In the way writing was the premiss for the appearance of grammar and logic we now see the contours of a future where informatics and cognitive science take the lead in making a framework for the way we think and express ourselves.

If one accepts my theory of externalization then the idea of artificial intelligence could be understood as a first phase in a process of externalization; a phase where computers are used to describe and simulate processes of our pre-computer (i.e. "natural") intelligence. But very soon, and probably already, our own intelligence will enter into a kind of coevolutionary process with its externalized computer simulation. In the second phase all comparison between artificial and natural intelligence is very difficult, in the same way as it is very difficult today to study genuinely oral cultures.

To make or change a natural language one is dependent upon the agreement and adjustments of the members of a linguistic community. In fact to construct a natural language is identical to the construction of a linguistic community. With computers, it is possible to settle a kind of linguistic convention by means of some key-strokes. Language engineering has become a possibility. The conventions made up as an agreement between the programmer and his/her computer can quickly be spread through software distribution and indirectly have consequences for large human language communities.

Language has always been more than a tool for conversation or inter-human messages. Language is a way of organizing complexity through comprehension and design. Language has never been a purely inner activity, neither of an individual nor of several individuals communicating. Language is linked to our material projections onto the world. It is a way of living in the world. We try to make our world intelligible through making it readable. In fact we transform our environment more and more according to our linguistic vision of the world, so most of our living becomes a reading of our own texts. Computers and telematics are pushing the evolution of culture a great step forward in just this direction.

The dominant rhetoric of development and progress is obsessed with the idea of technical inventions as problem solvers. One aim of the article has been to argue for the necessity to look at computers in general and artificial intelligence in particular, not so much as devices that *solve* our current problems in a faster or more "intelligent" way, but rather as a technology that will *transform* our problems in the way musical notation transformed music. In the same line: it makes sense only to a very limited extent to say that the function of writing has been to solve the "problem" of memory in illiterate cultures. Illiterate cultures are unaware of that "problem" in the same way as we may be unaware of the future "problems" that the computers of tomorrow are going to "solve" for us. An alternative way of looking at technical progress might be the following: first we invent the "solutions", then we invent the "problems", and only finally do we do the "problem solving".

Social Science in the Information Society

Current research in social science in the sub-field of information technology and society is largely lacking theories and concepts for understanding what is happening at a general level. The majority of social scientists working with computers receive their research grants from industry or technically oriented research councils. Often this "social science research" takes the form of assistance to engineers engaged in designing more "human" computer systems. It is high time that large, international research efforts are dedicated to the basic understanding of what is happening to human culture in face of new information technologies.

It has become commonplace to talk and write about the *information society*. Tacitly it is assumed that to understand the information society is to understand the role of advanced information technology in society. But all societies through all times have been information societies. Computers and other information technologies have just forced us to realize it in a new way. To understand our present information society we need to rewrite our cultural history from an information technology point of view. The present article can of course do nothing more than to scratch the surface of such an endeavour.

Acknowledgement. The list would be too long if I should acknowledge all those who have contributed to the present ideas, so I restrain myself to those who have read various versions of the present manuscript and whose comments have been incorporated, namely Jeanne Bamberger (MIT), Tamar Bermann (AFI, Oslo), Robbins Burling (University of Michigan), Tellef Kvifte and Viggo Vestel (University of Oslo). Thank you.

References and Further Reading

Bateson, Gregory (ed) (1973) The logical categories of learning and communication. In: *Steps to an ecology of mind*. Paladin, London, pp 250–280
Bateson, Gregory (1979) *Mind and nature*. Dutton, New York
Cattin, Giulio (1984) *Music of the Middle Ages I*. Cambridge University Press
Dal, Erik (1956) *Nordisk folkeviseforskning siden 1800*. Copenhagen (in Danish)
Dreyfus, Hubert (1979) *What computers can't do*. Harper and Row, New York
Geertz, Clifford (1973) *The interpretation of cultures*. Basic Books, New York
Goody, Jack (1977) *The domestication of the savage mind*. Cambridge University Press

Hindley G (ed) (1971) *The Larousse encyclopedia of music*. Hamlyn, London

Holbæk-Hansen L, Håndlykken P, Nygaard K (1975) Systems description and the delta language. Norwegian Computing Centre publ. no. 523, Oslo

Kvifte, Tellef (1981) On variability, ambiguity and formal structure in the Harding fiddle music. In: *Studia instrumentorum musicae popularis VII*. Stockholm

Kvifte, Tellef (1989) *Instruments and the electronic age: toward a terminology for a unified description of playing technique*. Solum, Oslo

Naissance de l'écriture. Cuneiformes et hieroglyphes (1982) Catalogue d'exposition, Paris: Editions de la Reunion des musées nationaux

Parrish, Carl (1959) The *notation of medieval music*. Norton, New York

Sinding-Larsen, Henrik (1983) *Fra fest til forestilling*. Magister thesis, Department of Social Anthropology, University of Oslo (in Norwegian)

Sinding-Larsen, Henrik (1985) Le rite et le jeu – deux modes d'expérience dans la fête. In: *Le carnaval, la fête et la communication, actes des premières rencontres internationals Nice 1984*. Editions Serre/UNESCO, Nice

Sinding-Larsen, Henrik (1987) Information technology and the management of knowledge. *AI and Society: Journal of Human and Machine Intelligence* 1 (2)

Sinding-Larsen, Henrik (ed) (1988) *Artificial intelligence and language: old questions in a new key*. Tano a/s, Complex 7/88, Oslo

Winograd, Terry and Flores, Fernando (1985) *Understanding computers and cognition*. Ablex, Norwood, NJ

Notes

1 It is important to realize the difference between the tempered scale as an acoustic phenomenon and as a phenomenon of human aesthetics. There are no "false notes" in the physical realm of acoustics. But through culturally specific socialization, we may learn to perceive and judge a certain set of tone intervals as correct. This is forcefully done in the case of Western music because the tempered scale is *physically embedded* in many sound-producing instruments (e.g. the piano).

2 In fact, the knowledge engineer will usually not use a programming language directly, but rather a set of description tools called "systems description languages" or "knowledge acquisition tools". As the end product in any case will be a program in some programming language, all these other languages will have to approach the same overall logic as the final programming language.

Chapter 15

Intelligence and Creativity

Lars Gyllensten

This chapter is concerned with the question of intelligence which has implications for developments in the area of the intelligent machine. Does the speed of a calculation belie intelligence? Surely finding a simple way to a solution – something a computer cannot do – shows more intelligence. Compare computer memory and human memory: we may not have a computer's memory for fine detail, but this is because we select what we feel is relevant to us. A computer cannot perform this function. Consider the computer and intuition. At the age of 12, Gauss discovered by intuition the formula for the sum of an arithmetical sequence. Could a computer ever do this? Intelligence is more than the ability to calculate and build up complicated scenarios using data and a given strategy. This is a reductionist and defeatist definition. An element of creativity is essential in the concept of intelligence. In its turn creativity must include elements of systematic intelligence: critical consolidation, attempts to incorporate creative ideas in a standardized whole and to assess their relevance. The fascination with AI lies in the hidden paths along which the brain moves when it proceeds without really knowing what is happening and what it is up to.

Let me begin with a little intelligence test. It appears in many versions, but the point is always the same. Let me pose it as follows.

Bill and Ben belong to a tribe of natives on an island in the Pacific. They are cultivated gentlemen, well aware of how two cultivated gentlemen should behave when they encounter each other – which is to say they should rub noses. They are now out for a walk, proceeding each from his own direction along the same path. In other words, they will meet. Bill is trudging along at 3 kilometres an hour; Ben, who is the younger and fitter, is doing 5 kilometres an hour. A cheeky fly, starting from Bill's nose, flies at a speed of 13 kilometres an hour towards Ben's nose, alights on it, flies back, and continues in this way for as long as he can. But when Bill and Ben meet, and rub noses, the fly meets a fearful end. The question, now, is what distance the fly has had time to put behind it, shuttling to and fro, before it dies. The original distance between the two men was 20 kilometres.

I have read somewhere that this problem was put to one of the greatest mathematicians of this century. He produced the answer in less than 30 seconds, and whoever had posed the question complimented him on this: "That is exactly what I would have expected of you. The two natives are approaching each other at an aggregate speed of 8 kilometres an hour, from a distance of 20 kilometres. They will therefore meet after $2\frac{1}{2}$ hours. In that time the fly, with its flying speed of 13 kilometres an hour, flies $32\frac{1}{2}$ kilometres. I know that you worked it out in this way. But a lot of other people, not arriving at this simple solution, become involved in tortuous calculations of the sum of an infinite, convergent series."

"Yes, well," replied the distinguished mathematician, "the fact is that I calculated the sum of the infinite, convergent series!"

And this, indeed, was an impressive performance by the skilled mathematician, to compute the sum of the series in such a short time in his head. It bears witness to a rapid, high and efficient intelligence, and to a practised mathematical competency. If he had had a well-programmed computer at his disposal, the calculation could have taken place still faster, using the same method.

These are intelligent performances, highly intelligent if you like. But is it not still more intelligent to work out the answer the simple way? What's the difference? Perhaps that the mathematician and the well-programmed computer are led to follow an accustomed pattern. From a sort of mental laziness, they slip into the familiar routine of "convergent series", and fail to look with fresh eyes at the problem as a whole. Would a computer, a software program, ever be able to do this? That Minerva, like Homer, nods from time to time we know, and that even a distinguished mathematician can have his stupid moments is no matter for surprise. Let him who is without blame cast the first stone.

But can a computer, with its built-in programs, ever escape from its own accustomed lines of thought? And what, in that case, would the necessary conditions have to be for such cheek?

I mentioned that this test of intelligence appears in many guises. The one I gave you just now I thought up myself – for the simple reason that I can't remember the original version. I don't remember the scenario, or the distance, or the speeds, whether it was a house-fly or a horse-fly. Nor did I mention the name of the distinguished mathematician – and for the same reason, forgetfulness. I remember in fact practically nothing, only the actual point of the story. How should we regard this, my memory and its lacunae? Is it that my memory is weak and stupid – unable as it is to recall the simplest data, which the simplest computer could have stored? Or is my memory wise, weeding out everything except the point itself, and saving its capacity, and its ability to take a broad view, for the essentials? A question consequent upon this – if one's memory claims to be intelligent, not stupid, when it forgets – is how does it know what is essential and a possible "point", and how does it know that it will not need the elements it weeds out?

Can a computer, with its built-in program, sweep out of its memory the data with which its memory should not be burdened? And how is it to be programmed to know what is worth saving, and what cannot be required at some time in the future? Can a computer have intuition, assuming that it is intuition that decides what should be saved and what should be thrown out? Or can a computer take risks, chance its arm – if this is what it comes to when the memory's files set their priorities?

Let me move on to another intelligence test, again something that many of you will recognize.

Carl Friedrich Gauss, who bears the honorary title of "Mathematicorum Princeps", is one of the greatest mathematicians of our age, and was suitably precocious as a child. When Gauss was about 12 years old and attending a class in arithmetic, the teacher set his pupils the task of reckoning out the sum of all integers from one up to 100. The good teacher had counted on this task to keep his adepts busy for the greater part of an hour, giving him a chance to relax. Gauss, however, came forward almost immediately, put his slate with the answer on the teacher's desk, and announced: "There it is!" The other boys counted and counted in the sweat of their brows, and in due course handed in their slates with their answers. When, finally, the teacher distrustingly examined the piles of slates, he found that a few had calculated correctly, but that the majority had committed one or another error, of various kinds. Gauss, however, had given the correct answer: 5050.

As the young genius explained: "If you write all the numbers in succession after each other, and the same row backwards beneath the first row, you get 100 pairs of numbers, and in all pairs the total is 101; 100 times 101 is 10 100, which is the sum of two such series. Half of that is 5050, which is the sum of all the figures up to and including 100." The 12-year-old Gauss had discovered immediately and off his own bat the formula for the sum of an arithmetical sequence.

What would a computer have done – which was programmed to add, but did not have baked into it the formula for the sum of an arithmetical series? It would naturally have set about the task like the other schoolboys, although it wouldn't have made any mistakes. It is, of course, intelligent to be able to put together so many numbers, one after the other, routinely, and reach a correct result. But it is more intelligent to break out of the rut, look at the situation with fresh and unconventional eyes, and discover how one can very simply add a succession of numbers in an arithmetical series, without having to put all the numbers together, one after the other. And so cruel are we in setting marks that what is intelligent appears rather stupid when it is confronted by something still more intelligent.

Let me try your patience with yet another familiar anecdote relating to ingenious behaviour, probably the best known of all – Columbus and the egg. You will recall that Columbus and a gathering of learned men were assigned the task of standing an egg on end, on its pointed end at that. The learned gentlemen pondered and puzzled, tried and failed, time after time. The egg kept turning over, and lying down on its side. Columbus gave it a gentle tap, producing a small dent in its pointed end, and an edge to the shell on which the egg could stand.

How would an intelligent computer have proceeded, a very learned computer with a program inside it that was well schooled in physics, on a level with what the most learned of these learned men could bring to bear on the problem? It would probably have calculated the egg's point of gravity, and its vertical projection in the pointed shell of the egg, computed the torque, and performed other mathematical calculations; deliberated these, and indicated how vibrations should be avoided in the substratum of the egg; made corresponding computations of the air currents and other factors that could disrupt the egg's balance; and, perhaps, have been able to describe a physical setting-up of the egg that would make it possible to keep the egg standing on its edge for a moment. It would, most certainly, have provided an intelligent analysis of the problem, and the necessary conditions for its solution.

But what did Columbus do? He solved the problem by a piece of cheek, an anecdote. One can, of course, ask whether he really solved the problem, or revolted against it. We can perhaps say that in fact he transformed the egg into something else – a cracked egg – and thus modified the premises set for the task. But it was, surely, an intelligent move that he made. And it has always been regarded as such.

How would a computer have had to be programmed to arrive at such a breach of convention? The examples of greater or lesser feats of intelligence that I have exemplified have one or two features in common.

One factor in the more intelligent of these solutions to the problems quoted is that they are not trivial. They contain an element of surprise, not to say wit. Inventive problem-solvers see their tasks in an unconventional manner – from, as it were, outside. They discover patterns or possibilities that are not inherent in the problems as set, either explicitly formulated or implicit. Their solutions afford us an "a-ha!" experience.

I should like to put a still finer point on their characteristics, and claim that there is an iconoclastic element to original, intelligent problem-solving. The cracking of the egg is symptomatic – perhaps also of the memory's clearing out of the bulkier goods in its store. Here, someone is breaking out of the close-to-hand, tautological routines, striking out over virgin terrain where no path has been marked.

I should like to suggest that the "a-ha!" experience that I mentioned is closely allied to an aesthetic experience or value judgement. And I would offer the hypothesis that an aesthetic factor is incorporated in the intuition or chance-taking that in the creative intelligence creates the new and ingenious solutions. Not for nothing do we speak of elegant solutions to problems, elegant theories, elegant programs and methods.

My intention with these fairly simple examples of intelligent performances has been to lead to these generalizations – on the break with routine, on the non-tautological, on the iconoclastic, on elements of surprise, and the aesthetic experience of the whole. Obviously, my tiny selection of examples cannot support such wide-ranging descriptions, such general hypotheses, regarding how intelligent work takes place. But if one reflects upon one's own experience, from reading, or from one's own exhilarating moments, in which one has come upon something intelligent, I am convinced that one will often discover such characteristics as I have tried to illustrate. Perhaps they are part of most intellectual performances that do not consist solely of humdrum routine.

One may object that what I have quoted as examples of intelligent thought and its properties in fact relate to creativity rather than intelligence. Many psychologists have been concerned to assert a difference in principle between these two abilities. They have also tried to demonstrate the differences by means of psychological tests, showing that we are dealing here with two different talents which are not necessarily correlated with each other. One is, of course, entitled to define one's concepts as one pleases, and to set up an operationalist definition of intelligence, trivializing it to mean a repetitive and unindependent ability to follow imprinted rules. To restrict the concept of intelligence in this way, so that it simply designates in principle an ability to master some sort of multiplication table, or to build up complicated scenarios with the data and the strategy given means that one has resorted to a reductionist or defeatist definition, and one that appears unconstructive and little capable of development. Nor does such a definition fit what one usually means by intelligence in everyday speech. Our conclusion is that an element of creativity must be involved in the concept of intelligence, if one is not to end up in sterility.

Anything worthy of the name creativity must also include elements of what we can call systematic intelligence – critical consolidation, an effort to incorporate the creative ideas in a structurized whole, an assessment of their relevance, etc. A whole number of the tests I have seen of so-called creativity have contented themselves with recording all manner of whims and fantasies, as long as they are original and unexpected. This also is a form of reductionism. Spectres of the brain, nonsenses and conceits that cannot be put in any constructive context hardly earn the name creative. As a famous Swedish writer has put it, "You're not a genius just because you're mad."

As will have become clear, I have dissected out such components underlying acts of advanced intelligence as are not verbalized or in any other way formalized – for example, an unconventional break-out from a routine system of rules or patterns, an aesthetic overall view ("elegant solutions"), the taking of a chance. Such non-verbalized elements of creative work are customarily called intuition. There is a wealth of testimony to the importance of intuition in all fields of intellectual activity – in art and literature, in technology and the sciences, not least in mathematics. Many of Gauss's discoveries, for example, were made intuitively. The evidence and the deductions came afterwards, in a laborious work of search. The Indian mathematician Ramanujan is another example. He was a natural genius, who grew up in fairly simple circumstances, without the broad schooling in mathematics that belongs to an advanced education in the West. He made a great number of mathematical discoveries, many briefly noted down as end results, and without their proof. The speed with which he detected mathematical contexts, for example in the theory of numbers, is legendary. It could happen in an instant, so quickly that he must have in some way "seen" the result, without needing to count. Mozart tells us something similar of the way in which he composed. His works, even the major ones, came to him sometimes in an experience of the whole, in which everything was clear to him right from the beginning, instantaneously, so that the only thing he had to do was to note it down in retrospect – if the word "only" is in place here.

Ramanujan's contributions to mathematics include the discovery or invention of serial developments, for example for the calculation of π. Ramanujan was only just over 30 when he died, in 1920. In recent years, his work in this respect has been worked over by others, and made available for the calculation of π to over 130 million decimal points. Such calculation presupposes a modern supercomputer, which neither existed nor was conceivable in Ramanujan's day. To give you some idea of the import of his achievement, I can mention that π to 39 decimal points is sufficient to calculate the circumference of the universe to an accuracy on a par with the measurements of the particles in an atomic nucleus. The feat of programming the computer, and the computer's work of computation, are naturally admirable, or at least awesome. But the great intellectual achievement is, of course, Ramanujan's.

Let me conclude with another example from the world of mathematics of the difference between, as it were, a pedestrian contribution, and its intuitive preconditions and expectations. There is an old topological problem that has to do with the colouring of maps. Assume that we have a map, on a flat surface. The map can look any way you like, cover as many areas as you like, and be of any shape you like. Our task now is to colour these areas so that no areas adjoining each other are given the same colour. People have long been convinced that no more than four colours are ever needed. No attempts to draw a map that would require further colours have succeeded. It has also been possible to demonstrate that four colours are sufficient for certain specific types of map. However, no general proof of this has been produced. A few years ago, a number of mathematicians succeeded in proving that four colours are always enough. They used a modern, high-power computer, and succeeded in testing a large number of representatively selected types of map. Their computations were extremely comprehensive. Their proof was *per se* interesting. Their programming and computing were impressive. But the enthusiasm this feat excited among their mathematical colleagues was very modest. Their proof lacked the elegance and generalization that could raise it from a skilful exercise in the art of using an advanced multiplication table to a high-class intellectual performance. The intellectual criterion was not fulfilled. The intuitive conviction and chance-taking that four colours are sufficient received a response that was an anticlimax.

There is an ancient antithesis between what we call talent and what we call genius – between the reproductive and the creative intelligence. Between them there is a sort of no-man's land. Here, between the trivial and the creative, the majority of our intellectual inputs are made. By means of this *causerie*, I have tried to point to some topographical characteristics of this landscape. I will end with this question: is it not there, in that territory, that one is moving in the sophisticated and ambitious attempts now being made to create programs and computers that are to resemble human intelligence? In that case, the task will be to map the terrain and, we may hope, discover the hidden paths along which the human brain moves when it proceeds without really knowing what is happening and what it is up to.

Translated by Keith Bradfield

This article is published in a Swedish version in Georg Klein (ed.), *Om kreativitet och flow*. Brombergs, Stockholm, 1990.

Chapter 16

On the Views on Labour Reflected in Chekhov and the Bible

Agneta Pleijel

In earlier industrial societies work in industry was closely linked to a morality of duty which was both individual and social. But the status of work today and the moral system which gave it its status have undergone considerable change. The Book of Genesis can be seen as the first gospel of labour, but what is our view of the meaning of work today? In *The Three Sisters* Chekhov has shown with both tender irony and deep seriousness that the meaning of work cannot be separated from the meaning of life, and attempting to arrive at a new view of work therefore always involves attempting to arrive at a new view of man.

I should like in this chapter to dwell upon two things: the identity of man, and man's work, or labour. This I will do via a reading of Anton Chekhov's *The Three Sisters*, which was first staged at the Moscow Art Theatre in 1901, sixteen years before the Russian Revolution. I do not intend to offer any exhaustive analysis of that play – far from it. And my perspective is limited: I am writing against the background of the sporadic discussion in recent decades of work in our time, and the changes that have been noted in a single cultural area, that of northern Europe, where work has long been regarded as almost the only factor to have created a sense of human identity.

This, obviously, is no longer the case: man has to seek his identity elsewhere than in his labour. But where? Everywhere, people are groping for new value systems, a new ethics. So far as I can see, this is due largely to the impoverishment of the traditional type of work, and the moral system it entailed, without any new moral system having emerged. Work in industry and the morality of "duty" were closely interwoven. Both are now undergoing such radical changes that a new generation has little or nothing to learn from the older.

Let me therefore resort to a source that has provided the basis of our civilization, and, by way of introduction, to Chekhov's play, try to summarize what is said there of the identity of man and his work. In the Old Testament, we read that God created man in His own image. He was to be fruitful and multiply, subdue the earth, and have dominion over the fish of the sea and the fowl of the air. The Book of Genesis can be seen as the "first gospel of labour", according to Pope John Paul II, who also wrote an encyclical on the subject.

We find in the New Testament a continuing reflection upon the basic terms established in Genesis. Let me sum up. God, through the process of the Creation, is a worker, constantly active. Man, as His image, is also a worker, continuing during his earthly life God's creative process. Christ, in the Gospel according to St John, says: "My Father worketh hitherto, and I work" (5:17). In the Gospel according to St Luke we read: "For what is a man advantaged, if he gain the whole world, and lose himself, or be cast away?" (9:25).

In other words, man shall not only fill the earth and subdue it, but shall also do it in such a way that he "gains himself", understands himself and his role in the creative process. Work and creation are not an objective but a subjective process. Work, according to the Bible, is a fundamental dimension of human life. Its purpose is for man to understand himself. The whole time, the aim of his work is ultimately self-understanding. I offer these quotations to draw attention to a fundamental discrepancy between this subjective, Biblical view, and the objective view of work that we today apply, almost without exception: work is seen in terms of technology, machinery, capital and material results.

According to the Bible, life and work on this earth constitute a learning process. If we broaden this perspective beyond that of the individual, human history can be seen, according to this view, as a gigantic work process, and the earth as a huge workshop. The one and only object of this process is human maturity. We know that history, according to Genesis, began with a Fall from grace: man ate of the fruit of knowledge. He thus became capable of distinguishing between good and evil. His *choice* was anchored in history, as an inseparable element of human identity. It was, indeed, at this moment that history actually commenced. Man is anchored in *time*. Having eaten of the fruit of knowledge, his life became finite: his life on earth was to end in *death*.

I do not entirely understand the wrath of the Lord at the Fall. After all, man's ability to distinguish between good and evil – which is to say his ethical dimension – is a necessary condition for his being able to function as the image of God. He is *free to choose*, in other words a free and creative being. Perhaps, however, the wrath of the Lord is simply a necessary condition for His being able to stipulate the necessary conditions: man, according to Genesis, shall eat bread "in the sweat of his face"; he is required to secure his livelihood and his life by labour. He is also to win maturity. Life is a learning process.

And what is promised by way of reward for his labour and his maturation? The following: "Nevertheless, we, according to his promise, look for new heavens and a new earth, wherein dwelleth righteousness" (II Peter 2:13), or (following the Book of Revelations) "And I saw a new heaven and a new earth" (21:1). In the process of secularization that our civilization has gradually undergone during the past two centuries, which is to say precisely during the epoch of the Industrial Revolution, it is only natural that people should have to an increasing extent placed this promise in *time*. In the secularized version of Christianity that Marxism in reality constitutes, God's promise has been transformed into a worldly Utopia. The new heaven and the new earth are to arise here, among us, only at a later point in time, when righteousness will prevail.

With this anchorage of the entire process in time, however, something happened to the Biblical message. The whole process of maturation, the concept that man's work related ultimately to his self-understanding, was increasingly erased. The great goal – the maturing of each individual life – was transformed, as I see it, into something different: material justice within the human collective. This was a grand idea: Christianity is in many ways a starting-point for our concept of equality. But something was lost en route. And when man himself became a means for the realization of the Utopia, as during various phases of Communism, the entire idea of man himself as the goal of the Utopia was emptied of all content.

The struggle of the labour movement in Sweden too often came into dire conflict with Christianity, and thus also with the view of labour reflected in the Bible. When the spiritual dimension disappears, however, something happens. In place of a subjective view of work, an objective and technical view emerges. In these brief lines, I am naturally not attempting to outline the historical development of the concept of labour, or work. I am concerned, simply, to underline one specific aspect. Nor do I wish to claim that a subjective interpretation of the concept of work must necessarily be associated with a religious view of man (although it undoubtedly makes it easier). For those of us who find difficulty in establishing or contenting ourselves with the concept of another world in which God's promise of a new heaven, a new earth, and righteousness will be fulfilled, I would recall the view expressed by Søren Kierkegaard.

Kierkegaard's entire work can be seen as an ongoing reflection upon what the Bible has to say of man, his role in the world, his choice and self-understanding, and the individual's relationship with others. Kierkegaard has interpreted eternity as something that is encapsulated in time: the moments of clarity when man sees himself and understands who he is. Such moments of harmony and clearsightedness exist. In such "Kierkegaardian moments" we see clearly what is wrong with the circumstances in which we live, what it is that runs contrary to our human nature, creating disharmony and feelings of meaninglessness and lack – from the circumstances of our private lives to the broader contexts that affect most of us, such as the labour and management organizations, technological development, the assertions of power.

And now to Chekhov. What I have seen more clearly than ever before on re-reading *The Three Sisters* is that the entire play is a sort of dissertation on the passages I quoted just now from the Bible. Its two fundamental themes are the questions of man's identity in relation to his work, and the question of the future. Its characters live as Chekhov himself did, and as we do in our secularized contemporary society. But the play's dimension in depth arises from the way in which the text processes, and counterpointedly returns to, the statements concerning man made by the original source, the Bible. The play is enclosed within two Biblical paraphrases, the one introducing, the other concluding it.

Right at the beginning, a bell chimes: we find ourselves in *time*. This is followed by the joyful lines of the youngest sister, Irena, describing the wonderful mood in which she had awakened that morning: "I suddenly felt that the whole world was clear to me – I thought I knew how life has to be lived. Dear Ivan Romanitch. I can see it all. A person has to work, whoever he happens to be, and labour in the sweat of his face; it's the only way a person can find the content and meaning of his life, happiness, satisfaction."

The morning, then, of the Creation, in Genesis. The play ends with a similar paraphrase. It is the oldest sister, Olga, who right at the end of Act IV, after a great deal of disappointment and disillusion, cries out: "There will come a time when people will understand what it was all about, what was the point of all this suffering, and what was concealed from us will no longer be concealed. In the meanwhile, however, we have to work . . . we have to work, quite simply, we have to work!"

Olga's words contain a negative reference to the phrase "And I saw a new heaven and a new earth" in Revelations. But we can also see them as a direct paraphrase of the words of St Paul: "For now we see through a glass, darkly; but then face to face" (I Cor. 13:12), with its continuation: "now I know in part; but then I shall know even as also I am known."

Both Irina's introductory and Olga's concluding paraphrase make it clear that Chekhov, to the same degree as the Bible, relates the meaning of human life, and man's understanding of himself, to his doings, to his work. None of the characters in the play reach this far, but it may nonetheless be worth analysing what it is that they associate with work, what "working" entails. It is often suggested that Chekhov's *The Three Sisters* is about man's vain longing for something other, but indeterminate, as expressed in the mournful refrain "To Moscow, to Moscow!" I will try to show that Chekhov, in *The Three Sisters*, dwells consistently upon something far more concrete.

Four Acts – four studies in a cycle of people's lives. In the centre the three sisters Olga, Masha and Irina, their brother Andrei, and his fiancée Natasha, whom he marries. Also, Masha's grammar school teacher Kulygin, and the sisters' old and trusty servant Anfisa. The rest of the cast is made up of officers from the company assigned to the little provincial town, so infinitely far from Moscow. It includes Lt.-Col. Vershyinin, in love with Masha; Baron Lt. Tusenbach, who proposes to Irina; and Staff Captain Solyonyi, also in love with Irina. At the end of the play, when Irina has accepted Tusenbach, he is killed in a duel with Solyonyi. Finally, the aged military surgeon Chebutykin also appears.

On the surface, little more takes place than has been suggested above except that the sisters' dream of getting to Moscow is gradually extinguished, and that the company leaves the town, and moves on. Beneath the surface, however, Chekhov is describing an entire social development and its consequences. Most of the characters belong to the old social order; they belong to a land-owning class, which is being confronted with a new type of society. They dream about taking a job. Irina in Act I: "You could not, in the most blazing heat, long more for water than I long to work." Tusenbach: "A great healthy storm is blowing up, it will blow our society clean from sloth and indifference, clean from all prejudices against work, and from rotting boredom. I will work, but in twenty years, in thirty years, everyone will work. Every single one of us!"

This circle of people suffers – and we cannot ignore the fact – from a bad conscience, because they know they are living on the work of others. We are concerned here, at any rate, very much with the social movement that began in Russia in the second half of the last century. Of greater interest for our purpose, however, is to study what they themselves hope they will gain in positive terms by working. For Irina and others it is a matter very largely of *community with others* – the chance to escape from the coolness between people that Tusenbach remembers so intensively from his upbringing in a noble family in St Petersburg. To Masha's husband, the teacher Kulygin – a bore in the eyes of the other characters, but one into whose mouth Chekhov puts a number of truths – work seems to be a matter of *avoiding a fragmentation of the self*: "The Romans were healthy because they knew how to work – and how to rest. They had their *mens sana in corpore sano*. Their souls and their bodies developed in the same direction." Vershyinin, for his part, dreams of a future in which everyone works because he has a vision that more and more people, by education and training, will become wiser and more sensitive. His dream of the future is the whole time bound up with the idea of *education, of training*. In this garrison town he has found three people, namely the three sisters, who are sensitive, educated, and broad-minded. In his eyes, many more people will become, in the future, just as they are.

Even this brief selection of propositions from Act I reveals a broad spectrum of ideas relating to work. It confers a sense of community, it permits spiritual growth, it helps us to forget ourselves (bridging the existential gap of which Sartre was speaking when he underlined that man is the only creature in nature who is aware of self). Work is to confer happiness. Vershyinin, it is true, does not naively believe, as do Irina and Tusenbach, that happiness will necessarily be achieved during their own lifespan. In "two hundred, three hundred, yes, ultimately a thousand years" there will, however, be a new and happier life for everyone. "We," he says, "will no longer exist, but it is for that life that we are now alive, that we work, and suffer; it is we that are creating it – and in that alone lies the purpose of our existence, and, if you will, our only happiness."

Today, of course, we can claim that Chekhov's characters are idealizing work. They hardly differentiate between different aspects of the concept. We might say that they are outlining the contours of the secular Utopia: through work, sacrifices and disregard of self, and of one's own happiness (Vershyinin), the kingdom of joy will finally emerge – "a new heaven and a new earth" on our own planet. Chekhov, of course, sees all this with the loving irony that is his distinguishing characteristic as a writer. There is a strong element of comedy in the longing of these idlers for work. However, I do not believe that it is by chance that what they long for is "work" – not "love", "parties" or "war". Chekhov's irony is, indeed, loving. And beneath it is a serious intent.

His characters idealize above all physical labour. The new type of work in industry – which, after all, was the "work for everyone" of which Tusenbach speaks – was not as it seemed in their dreams. That we know. And that Chekhov also knew. Even in Act II, the disappointments are beginning to be felt. Work is mechanical, repetitive, routine. Irina, working now at the Telegraphic Office, says: "I've got to look for another job, this is not for me. All that I so fervently desired and dreamed about, there's not a trace of it. It's a job without poetry, without thoughts." Olga, who is a teacher, gets headaches from the days she spends in the school. And yet their dream of work remains alive and intact within them, as if they had not seen the contradiction. What sort of work *is* it then of which they are dreaming? Here, in Act II, we are already halfway into a new society, a new moral system. Let me just point to some of the aspects that Chekhov has observed, and to which he discreetly draws our attention. *The Three Sisters* has one, and only one, main character – in the sense that she stages and illustrates the transformation that takes place. This is Natasha, the brother Andrei's wife, who is sometimes regarded as playing a secondary role. She deserves, however, a place as the main character in the play – the New Age. She is of a different class from the sisters, from the bourgeoisie or merchant class. Gradually, she pushes out the sisters, literally driving them from their apartments to make room for her children.

When we first meet her, she is – by the sisters' standards – vulgarly dressed, in a pink dress with a green waistband. Her lack of taste, however, is very much bound up with her pronounced attentiveness to her outward appearance. Chekhov gives her many lines that relate to this attitude. She worries about what is "right" or "wrong" in her dress. She is always looking in the mirror. The sisters are her exact opposite, not caring how they look. They are unhappy but "genuine", in the sense that they still exist in an environment that accords them a self-evident value. Natasha is uncertain in this environment, and therefore false; she is forced to play a constant double game. The sisters know how to behave. Natasha does not, and half her lines are therefore concerned with upbringing, table manners, the "correct" way to health, and so on.

In her train we see a modern fixation with the outward role: the dependence upon books on etiquette, trendy advice on health, pompous views on how to bring up our children, recipes and tips on how we should be feeling, how we should make ourselves up, how we should eat – an entire world of rules as to how we should be when we don't know who we are, or indeed if we are anything at all. The advice given in weekly magazines, the consumer information that constantly confronts us, the continual playing of roles – Natasha is not for one moment authentic. In her, Chekhov has captured ourselves, and the modern world's rhetorical echo chamber. And more than that, he shows us how it – or Natasha – is gaining ground, and finally, paradoxically enough, power.

At the same time, an old system of moral values is being abolished. In Natasha's life falsehood and truth are of subordinate importance, since her social role is all-significant. This enables her, without any great qualms of conscience, to deceive Andrei with Protopopov, and even bear his child without divulging who is the father. Conscience appears to have lost its role. Instead, it is the role that has taken possession of the person. Chekhov does not assign values: he simply records events. What he sees, leads straight into our own age. Andrei is changed in the course of his marriage. He ceases to dream of being a free intellectual, or a university professor in Moscow. He enters, instead, the civil administration. He becomes a bureaucrat, an administrator, a member of the local council. He joins the new, and expanding, stratum of bureaucracy that "represents" us, that "plays our role" for us. (And, symbolically enough, Protopopov, with whom Natasha deceives him, becomes his superior.)

At the same time, and in close conjunction with this societal change, the concept of an occupation, of a job, of knowledge is emptied, in the play, of content. This is very clear in Act III, in which is introduced something I should like to call the "theme of oblivion". One of the characters who really has a profession is the doctor, Chebutykin. But in Act III he gets royally drunk, blasting off against the contemporary view which holds that he should be able to treat "every disease under the sun". Instead of being a physician, subject to the conditions of life and death, and in no way almighty, he is required to be an "expert" whose social standing is dependent upon his *success*. One of his patients has died. He regards this as his own fault, and feels it is because he has "forgotten" what to do.

His "role" – as I interpret it – of doctor leads to his feeling that he personally has ceased to exist: "Perhaps I don't even exist – I just imagine that I'm here, and that I eat and sleep." His profession is becoming a role, and his knowledge consists of playing it well. In the same lines, Chebutykin recalls that he has heard people around him discoursing on Shakespeare and Voltaire. No one had read them, it was all pretence. "The vulgarity of it! The cheapness," he exclaims. "I know absolutely nothing – I've forgotten all I knew – I don't remember a thing – absolutely nothing."

This entire passage is intimately related to Natasha, and the New Age. In this same Act, Irina also complains over oblivion: "Where has it all gone? Where is it? Oh heavens, oh heavens! I've forgotten everything, I've forgotten . . . It's all mixed up in my head . . . I can't remember the Italian for window or ceiling." And this immediately after noting how Andrei has altered in his marriage, and immediately before her own complaint that her job at the Telegraphic Office is destroying her: "I feel that I am getting further and further away from the life that is *real* and beautiful" (author's italics).

In Act III, work fails to bring the characters closer to reality. On the contrary. Their lives appear to degenerate into a playing of roles, and representation. This leads to feelings of emptiness – or alienation, to use a word, popular in recent decades, intended to capture the phenomenon of a person's work not reflecting his or her being.

In this same Act, the play's only direct confrontation occurs between Natasha and one of the three sisters, Olga. This concerns Anfisa, their faithful servant. Natasha wants to dismiss her. Anfisa has become too old and incapable. She is no longer useful. "There shouldn't be people in a house who aren't needed." Olga objects. Olga cannot forget all the years that Anfisa has been with them, and she is upset by Natasha's brutality. Natasha's reply relates to another of the realities of the New Age: the division of labour, the partition and carving up of work that is required when no one can longer have any overall view. "It's the school for you – and the home for me," rules Natasha. "If I say anything that concerns the servants, I know what I'm talking about."

Her ethics are utilitarian; administration, without the admixture of unnecessary feelings; the objective view; and logic. Feeling has been replaced by duty. This Act, in which two eras are literally opposed in the characters of Olga and Natasha, is dominated by the great fire that has broken out in the town, rendering many people homeless. Olga pours cast-off clothing over those who have lost their belongings, while Natasha drily observes: "We must always help the poor – that is the duty of the rich." Natasha is content once it is said that "they" – the public sector – are planning some charity event for those impoverished by the fire.

What we are witnessing is the delegation of responsibility. Olga is prepared to assume personal responsibility, as a feudal moral order required: Natasha is content for it to be delegated. I draw attention to this not in order to idealize any sort of feudal ethic, but to underline that Vershyinin's dream of the future – his belief that work plus education will create good and wise people – is soon punctured in the play. What can be glimpsed on the horizon is not a society of education and spiritual growth, but that of a utilitarian ethic, the playing of roles, the delegation of responsibility. Even if he may be mistaken in his hope for the future, he nonetheless sums up the situation in a way that I believe to be valid even today: "In the old days, the human race engaged in war. It filled its time with battles and attacks and victories. But all this belongs to the past, and it has left a great vacuum that we are for the present unable to fill. But humanity is seeking, and it will naturally find. Oh, may that day soon be here!"

And so this class of warrior nobility, and with it the moral concepts and ethics of the old society, departs from the stage in Act IV of *The Three Sisters*. The New Age lies ahead of them. And that New Age now lies behind us. We have witnessed what Chekhov so clearsightedly registered, namely how little happiness the era of mass industrial labour brought with it. We are again faced – like Vershyinin – with "a great vacuum that we are for the present unable to fill". Nor are there lacking today the encouraging ideologies that assure us that infinite happiness awaits us just around the corner. A new technology is relieving us of the scourge of physical labour. Man will be eating his bread without effort, without sweat. The important thing is no longer work but "leisure", and the politicians are doing everything in their power to "fill" it for us.

Little is now said of the value and dignity of human labour; such things are out of date. Some people, it is true, sense the awesome meaninglessness concealed beneath the shiny surface of this splendid leisure. Honest physical toil is the subject in some quarters of nostalgia; this is, most certainly, because it was performed in a society that could clearly point to its "meaning", for example in the form of a hope that things would change for the better. But for many people – and their numbers are increasing – the Western world is now being drained of all meaning. Not long ago I read, with mixed feelings, Bertrand Russell's excellent essay "In Praise of Idleness" (1932). In it, Russell notes that people work far too much – a relic of the old slave morality. They should take life easy; it should be possible to distribute the work between people far more sensibly.

This is wise and true and reductions in working hours and "job rotation" are phenomena that were under discussion in our society not that long ago. But since 1932, when Russell wrote his essay, the pendulum has indeed swung: the people who then had the privilege of being able to "idle" are now the very same people who have the privilege of a meaningful job that devours them hair and hide, or body and soul. Conversely, the people who at that time were working themselves to death are now the selfsame people whose leisure the politicians are striving to fill.

Despite, however, the swings of the pendulum, all these issues are part and parcel of the same discussion, the same great fabric of questions that we must reduce to the most elementary of all: who is man? What is he, and what is he doing on this planet? This sounds very solemn and high-minded, as it naturally does when I suggest, also, that we have to take the insights formulated in the Old and New Testaments seriously: man is, by nature, a creator. He expresses himself through his work, and through his actions.

Work is in the deepest sense man's language: it is what puts him into communication with the world, and with other people.

If we look at it like this, then it is self-evident that we are concerned not just with any work, but precisely that which has as its objective man himself, and his development and maturation. In the work he performs he has to have an opportunity to take responsibility. He has to have the opportunity to choose between good and evil, and to see his own life as an accumulation of experiences and insights through which he becomes participant in and connected with the lives of others.

If Chekhov sees his characters with tender irony, he nonetheless takes them deeply seriously when he allows them – despite all the disappointments that work has brought them – to maintain, nonetheless, their longing for work, in the closing lines of *The Three Sisters*. Without themselves realizing it, it is in the Biblical sense that his characters are longing – for the work that cannot be separated from the meaning of life, and constitutes a language between themselves and the world. The comedy, or tragi-comedy, arises largely from their at times confusing this with a work of an utterly different and reductive kind – just as we do. What we lack is thus not, primarily, a new view of work (or at least, this is not enough), but another view of man.

Note. The quotations from *The Three Sisters* are from Michael Frayn's interpretation of the play (1983, 1985, Methuen, London).

Translated by Keith Bradfield

Chapter 17

Rameau's Nephew: A Dialogue for the Enlightenment

Herbert Josephs

Diderot's body of writings – including his translation of Shaftesbury, his biography of Seneca and his dialogues – is described as a persistent search for the vital interlocutor, for that other who might stimulate his imagination and onto whom he could project his ideas. To Diderot the dialogue was far more than a narrative strategy or a component of rhetorical technique: he had an aversion to literary speech limited to a single voice. None of his writing is farther removed from monologue than *Rameau's Nephew*, and it belongs to the dimension of the ambiguous, the uncertain and the paradoxical. If offers a world where new questions are generated and where isolated thought is changed into genuine dialogue.

Rameau's Nephew has often reached its public in unintended guise. Since its initial appearance in France in a translation of Goethe's translation of the original manuscript, through its frequent appearances in our own times on the French stage, Diderot's masterpiece has resisted classification within a literary genre. The Encyclopedist's vivid portrayal of an imagined encounter between himself and the nephew of the celebrated composer has been variously read as philosophical dialogue, as literary satire with polemical intentions, or as another of Diderot's experiments in fiction, depicting the author's psyche divided against itself. *Rameau's Nephew*, with its gesticulating protagonist miming satires, dreams and musical performances, has repeatedly challenged the theatrical imagination to attempt its performance; its nature, however, as a work of imaginative fiction has most often seemed to protect the dialogue from translation into the more physically compelling but also more physically limiting medium of the public stage.

However distant from Diderot's intentions and achievement was Hegel's commentary on the divided and alienated consciousness or any of the modern adaptations of the dialogue for the theatre, the diverse responses elicited by this plotless narrative of a hypothetical café encounter, all recognize implicitly that with *Rameau's Nephew* Diderot had not offered to himself or to his eventual reader simply a series of philosophical statements bound and supported by the fictional framework long familiar to the tradition of philosophical dialogue. He had drawn the character of the nephew, of *Lui*, named only obliquely in the dialogue, from one of the milieus he occasionally frequented and had transformed him into a dazzling figure of fantasy. At the same time, however, this unforgettable literary creation, the bizarre but attractive image of artistic failure and social roguery, was shaped by the *philosophe* into his most complete fictional representation of the mental energy that triggered into activity his essentially dialogic intelligence.

From his translation of Shaftesbury, which he had described as a conversational exchange with the British author, to his biography of Seneca, written shortly before his death and likewise conceived of as a conversation with his historical subject, virtually the entire body of Diderot's writings demonstrates a persistent search for the vital interlocutor, for that fascinating other who might stimulate his imagination and onto whom he could project ideas and feelings in search of a character. This same process reveals as well his unconquerable aversion for any of the inherited forms of either philosophical or literary speech limited to a single voice. Whether in his earliest exercises in imitative writing or in his most adventurous experiments in new fictional forms for philosophic discourse, it is apparent that the dialogue was for Diderot always far more than merely a narrative strategy or a component of rhetorical technique. And none of his writings is further removed from monologue than *Rameau's Nephew*.

Transforming the familiar into the allegorical, Diderot created for his fictionalized conversation a symbolic decor at the Café de la Régence, and staged his imagined encounter with Rameau as a kind of verbal chess-game. In a characteristic act of narrative *dédoublement*, he pitted against each other a high-minded representative of the ideals of the Encyclopédie, *le philosophe*, and Rameau, a discomforting original, a sensitive aesthetician, a perversely entertaining moralist but also a mediocre musician, social parasite and outcast, reduced to an artistry of brilliant mimicry by his dependence on a soulless milieu of financiers and actresses. The dialogue would seem to be neither more nor less than an imaginative rendering of a confrontation, enacted in a manner characterized by polite aggression and defensive positioning, between the Encyclopedist and his enemies, the anti-*philosophes*. The character designated either as *Moi* ("I") by the author or as *Monsieur le philosophe* by his interlocutor, appears to espouse the Enlightenment belief in the powers of rational inquiry to understand, to order and finally to master and control the objects of human knowledge. He is the proponent of a moral system founded on the supreme value of virtue; his mission is that of upholding and transmitting belief in some native moral instinct that he endows with the transforming force of the sacred. Rameau's nephew, however, poses as the exception to the *philosophe*'s definition of the human, for he is a creature in whom that universal moral fibre, for some reason never quite clear to him, has always failed to resonate. Rameau is assigned the role of the disenchanted mind, the cynic committed to an unmediated contact with material reality, bitter though this contact often is for him. Questions of truth and beauty, of identity and social posturing, of eternal ideals and hedonistic pleasures are raised, debated, dropped and again raised, always shadowed by some haunting concern shared by both parties to the debate. The exchange, often familiar or ironically proper, but always intense and rapid, dramatizes the shock of value systems: the discourse of the *philosophe* is structured by eternal ideals and by a belief in the happy life constructed on supports of virtuous action; his arguments are buttressed by a rhetoric celebrating wholeness and unity and by the self-satisfied abstractions of theoretical reason. The life-style of *Monsieur le philosophe* is offered as judgement of the nephew's cynical, proudly self-mocking parasitic existence, guided only by a vision confined to the present and the practical, his lost integrity dissolved by a life of pandering into shapeless multiplicity.

And yet, this provocative encounter, whose rhythm of exchange continually opens onto horizons of change and uncertainty, is initiated by what appears to be a narrative manner more traditionally associated with closed story-telling strategies, directed by an authoritative voice towards the revelation of known truths. In a few incisive brush-strokes, the narrator offers first a sketch of his own mental habits, the circumstances and setting of the encounter, and then a more extended portrait of his eccentric protagonist, Jean-François Rameau. But even the opening lines of *Rameau's Nephew*, which take us from the gardens of the Palais-Royal to the neighbouring Café de la Régence, are propelled by the metaphor of dialogue, the author/narrator presenting himself as engaged in the repeated act of mental libertinage, in fickle pursuit of tempting ideas. In a phrase that has become emblematic of Diderot's tirelessly inquiring spirit, the narrator acknowledges that "my thoughts are my whores". And it is with a mixture of delight and caution that the narrator advances towards his encounter with the illicit pleasure of contact with the unconventional and with the free play of ideas. His grandest moment of intellectual free-thought begins, however, only with the arrival of his chosen interlocutor and with the narrative stride that carries the author from monologue into dialogue.

Rameau's nephew, somehow always "other than himself", immediately appears to have inherited the dialogue's burden of maieutic function; he is the "original", defined by Diderot as that "grain of yeast that ferments and restores to everyone a bit of his natural individuality". What Rameau has to offer is not so much the guarantee of ever uttering a single truth as the promise of dissolving with his incisive critical thrusts the barriers erected to conceal the fragility of what so effortlessly passes as the truth.

And what had at first seemed to represent an ultimate voice of authority, some prevailing narrative presence that would establish value in the midst of debate and propose solution at the conclusion of conflicting argument, is suddenly withdrawn and absorbed into the persona of the rationalist Encyclopedist *philosophe*. For *Rameau's Nephew* is no renewal of the age-old act of Platonic ventriloquy, alternately giving speech and silence to some fictional marionette. The voice of Rameau's nephew will remain irreducibly foreign, the dialogue will remain a genuine exchange, and not merely another of the traditional literary masks for what is finally always monologue. And it is not only Rameau but the *philosophe* as well who will function as the provocative midwife, the energizing "accoucheur", forcing into existence from beneath the nephew's own functional mask of cynical doubt the disjointed, dissonant strains of an alienated consciousness.

Once the two discourses are set in opposition to each other, and whatever the rhetorical powers deployed on either side of the exchange, whatever fructifying, fermenting effect the prodding and position-taking may have on both adversaries, no agreement will be forced upon either of the interlocutors. No sooner does one theory sound with the ring of validity, than it is thrust back into the relentless, questioning light of scepticism and thus into the ceaseless movement of dialogic thought. And if the exchange between the public-minded *philosophe* and the debased panderer often uncovers a sophisticated play at power and control, of evasive masking and sadistic unmasking, if outrage over servile abjection and satiric mockery of pompous moral idealism seem to vie with each other for momentary advantage, what remains constant is the energy of criticism, the intellectual vigour that forces an inversion of every position, that uncovers every position, especially the most cherished, as mask, and that promises at least, perhaps at most, the renewal of its own creative vitality.

For, over-arching the exchange, guiding its direction and allowing it to generate its own inner change, is the voice of the narrator, reappearing infrequently but pointedly to reaffirm his presence, to dramatize and represent his own reflection. But while he lifts the veil of narration to reveal authorial control, he never absorbs either of the interlocutors into some pre-established order of things. Diderot's voice is never simply that of the master, the teacher, the controlling force that has brought two conflicting discourses into confrontation only to reveal and affirm with finality the validity of a truth held prior to dialogue. Diderot's narrator is, if anything, the mystifier and illusionist, occupied primarily with creating and preserving space within his fictional exchange for uncertainty, sweeping aside the rational premises, the logical conclusions and the abstract classifications of Enlightenment ideology and, no less urgently, giving the lie through an inner dialogue that explodes outward, to the comforting but finally unacceptable fantasy of a unified and coherent self.

As a result, *Rameau's Nephew* will never truly leave the dimension of the ambiguous, the uncertain and the paradoxical. In those remarkable pages where the nephew seems to have abandoned his interlocutor to step upon the more purely fictional stage for his perplexing performance in mime of the rapturous melodic beauty of the new Italian lyric opera that seems to become a representation of the processes of nature in ebullition and of some mysterious universal harmony; or in his satiric enactment of the varied positions of mutual dependence that is universalized into the beggar's pantomime, the "grand branle de la terre", the nephew's personality is broken down into a compelling and illuminating but frightening and ludicrous multiplicity of forms. And the ambivalent reactions of attraction and repulsion, of awe and horror, amusement and admiration, are transferred from the narrator to the reader. We become witness not solely to the bizarre conduct of this curious phenomenon, but as well to the anxiety provoked in the detached, reflective *philosophe*, disoriented by the mixture of aesthetic sensitivity and moral perversion contained within a single being. Rameau's eruptions into a proliferation of forms has the effect of emptying the dialogue's intellectual space of all those fictitious models of wholeness that somehow join together the conflicting polarities of the rational and irrational, the natural and the civilized, the individual and the social. But as Diderot will later deny mastery, both socially and intellectually, to the Master in *Jacques the Fatalist*, in *Rameau's Nephew* he denies conclusiveness to his ending as well as, to his story-teller, the authority and ironic detachment common to other narrators of his age.

Rameau's Nephew, then, in its final epistemological stance, and in its ultimate formal openness, rejoins the scientific philosopher of Diderot's earlier *Pensées sur l'Interprétation de la Nature*; all knowledge is at best reducible to the status of the tentative, to the hypothetical, subject to modification, revision and reversal by the equally tentative perception born of the following moment. The achievement of the encounter between the *philosophe* and the composer's nephew, when the adversaries take leave of each other, may be said, philosophically, to have, at most, provoked a cascade of thoughts, fragmented, undeveloped, each one retaining its status as potentiality, all of them mere gestures of a mind in continuous motion. There had been no coming to rest in stasis, no seeking of refuge permitted outside the disruptive dialogic rhythm set in action by the encounter with the "original". Firmly held truths, whether on matters of education or morality, on providence and determinism, genius and mediocrity, had generated their opposites until both positions were absorbed into contradiction and brought to an irreducible logical impasse.

As a literary experiment, *Rameau's Nephew*, a narrative without an ending, is a testimony to the refusal of conventional genre and a permanent challenge to the expectations of readers guided by their cultural forms to seek out the satisfactions provided by closure and certainty; as one of the most distinguished acts of Enlightenment intelligence, the fictional conversation is a unique monument to the force of interrogation and to the refusal of knowledge that tends to the totalizing and the absolute, that seeks assurance without deviation and certainty without suspension. For the most unconquerable of Diderot's enemies was neither Palissot nor Fréron, but an intolerance to ambiguity and paradox so stubborn as to appear endemic to the human mind. With *Rameau's Nephew* Diderot took on as adversary a world intolerant of dialogue itself. Resisting the mind's ineradicable temptation by absolute knowledge, by abstract finalism, by closure, he offered in exchange a vibrant mental world dissolving permanently into uncertainty, where new questions were generated and where sterile thought, secure in its own isolation, was changed into genuine dialogue.

Chapter 18

Literature, Reflection and the Theory of Knowledge

Allan Janik

Both humanists and scientists may think it absurd to suggest that literature can play a role in epistemology. But this is because literature has been consigned to a nebulous, non-cognitive realm of values, leading in the "fact"-worshipping twentieth century to the trivialization of studies which should illuminate the character of human life. The manifold nature of experience can only be captured significantly in narrative form, and by reflection, a mode of knowledge that involves epistemological pluralism. Literature has this ability and, through its capacity for concrete portrayal, it can also move us. Janik gives four examples: Aeschylus' *Orestia*, Shakespeare's *King Lear*, Diderot's *Ramean's Nephew* and the poetry of G. Trakl. His statement is: without literary reflection, the essential problematic character of human experience can only be superficially explored.

At first glance it will surely seem absurd to both humanists and scientists alike to suggest that literature can play a role in epistemology. This is principally because literature in the "fact"-worshipping twentieth century has been consigned to a nebulous, non-cognitive realm of "values". This distinction, once the pride and joy of analytic philosophers, in fact ushered in a reign of terror second to none in the humanities and the social sciences. Those disciplines became paranoid about not being like the physical sciences in subject matter and methods. And in seeking to emulate physics the humanistic and social studies tended to discard those narrative methods which are their actual strength rather than a weakness. It has taken anthropology a hundred years to discover this; while literary studies have not even begun to emancipate themselves from the desire to become literary *science*. In calling our attention to the role of imitation in history Karl Marx echoes Heinrich Heine's dictum that in all crucial matters what happens as tragedy is repeated as farce (i.e., as in the ancient Greek dramatic festivals in which the tragic trilogy was complemented by a comedy on the same theme). However, there is much to be said in this case for the reverse: what was a grotesque joke on epistemology, i.e. making all knowledge fit into the strait-jacket of physics, has bred the tragedy of *trivializing* those very social and literary studies, which should in fact illuminate the complex, problematic character of human life. In short, literary studies have tended to focus away from what literature and literature alone can illuminate: how human beings gain experience.

To be sure, experience is not *one* thing – indeed, it is not a *thing* at all; so it cannot possibly be one thing. The manifold nature of experience, then, can only be captured significantly in a *narrative* which reconstructs that experience. To understand such phenomena as cannibalism, buying shares of stock, rituals of anointing the dead, filing a divorce, concealing anger, etc., etc., we have to tell a story about the constellation of practices in which the one we would understand is embedded. These narratives may be literary, anthropological or religious in external form but their quality, and therefore their effectiveness, will depend upon their literary character. It is all too little reflected upon that the great social scientists of our century have been great story-tellers, even though they might not have seen their work in that light. Think only of Max Weber's story about capitalism and the Protestant ethic, Georg Simmel's philosophy of money and Margaret Mead's story of coming of age in Samoa – not to mention Freud's story about the Oedipus complex (even before the turn of the century Freud was observing that his case studies had the character of short stories). It has taken most of this century to battle our way to this perspective in social science. The next step is to recognize the full epistemological significance of what is *irreducibly* literary.

What can literature do that, say, moral philosophy cannot? Why do we *need* literature? Which is to ask: what do we lose if we ignore it? The answer to these questions is tied to a notion that we have been wrongly fighting against for most of the century. It is the notion that there are *many* modes of knowing which are not reducible to one another. The rejection of this Cartesian-positivist notion of the unity of knowledge has been the great triumph of philosophy of science in the last twenty-five years – although there remain any number of people who have not grasped its true force and significance. I refer to the path-breaking work associated with names like Kuhn, Winch, MacIntyre, Von Wright, to mention but the best known. Their work has among other things opened up the door for the notion that there is a mode of knowledge, *reflection*, which cannot effectively be based upon the sort of direct communication typical of scientific research reports. Briefly, the reason for this is that scientific reporting aims at developing solutions to problems; whereas reflection aims at understanding why we have the problems we do. The central insight here involves epistemological pluralism. There are problems, like those about the functioning of physical processes concerning the world which is *before* us; but there are also problems which arise because we have the sort of personality or enculturation that we do. But this way of formulating the distinction is misleading; for in the first case we can be said to *have* problems, in the second we *are* ourselves problematic but lack the possibility of observing our quandary from without. Literature enables us to get a hold of these latter sorts of problems, whose roots are obscure because they are *familiar and close to us* to the point that what is in fact problematic is something that is so obvious and taken for granted that we never even consider calling it into question. In this context what we most need is the capacity to reflect upon our situation. Because our very *identity* is involved, this reflection cannot take the form of an abstract critique, i.e. of the sort that philosophers of science produce; but must be concrete, i.e. have the power to *move* us. This is precisely what literature does best.

Let us consider four examples: Aeschylus' *Oresteia* as an example of the problem of essential contestability, Shakespeare's *King Lear* as an example of misguided questioning, Diderot's *Rameau's Nephew* as an example of the problem of dialogue across opposed perspectives, and Georg Trakl's poetry as a reflection upon the world-constituting character of language. This is not to say that these are the only works of that nature or that their significance is exhausted in this sort of reading – that would be absurd – but that they can be of crucial significance in areas, like working life, where their relevance is not at first glance obvious.

Aeschylus' problem in the *Oresteia* is eminently modern. Orestes finds himself trapped between conflicting moral obligations. He must *act*. Either he must kill his mother to be a good son to his father or he lets his mother live and leaves his father's murder unavenged. He must do one or the other; but both bring guilt with them. There is no finer example of what it means to live with an essentially contested conflict of justice. In the abstract, i.e. as posed as a problem in casuistry, for example, the question seems absurd. It is the sort of question that can only be posed in the concrete. It must be a problem for somebody in particular to have force and we must know that person intimately. That requires an elaborate texture of description, which Aeschylus weaves in stately resonating sentences and provocative metaphors, whose meaning changes subtly as the plot develops. The reader must experience the transformation of *persuasion* from a mode of treachery and deception to the basis of legality in the very language of the play.

In *King Lear* we have the example of the most common sort of mistake a man can make: asking – or better, pressing – a stupid question. Lear wants to know which of his daughters loves him most, so he is foolish enough to *ask* them with the promise of his kingdom as reward. The question is in fact wholly counterproductive; for it unleashes deceptive, treacherous and ultimately self-destructive acts. None of the stupidity in the question can be captured in a prose description (like this one!) because the question as I have posed it is an absurd one. It is problematic only in the actual context of a life story. The point is that nobody sees themselves as stupid – and this is precisely what has to be brought to life: our self-deception. The spectator must not simply witness Lear's stupidity – he or she must *experience* it (which is far more than merely an emotional matter) as a *real* possibility. Shakespeare's art is the irreplaceable mode of constructing that experience, of *showing* something that it is vain to put into scientific discourse.

In *Rameau's Nephew* Denis Diderot produces a masterpiece of moral, aesthetic and epistemological insight. In fact the dialogue is a way of getting even with Plato for his dismissive attitude to actors. Here a parasite confronts a philosopher with a fool's wisdom. The two could hardly be more different: a worldly-wise idealist and a failed artist subsisting as a professional flatterer. Yet, the two need each other. The moralist cannot pursue the ideal without distinguishing it from its counterfeit; but that means he needs sham to identify himself *against*. The idealist turns out to be a bit of a philistine whether he cares to or not. Similarly, the cynical parasite ridicules the honesty and thrift of conventional morality, which in fact makes his living possible. But again it is Diderot's language which brings this odd couple to life. They exist side by side, even as friends, as wholly incommensurable forms of life (i.e. ways of weaving together words and actions). By leaving the dialogue to be concluded in the mind of the reader Diderot forces him or her to reflect upon these two modes of living. It is in that sense a genuine dialogue in a way that much of Plato is not in that it presents a meeting of two genuinely opposed points of view, which nevertheless co-exist in society.

Finally, there is the case of Georg Trakl. His poems so violate standard grammar that this fact itself has been taken as a sign of mental imbalance; but there is much more to Trakl than such a facile explanation would suggest. His poems seem systematically to reject normal syntax and semantics. He evokes beautiful images only to transform them into pictures of horror, decay and emptiness. He juxtaposes imagery without concern for "logic". In his sentences it is problematic to discern what is the grammatical subject and what is the object, which adjectives agree with which nouns. Out of the ambiguity and silence of his bizarre world he shows us how ours is constituted (i.e. by a contrast, which is shattering to experience). Shallow optimism dissolves before an eschatological world picture; sanity melts into madness in such a way as to suggest that our *conventional* notion of sanity is itself a form of madness. The shockingly unconventional interweaving of imagery, sound and theme thus unmasks the vacuousness of conventional mores.

There are but a few dramatic examples of the role that literature can play in the epistemology of reflection. It would have been just as easy to choose Chekhov, Karl Kraus, Claderón, Offenbach, Strindberg or Molière to make my point here: without literary reflection the essentially problematic character of human experience can only be shallowly and superficially explored.

To return to my main point: if we want to appreciate the role of literature within epistemology, we must consider the relationship between literature and reflection. So we must return to the question: if literature *can be* epistemologically important – nobody would suggest that it *must be* – why is it that the fact is so seldom recognized? The answer cannot be simply that mainstream Anglo-Saxon philosophy in our century has rejected the idea; for philosophers, thank God, have no monopoly on wisdom. Indeed, the tradition of analytic philosophy rejects the notion outright. It is for this reason that Wittgenstein could write disparagingly of our culture:

People nowadays think that scientists exist to instruct them, poets, musicians, etc. to give them pleasure. The idea *that these have something to teach them* – that does not occur to them (*Culture and Value*, 36).

It is more that people have for the most part forgotten *how* to use literature as a basis for *reflection*; moreover, it is typical of Wittgenstein that he was only capable of reading this way: crudely put, every book was for him a potential Bible. Clearly, this very attitude to literature entails a highly critical approach. Not just any text can be approached this way – some texts should not be approached this way – indeed, that greatest of novels *Don Quixote* is in fact as radical an analysis of the illusory world that the *romance*, which has supplied the content, if not the form, of what most people take to be literature from Amadis de Gaul to Jacqueline Suzanne, plummets us into. Be that as it may, literary texts can be the raw material for reflection. Their epistemological significance has to be elucidated in terms of the concept of reflection. So it is necessary to raise two questions here: why do we reflect in the first place, and how can we go about it? The answer to the latter will bring us to the point of these musings.

Reflection is a certain kind of thinking but not all thinking is reflective.

Indeed, in the pragmatist tradition (James and Dewey and later less naively Heidegger and Wittgenstein) thinking is nothing more than a way of acting, a way of getting a job done in the concrete. On this view thinking is the result of rigorous discipline according to which *we learn what is the appropriate action in a given situation*. I have avoided the term "behaviour" and the constellation of terms around it because it connotes but one (questionable) way of construing the phrase I have emphasized for the most part simply by *suppressing* problems of meaning, reference, intention, etc., rather than asking how they can be understood pragmatically. Indeed, what distinguishes the Heidegger of *Sein und Zeit* and the Wittgenstein of the *Philosophische Untersuchungen* from James and Dewey is a clear tendency to avoid the behaviourism to which the former were tempted and to which so many of their disciples succumbed. Thinking, then, is the result of hard *drilling* (Wittgenstein's word is *Abrichting*, which could be translated as "dressage"). It is a matter of following a rule, i.e. imitating a model, blindly, which is not the same as mechanically; for it admits of variation. On this view thinking is a matter of acting quasi-instinctively, a matter of our responses becoming "second nature" to us. It has certain self-enclosed, monological character, even if it has to be learned from others because it is basically a matter of learning to follow orders. This is why coaches often insist that their pupils should not think but simply *do* what they seek to do, which is to say that the kind of thinking that goes into learning is *unreflective*. Reflection plays another role in our natural history. In fact it is nothing more than philosophizing in its everyday form. Reflection begins with a *surprise*. The hammer we seek in its normal place in our workshop is missing; we find ourselves in a position where we are obliged at once to perform and to refrain from performing the same act (whence arises tragedy); the amount of money that we have long lived upon becomes worthless in runaway inflation. In short, our accustomed practices no longer function, meanings become contested, we lose our identity. We do not know "instinctively" what to do. Where there was order there is *anomie*; i.e. because we no longer understand our situation we no longer understand who we are. The result is a kind of madness that becomes self-destructive or is mastered in reflection. Reflection, then, in its most important, figuratively and literally, its most *dramatic* form, is anything but a luxury; rather, it is a way of finding orientation in situations of ambiguity, chaos and defeat (Jaspers). This is in the most profound sense *why* we reflect – it is, of course, not the only situation in which we reflect but the one that best illustrates the role of reflection in life. The next question is *how* we can reflect.

From the start it ought to be clear that there can be no formulas for bringing ourselves to practical guidance. Nor can anyone else solve the problem for us; for the paradigm case we have described is one in which we cannot be said to have a problem but one in which our life itself is problematic (cf. Gabriel Marcel on being and having). By the very nature of the situation we need to go outside of ourselves. We need something like a mirror in which we can get that sort of glimpse of ourselves of our own involvement in action, our own thinking (cf. the trick of playing the piano and watching ourselves play the piano). What makes literature so special here – i.e. distinguishing it from, say, history or sociology, which can play a certain role but only on the basis of their narrative character – is that literary works address us *personally*. They further make the demand that we suspend our preoccupations with ourselves for the sake of immersing ourselves in a story. It is the personal character of this movement which lends literature its emancipatory role. This is not simply a matter of reading a text as we do, say, an advertisement, but of *confronting* the text (that hermeneutic can take all sorts of forms, including the bizarrely radical form associated with so-called "deconstructionism"). The existential aim of the exercise is to see something about ourselves which is in the best of circumstances obscure and has now become tormenting. The odd presupposition is: to achieve self-enlightenment we have to forget about ourselves. Whatever help we receive has to have the form of intellectual and moral midwifery, i.e. in making the birth pangs meaningful. In the moral sphere that we have been discussing the hermeneutic activity involves transforming strain, tension and ambiguity from something terrifying into an opportunity for growth. Hermeneutics as practised on myself or on another is a matter of learning to "suffer into truth", in Aeschylus' phrase. Reflection is a *catharctic* experience.

I have put the matter in existential terms because it provides us with a striking paradigm case. Naturally, not all malfunctioning practices bear with them the pathos I have described. And, of course, cultivated people (in the literal sense of those who have "grown", not necessarily those who have merely received an extensive formal education) learn the value of reflecting at leisure and not only under duress. Indeed, a balanced life has to be one which is opened to the possibility of radical disruptions and therefore involves being prepared to reflect radically. In short, I am suggesting that *Bildung*, hermeneutics and the classics are related to one another in much the same way that H.-G. Gadamer has described but I would understand these notions quite differently from how he does; for I would reject the idea of tradition as well as the notion of the classic as he would understand it. In addition, unlike Gadamer, I do not think that you can *say* an awful lot about this; rather, it has to be shown as Wittgenstein might put it. There is not much hope of convincing the sceptic here (but is there ever really? – cf. Quine). The point of relection upon literature is to lay bare a scenario whereby we find our way from illness to health, from misery to mere unhappiness in Freud's apt phrase. This is the role of reflection; literature is its indispensable instrument.

Chapter 19

The Chair of Tutankhamun

Thomas Tempte

Craftsmanship involves values, technical reasoning and a tradition that has changed little over the centuries. It can never be placed in opposition to new technologies. Craftsmen have used existing machines and designed new ones. In fact, the craftsman makes technical advance possible. However, the craftsman's workshop is not controlled by machines. His approach is different to the industrial approach. He applies all his faculties to performing a given task, and the work is not fragmented. The tradition of the craftsman is determined by aesthetics, tradition and taking the time the job needs. This is only possible when the craftsman is in control of his means of production. The integrity of the craftsman lies in the tools and machines he makes himself. To a craftsman a tool is an object that mechanically shapes the raw materials of nature into a desired form for a particular purpose. Therefore the computer cannot be regarded as a tool, but it could be a useful data machine.

In the early 1970s I went to an exhibition at the National Museum on the theme of two Pharaohs. There, in a display case, I saw a worn-down little white-painted backed chair. It was made 3000 years ago by a cabinet-maker for Pharaoh Tutankhamun (1350 BC). The chair had a strong fascination and attraction for me. It was displayed in a totally enclosed glass case and several times I had to stop myself banging my head against the glass as I examined it.

What was the fascination this chair held for me and why did I find it so absorbing? Was it because it could have been made in our times but with quite different intentions from the ones I recognized? What was the secret of this chair?

In time I acquired some pictures of the chair, which I tacked up by my workbench, where my gaze fell on them every day. Sometimes I took them down, held them in my hands for a while and then put them away because they were beginning to distract me too much.

Several years later I completed a study of ancient machines, tools and instruments. At the University of London museum I had examined chisels, mortise chisels and saws of copper from Egyptian tombs. After completing the reconstruction of an Egyptian turning lathe, I had some time to reflect. How could the workmen of ancient times have used cutting tools of copper? How could they have cut joints in ebony? My respect for the carpenters of ancient times grew in pace with my curiosity about them. Having spent so much time penetrating the craft traditions of several thousand years ago, I needed to have an answer. Tools which work well and effectively generate a sense of fulfilment and pleasure in the work and promote the desire to do the job. But they also bear witness to the wisdom and awareness of the craftsman. It was not enough for me to simply understand, I wanted to make something that they had made. And so the seeds of an idea germinated and I decided to make Tut's chair. The museum in Cairo sent me a single measurement: the height of the back of the chair. The Egyptian Museum in Stockholm furnished me with four monochrome transparencies. Drawing on the experience and sense of form I had from renovating numerous articles of furniture, I began to make sketches. But I had to have other kinds of experience which helped me over major thresholds of resistance.

Several years before, Åke Axelsson, a furniture designer, had exhibited his reconstructions of chairs from ancient times. He made these pieces of furniture from vase paintings and picture fragments, that is to say rather sparse reference material which needed a lot of insight and constructive imagination. His works revealed to me that there was more to the pictorial world of antiquity than was described in traditional art history. The second, and perhaps the decisive, event was that the curator of the Egyptian Museum came to see me at my workshop with an Egyptian folding chair in a plastic bag and asked me to restore it. The folding chair could have been contemporary with Tut's chair and shared much of its inner design language. Taken together, these two events gave me the courage to attempt to make Tut's chair.

The chair has both a complex and complicated technical design. It is a good example of the independent carpenter's craft inasmuch as the design determines the internal form while the outer shell is the product of art. These two main components merge in a very striking way.

The chair has a lower and an upper part which would not merge unless the artistic aspects of form and proportion had been resolved. The lower part of the chair consists of four columns on a square base. The square recurs in the front and sides of the chair. A tabouret of compatible proportions had been added with a back. The design is neither bold nor visionary, rather it is stable and requires a great deal of work. The back would be quite out of proportion but for the use of an extra support which forms a triangle, the most stable element in construction. This design means that the chair expresses an unusual kind of tension. In many ways this is a pure work of art. It is richly worked and carved. Its front and back legs and pendulous belly imitates the underbody of a lion. Its open latticework depicts lilies and papyrus flowers. The latticework serves to support the seat which, with its shaped side pieces, would otherwise be very fragile. Its ends are of straightforward end-grain wood which do not anchor the fibres securely. In the middle of this composition there are two pure design elements, the back and its fastenings of natural grain knees or brackets. The most characteristic aspect of this chair is the large amount of openwork. The lower frames of the chair form a network of ribs and both an open and closed space beneath the seat. One is reminded of a commode. The heraldic working of the back gives a simultaneous impression of a board and latticework. If the chair is turned round, the support at the back forms even more latticework. Taken together, these aspects of the chair create an atmosphere that may be termed an expression of technology. A study of the construction of the chair makes one understand why it is strong enough to sit on. One dares to use it because it is, quite simply, sturdy.

But the chair also has a heraldic and cultural content. We can assume that the chair was not seen as just a chair but also as an object which represented the Pharaoh in his absence.

The chair is a lion on its four paws. The paws do not touch the ground. They hover just above the ground. But the small capital-like heels with their collars stop the chair sinking too deep into soft ground. The latticework under the seat consists of two heraldic plants: the papyrus flower of Upper Egypt and the water lily of Lower Egypt. These are joined with a reef knot. The reef knot has magical properties in many cultures. It can be tied very tightly but is still easy to loosen. The hieroglyphic sign for air, which is simply our own windpipe, passes through the knot. Even the very air we breathe is subordinate to the Pharaoh. The bowl-shaped seat cups the buttocks. We should remember that in this culture, people squatted. The weight of the body was relieved slightly from the normal squatting position.

The frame of the back consists of thin, carved, closely spaced hieroglyphics describing the attributes of the Pharaoh.

The hawk in the centre is a hawk god, a type of god with which the Pharaohs were linked. At the shoulders of the god's wings there are two reversed glyphs signifying the entirety of heaven, a practical sign that is a rope noose framing all the names used to describe the Pharaoh. This sign could be enlarged or reduced depending on how much was to be written inside it. The god holds the world in his claws and the glyph for power and strength is under its wings. The Pharaoh is often pictured with this sign in his hand as a sceptre.

This is surrounded by the reverse glyph for power and health and under its tail feathers there is the glyph for power and wealth: a stylized basket full of gold. We can say that the cult content of the chair is closely related to its artistic content.

What, then, is the carpenter's contribution? It is the very existence of the chair. His contribution is the expression of all the proportions of the chair, the solutions of technical design problems, but, first and foremost, the time he has spent on it. Care is probably the message reflected in every part of this chair with its well-rubbed shapes which emerged during day after day of careful work. Has the chair any expression that can be attributed to the person whose hands and mind made it? I maintain that it has. A very special attribute, namely a creative and imaginative intellect, was required to give material form to something which was surely the object of numerous instructions from the many people involved. This was combined with a deeply personal and very sophisticated approach. Perhaps not particularly conscious or even formulated, or so much an expression of self (this was a collective culture), but deeply rooted in the craftsman. The personal ability and will to give shape to everyone's wishes, both one's own and others, in manageable materials, must have been evolved from an older tradition.

How long did it take to make this chair? Did they have templates which were used over and over again? Did they have any standard measurements or other modules?

I began to plan my reconstruction work by making a detailed analysis of the work operations and types of problem that would occur. From the craftsman's viewpoint there were two types of work operation: the straight-forward assembly and carving work: the second being dependent upon the first. There would be no carving if there was nothing to carve. The carpentry work needed no carving at all. My work needed only a saw, a handy little plane, a drill, a file and some cutting tools. The Egyptian carpenter had no more tools than these. The plane was not known at that time; they probably used scrapers, grindstones and files, but they developed great skill with their copper awls, a sort of cross-headed axe.

Of course I began to use my machines, but I soon had to give that up and found myself forced back to almost the same level of technology as my Egyptian predecessor. The only thing I used constantly as my band-saw, but that is no more than an ordinary motorized saw blade. It helped me save my wrists.

I found that my predecessor had a completely different view of forces and counter-forces than we have today – joints, open carving, angles, chiselled grooves, work done without any thought of using time-saving methods. The work was purposeful, and obviously aimed to create a genuine work of substance without using any short cuts. His eye and his feeling for proportion must have been very highly developed. He must also have chosen his wood with the greatest care.

The wood he chose was very durable and very uniform. I remember from my work on the museum's folding chair that the wood was very salty. The pieces may have been soaked in salt water for several reasons: to protect the wood from attack by insects (a major problem in Africa), and this treatment can help to stabilize the shape of the wood and make the wood less sensitive to changes of climate. The finished parts may also have been "seasoned" in this way. The craftsmen of ancient times worked mostly in unseasoned wood because unseasoned wood, even hard wood, is more easily workable, and wear on the cutting tools will be less. To avoid changes in shape, they may have then placed the finished parts in a salt bath. This replaces the sap that was in the cells.

He made the dowel holes far larger than we do today, and the dowel necks are different too. The absence of the vertical and horizontal is striking. The only things that are perpendicular are the sidepieces of the chair back seen from the front. And the only horizontal planes are the top of the back and the lower part of the front frame. Everything else falls and leans in different directions. The Egyptian sign for the horizon (heaven) looks like this.

A German researcher once made a study of the way that sign was written over two thousand years. He found that the signs were always slightly askew. Was this a general practice which we know nothing about or was it only a calligraphic oddity?

The seat of the chair has three different radii; one from the front, one from the sides and one at the back. Making a seat like that takes a great deal of time.

I believe that the entire chair was made by using the method of fitting, that is to say the parts are put together, measured, taken apart, adjusted, and assembled once again. This method, with its mixture of repeating work, constant attention, exactitude and care with parts that are constantly being worn down, and the risk of damage to the parts, requires a highly developed mind. The carpenter must have a clear picture of the final result in his mind's eye and, at the same time, feel that each little insignificant operation has its value in the context of the total work. This is mentally fatiguing. The same kind of emotional drain is experienced by a boat-builder laying a clinker hull. The craftsman needs some aids to help him if he is to maintain full concentration during such a protracted period of work. I believe the carpenter had some set squares and a little stick with some measurements carved on it, and perhaps some kind of proportion scale to stop him losing his way during his work.

The Egyptians worked in many types of wood, and the furniture which has been preserved is all in more solid and hard types of wood. Tut's chair is made in what is said to be cedar, probably cedar from Lebanon. The cedar is a coniferous tree, and coniferous wood is rarely very hard or dense, with the exception of trees which grow under special conditions or which are treated in some way or other. I should like to know how cedar from Lebanon was treated 3500 years ago to give such good and durable wood.

My reconstruction is in Swedish ash heartwood taken from a young tree. This is a very hard, tough wood, which is easily attacked by insects if kept in a humid atmosphere. To some extent the chair has a self-locking construction. No glue has been used. All the joints are fixed/locked with dowel holes which have been drilled at different angles to give greater stability to the structure. My chair is very stable.

To summarize: why did I spend so much time on furniture that is several thousand years old? Do I benefit from it in any direct way, or is it simply a hobby? Perhaps it is another way of contemplating one's navel?

The answer is, first and foremost, it is great fun. Time passes so quickly that I often forget to stop for meals.

Ever since my apprentice days I have understood that the craft occupations were doomed, and from the very beginning I reacted against this tragic stupidity. There is no strength in isolation and every committed craftsman needs support from a living craft, knowing that other people share my passion for my work. It is depressing to think that crafts are on the retreat, so I derived strength from the work that was done in times gone by. The most important benefit from communication with fellow-craftsmen is finding out about their reasoning and their values, and except in the rare cases where something completely new emerges, what they make is less important. It is the same with my colleagues who lived thousands of years ago. I have also gained great reassurance and security by realizing what an old and strong tradition a manufacturing craftsman can fall back on. The values, the technical reasoning and traditions appear to have changed very little over the centuries. If this can be made to stand out very clearly and is perceived as an asset, then the tradition serves as a good support. All the superficial values can be removed as a thresher separates the ears from the wheat.

Another experience I have gained is that craftsmanship can never be placed in opposition to new technology. For thousands of years craftsmen have used existing machines and designed new machines. Who invented the wheel, the lathe, the potter's wheel, the windmill, the spinning wheel, the stirrup, the scythe, the mower, the combine harvester, the turret feed and much more? The craftsman is never the enemy of technology but is rather the person who makes technical advance possible. However, the craftsman's workshop is not controlled by machines, but relates the capacity of the machine to the production in progress: in other words, the craftsman controls the machines.

Translated by Struan Robertson

Chapter 20

Semiotics and the Historical Sciences
Iurii Lotman

Lotman says that the science of history has been caught in an unfortunate position between the description of Hegel's idealism of the logical movement of history through great events on the one hand and the new school's picture of immobile history rooted in the practice and mentality of the collective on the other.

The latter school reacts against the former but they are fundamentally reunited in denying history and mankind the possibility of non-predictability, chance and freedom. Lotman argues against this kind of determinism and by using examples from film, mathematics and physics, attempts to find the place of open change in the system. In particular, he discusses Prigogine's analysis of dynamic processes which, when equilibrium is disturbed, give rise to critical points – points of bifurcation – with different possibilities for development. Such points of non-predictability also exist in history. A basic error of current historical science is the rejection of non-predictability. But the development of science is, according to Lotman, characterized by a high degree of predictability, decidability, while the history of art is characterized by non-predictability.

The transformation of an entire group of the humanities in relation to the establishment of semiotics as an independent discipline has yet to sufficiently impress history as a science. However, the very nature of history makes the introduction of semiotic methods into it particularly important. History occupies a special place among the sciences, and whether it can be considered a science at all is an issue which has been raised again and again – not without reason – and as such has never been finally resolved. The historian, who is less inclined to theorize than to do research on concrete material, usually tends to be satisfied with Ranke's formula: the goal of historical research is to establish the past *wie es eigentlich gewesen war*. In spite of all its naive clarity, however, this task has turned out to be an utterly difficult, if not impossible, one. The notion of "establishing the past, *wie es eigentlich gewesen war*, means to activate a procedure common to all science: the elucidation and gathering of facts and the establishment of lawful connections between them. The facts, which exist independent of the historian prior to his analysis, are assumed to be something primary. This is the given. What, then, is the situation of the historian?

The historian is doomed to deal with texts. The text stands between the event "in itself" and the historian, and this changes the scientific situation in a fundamental way. The text is always created by someone and constitutes a situation which has been translated into some kind of language. One and the same reality, which has been codified by different means, will produce different–sometimes conflicting–texts. The extraction of events from a factual text, from a story about an event, constitutes a decoding operation. Thus, the historian begins, consciously or unconsciously, by subjecting his original material–the text–to semiotic manipulations. Therefore, if these operations occur without the researcher's awareness of them and with his conviction that the document is authentic, and he considers his knowledge of the language and intuitive sense of authenticity which his work experience has fostered to be sufficient to be able to understand the text, then, as a rule, there is a substitution in the historical auditorium for that "natural awareness", which upon closer scrutiny proves to be the awareness of the historian with all its cultural and historical prejudices.

From the perspective of different cultures, of different genres, even from the confines of a single culture, one and the same actual event may seem worthy of a written record, of being turned into a text, or it may appear not to deserve this. Thus, both in Scandinavian medieval and in Russian chronicles, armed conflicts, feuds and bloody incidents are recorded. And if nothing like that had occurred, then no *events* at all would be considered to have happened. In the Icelandic sagas such events are viewed in terms of "all was quiet", while the Russian chronicler would indicate such events in his yearly chronicle by an empty space or by writing "peace reigned".

The conception of what constitutes a historical event is dependent upon the type of culture involved and is in itself an important typological indicator. Having selected his text, the historian thus has to make a distinction between what constitutes an event in the text from his own point of view as a historian and what is an event worth remembering in the eyes of the author of the text and his contemporaries.

The historian is consequently caught in a curious situation from the very beginning: in the other sciences the researcher begins with the facts, while the historian acquires facts as the result of a specific analysis, and not as the starting point of that analysis. The matter becomes even more complicated when it comes to the establishment of conformity to law.

The fact that historical research is initially based on a text has a variety of consequences, which in a most direct way influence our conceptions of what the historical ties between events are. Every text, first of all, is an utterance in a natural language and is thus inevitably organized according to the laws of the syntactic structures of that specific language. In his "Quest for the Essence of Language", which emphasizes the iconic characteristics of natural languages, Roman Jakobson has pointed out that the listener has a tendency to apprehend formal connections as connections of content and thus to transfer the linguistic structure on to the structure of the object. Jakobson writes:

When discussing the grammatical universals and near-universals detected by J.H. Greenberg, I noted that the order of meaningful elements by virtue of its palpably iconic character displays a particularly clear-cut universalistic propensity . . . Precisely therefore, the precedence of the conditional clause, with regard to the conclusion, is the only admitted or primary, neutral, nonmarked order in the conditional sentences of all languages. If almost everywhere, again according to Greenberg's data, the only, or at least the predominant, basic order in declarative sentences with nominal subject and object is one in which the former precedes the latter, this grammatical process obviously reflects the hierarchy of the grammatical concepts. The subject on which the action is predicated is, in Edward Sapir's terms, "conceived as the starting point, the 'doer' of the action" in contradistinction to "the end point, the 'object' of the action." The subject, the only independent term in the clause, singles out what the message is about. Whatever the actual rank of the agent, he is necessarily promoted to hero of the message as soon as he assumes the role of its subject. "The subordinate obeys the principal". Notwithstanding the table of ranks, attention is first of all focused on the subordinate as agent, turns thereupon to the undergoer, the "goal" of his action, the principal obeyed.[1]

We have to note that Jakobson actually speaks about two different cases here. In the first part of his discussion, he points out that the grammatical structure of the text iconically reflects an extra-linguistic reality and, in the second part, notes that in language causes and conditions precede results and consequences. For us, however, the end of the statement is more important, since it says that grammatical structure predetermines the distribution of roles in the content of a proposition, i.e. *language subordinates reality* to its organization.

We could add even further examples of the fact, that the very necessity of grammatically organizing a text has an influence on what this text is capable of saying. But the laws of text construction on the level above the phrase, i.e. the laws of rhetoric, are more important. As soon as we transcend the limits of the phrase into the broader elements of the text, the correct construction of this text implies a sense of topic. The topic has its own logical laws. In order to tell about some event, it has to be organized according to the laws of this logic, i.e. the episodes have to be arranged in a definite plot sequence, the plot has to be brought into an extra-textual reality, and simultaneous events, which may not be connected, must be re-organized into a consistent and connected chain. Thus, the necessity of the historian to rely on texts and of the texts to retell the events according to the laws of linguistic and logical, rhetorical and narrative constructions results in the extra-textual reality falling into the researcher's hands in an obviously distorted shape.

Finally, on the highest level, the text is ideologically codified – laws of the political, religious, philosophical order, genre codes, considerations of etiquette, which the historian has to reconstruct on the basis of these texts, while at times falling into logically vicious circles – all this leads to additional codification. The difference in the levels of consciousness and goals of work between the author of the text and the historian who reads it creates the highest threshold of decodification.

The historian's work with the sources is the labour of a decipherer.

It is an attempt to overcome these difficulties in the science of history outlined above that is to a certain extent responsible for the emergence during the last fifty years of the French historiographical tendency, which has now consolidated itself in the school of *l'histoire nouvelle, l'histoire de la longue durée.*

The direct impulse behind the emergence of scientific quests in this direction was the obvious crisis in the political history of the positivist persuasion, which already during the second half of the nineteenth century had experienced "compilationism" and theoretical destitution. The attempt to save history from the deeds of rulers and the life stories of great men gave rise to an interest in the life of the masses and in impersonal processes.

While enumerating the predecessors of these views of history, Jacques Le Goff calls to mind Voltaire, Chateaubriand, Guizot and Michelet.[2] To this list we ourselves could add Leo Tolstoy, who stubbornly repeated that real history occurs in individual life and in the unconscious movements of the masses, and who never tired of ridiculing the apologies of "great men".[3]

However, the movement of *l'histoire nouvelle* had a more serious intent than the wish to dissociate itself from an already discredited scientific eclecticism. One of the basic impulses was the effort to get outside the bounds of the vicious circle, which we discussed above. This led to a criticism of the very notion of "historical fact" and the attempt to deliver history from "historical personalities". This is the context of Lucien Febvre's and Marc Bloch's famous slogan: *l'histoire les hommes, non l'Homme*. The demand to study the impersonal, collective historical impulses which determine the actions of the masses who are not aware of the forces acting upon them defines the innovative theme of this school and carries the historian far beyond the limits of the usual traditional subjects in research. In this connection, we may point to the works of Le Goff, Delumeau, Vovelle, Aries, as well as Carlo Ginzburg among the Italian historians.

The effort to avoid the usual sense of plot in historical narrative is no less noticeable. The urge for "a history of great duration" or, in the more daring words of Fernand Braudel, *histoire presque immobile*, or even more decisively, *histoire immobile* (Emmanuel Le Roy Ladurie), is actually tied to this. True, this kind of extremism has not found support. But the urge to bring history and anthropology together, to focus attention on the slower-moving processes, clearly reveals a wish to avoid the dangers of narrative history. Instead of this, the description of certain historical continua is coming forth. In the end history begins to look like some kind of geological process, which affects people, though without people's help.

The tendency of the "history of great duration" (or "history of extended breathing", as it is also called) brought fresh air into the science of history and added richness through research studies which have already become classics.

However, all the principles of this school were not accepted without objection. History is not *just* a conscious process, but neither is it *just* an unconscious process. It is the mutual tension between both of these. *Histoire de la longue durée* developed under the sign of a broad scientific synthesis. Both the name of the journal *Revue de synthèse historique* and the title of Berr's work, "L'Histoire traditionelle et la Synthèse historique", published already in 1921, amply testify to this. This was also emphasized by Marc Bloch. But it is obvious that the synthesis which developed on the basis of economics and sociology completely passed over linguistics, in spite of the fact that the most revolutionary changes at this time occurred in this very discipline. However, after Jakobson's historical contacts with Lévi-Strauss, in the latter's works anthropology and ethnology have borrowed support from linguistics to become one of the most significant scientific events of the ending century. The French historical school hardly "gave notice" to this event. At the same time French structuralism was developing in the atmosphere of synchronic analysis and did not intrude upon the "foreign" territory of the historians.

In this connection it would be very appropriate to draw a parallel to the history of language. The history of language, at least the languages of written cultures, develops from the tension between two poles: the living spoken language and the traditions of the written and printed word. Boris Uspenskii, professor of the history of the Russian language, writes:

Literary language tends toward stability, living speech toward change. This is also where the continuous distance between literary language and living speech originates, in the creation of a kind of constant tension between poles, like a field of force. The degree of rupture between literary language and living speech is incidentally determined by the *type* of literary language.[4]

"One could say, that the difference in character between the evolution of the system [of the living language] and the norms [of bookish language] boils down to the difference between a discrete and continuous development." Uspenskii explains: "in contradistinction to the evolution of a system, the evolution of norms–including those of the written language, i.e. the norms of literary language–does not have a continuous but a discrete (graduated) character." And further: "Thus, if we understand the history of language as an objective process which in principle is independent of ties to the spoken language, then the development of literary language is directly dependent upon the changing circumstances of the bearer of the language."[5]

The history of language–a typical collective and anonymous object–is a process of *la longue durée*. But the history of literary language is the history of creativity, a process tied to individual activity and with a very low degree of predictability. If "political history" neglected one side of this double-sided process, the "new history" neglects the other side. Just like the history of language, any dynamic process which is completed with the participation of a human being oscillates between the pole of continuous slow changes that are characteristic of the processes mostly uninfluenced by human consciousness and will, and often enough unnoticed by the contemporary because their periodicity is longer than a generation, and the pole of conscious human action realized through personal wilful and intellectual efforts. It simply is not possible to tear one side from the other; it would be like tearing the north from the south. Their opposition is a condition of their existence. These are, moreover, tendencies which are realized on all levels.

And just as one could discern blocks of anonymous collective processes in Byron's brilliant individuality, one may find elements of creative uniqueness in the production and personality of any representative of Byronic European "mass culture" at the beginning of the nineteenth century. Nothing that is done by people and with the participation of people can avoid belonging to the anonymous processes of history and can avoid being part of the personal sphere either. This is determined by the very essence of man's relation to culture – the isomorphic relation to the universe of culture and the simultaneous necessity of being just a part of it. The question of which of the two possible hypostases will encompass this or that historical element is, moreover, dependent not upon the immanent essence of this element, but upon the position of the historian writing about it. Is Beau Brummell a fact of mass culture, to which we prefer to relegate him in that usual contempt for such manifestations as fashion, or is he an individuality who has left an imprint on the anonymous, "slow" history of the times? The simple transfer of a fact from one line of connections into another may change the traditional into the individual.

The difference in participation of conscious human efforts on various levels of the total historical process is important both for the differences in the evaluation of the role of chance on the one hand, and for the creative possibilities of the individual on the other. The task of "liberating history from great men" may turn into both a history without creativity and a history without thought and freedom – freedom of thought and freedom of will, i.e. the possibility to *choose the paths*. On this road, Hegel and the historians of "the new school", who are complete antipodes in all other respects, surprisingly converge. Hegel's "historiosophy" is based on the notion of a motion toward freedom as the goal of the historical process. But the primordial predestination of this goal aborts the question of freedom, and this is clearly the consequence of the German philosopher's reasoning. There is no coincidence in Hegel's conviction that "the world of reason and self-conscious will has no room for chance". There is a direct link between the denial of the role of chance in history and Hegel's idea that the realization of the "world of reason" represents the last act of world history, completing its movement after having reached self-cognition. In the introduction to *The Philosophy of History* Hegel wrote:

the principle of *development* has further implications, for it contains an inner determination, a *potentially* present condition which has still to be realized. This formal determination is an essential one; the spirit, whose theatre, province, and sphere of realization is the history of the world, is not something which drifts aimlessly amidst the superficial play of contingent happenings, but is itself the absolute determining factor; in its own peculiar destiny it is completely proof against contingencies, which it utilizes and controls for its own purposes.[6]

This way of thinking finds a logical ending in the picture of an unconditional and predestined incorporation of the particular into the general: "The principles of the national spirit in their necessary progression are themselves only moments of the one universal spirit, which ascends through them in the course of history to its consummation in an all-embracing *totality*."[7]

Thus, freedom of the individual is not the same as the choice of an alternative path, but the free merging of one's self with the necessity of world development.

For Hegel the spirit realizes itself through great individuals; for the "new history", the dominating anonymous forces in historical development realize themselves through unconscious collective manifestations. In both instances, historical action is action freed from choice.

Is that the way it really is?

Let us temporarily leave the question of how man's intellectual capabilities and moral responsibility appear from this point of view, and look at the issue from another angle. Indeterminacy is a measure of information. Minimal information consists of the choice of one out of two equally plausible possibilities. In proportion to the exhaustion of the indeterminacy reserve, the information value of the process sinks to reach zero at the point where it has become completely redundant, i.e. fully predictable. Let us imagine a stone, travelling along a certain trajectory. If we could compute all the factors affecting it already before the throw and completely exclude the possibility of new factors entering into play during the course of its flight, then it would be possible to predict the place of impact before the stone was thrown. Hence, in order to determine where in time and space our stone would be, an actual throw would be totally superfluous. But let us change the conditions. Suppose that we cannot compute *all* the factors that will occur in connection with the motion of the stone along its trajectory. Then the exactitude of our prediction will grow with each moment, just as the redundancy of the text will increase progressively (we regard the trajectory curve outlined on the screen by the device synchronically tracing the flight of the stone as a text). The redundancy is in reverse proportion to the information, which will decrease in relation to how far the stone has flown and to the decline in possible alternatives as the remaining motion becomes less and less. Of course, if the stone could choose its path at every particular moment of its motion, the information potential of its flight would be preserved.

The documentary history of mankind has already lasted thousands of years. If the historical process did not include mechanisms of unpredictability, i.e. did not encompass chance not as "an embroidery throwing light from above on the canvas of constantly active factors" (Febvre's expression in his response to Braudel's book *La Méditerrannée et le Monde Méditerranné à l'Époque de Philippe II*), but as an important functional mechanism, then history would have been superfluous long ago, and we would have been able to predict its future development. As we know, this is not the case. Not even where the role of the individual personality is insignificant and the previous condition of the system is sufficiently well known (for instance, in the history of economics during the last three centuries, in the history of individual languages, in the history of technical inventions or everyday customs) has the prognostication been marked by successes, but by resounding defeats. This is especially true when it comes to the history of man's creative individuality, which the *histoire nouvelle* lost together with the cult of great men.

The reader must not misunderstand me. The work of the *histoire nouvelle* school has been perceived as a fresh wind in contemporary historiography, and the reading of works by Braudel, Le Goff, Delumeau, Vovelle and others represents not only a professional but also an aesthetic experience for the specialist, because the beauty of precise thinking is no less a beauty. The criticism of some aspects of the methodology in this research is called upon simply to point out the necessity of moving further, and not at all to erase the road already covered.

Behind the methodology of this school one can discern the century-old scientific psychology, which was based on the conviction that where determinism ends, science will also end. From the proverbial "Laplacian demon" to Einstein's conviction that "God does not throw dice" runs the tendency to rid the world of chance or at least to expel it beyond the boundaries of science. In the special section on chance in his book *Sciènce et Méthode* Henri Poincaré wrote:

We have become absolute determinists, and even those who tend to reserve the right of free will for human beings give unlimited range to determinism in the inorganic world. Every phenomenon, regardless of its importance, has its cause; and a spirit that is infinitely powerful and infinitely knowledgeable about the laws of nature would be able to predict such a phenomenon from the beginning of time. If such a spirit existed, one could not gamble with it without losing all the time.[8]

And despite the fact that further on Poincaré stipulates the actual impossibility of differently considering the multitude of factors as probable, the spirit of the Laplacian demon does not leave him: "If we knew exactly the laws of nature and the initial state of the universe, then we would be able to predict exactly any subsequent moment of this universe."[9]

As far as the historical sciences are concerned, the special circumstances at work here make it necessary for the historian to choose between an extra-scientific substitution of history for biographies of "great men" and a strict determinism. We have already seen what deformation the extra-textual reality is subject to, when it changes into a text – into a source for the historian. We have also seen by what means the historian attempts to escape this danger. There is yet another source of deformation of reality, but now that the creator of the document/source is no longer at hand, it is the result of the actions of its interpreter-historian.

History develops along a time vector (arrow), whose direction is determined by the movement from the past to the present. But the historian looks at the texts he is studying from the present to the past. To a majority of writers, who have examined the epistemological side of the historical sciences, the identity of the forward-looking and the retrospective outlooks appears as such a self-evident truth that the problem never even becomes an object of examination. The conception is that the chain of events does not change in essence, whether we look at these events from the direction of the time arrow or from the opposite point of view. Furthermore, to those who see a movement in history toward a definite goal, this outlook appears natural, while their opponents (see, for example, Toynbee's criticism of the "new history" school) perceive it as a methodologically convenient device.

Marc Bloch gave two chapters of his final book symmetrical titles, "To understand the present by means of the past" and "To understand the past by means of the present", thereby in a way underlining the symmetry in the direction of time for the historian. He was also of the opinion that the retrospective view allowed the historian to differentiate between essential and accidental relationships: "Provided that history will be re-established later in its real movement, it is more advantageous for the historians to begin reading it, as Metland expressed it, 'backwards'." And further: "By mechanically moving from the more distant to the closer, we always risk wasting time on the study of the origins of and reasons for such phenomena which might appear to be imaginary on closer examination".[10] In comparing the past as it is recreated by the historian with the motion picture, Bloch makes use of a metaphor: "In the film he [the historian] is watching, only the last scene will remain intact. In order to re-create the faded features of the other scenes, the film reel will have to be unwound in the opposite direction from that in which the film was shot."[11]

It would probably be immediately observable that all the scenes in this film with the exception of the first would appear totally predictable and thus totally superfluous. But this is not the point. It is more important to note that the very essence of the historical process is distorted. History is an asymmetrical, irreversible process. If we use Marc Bloch's image, then this is a strange film in so far as it won't bring us back to the initial scene after the film has been set running in the opposite direction. Here is the root of the discrepancies. According to Bloch–and this is a natural consequence of the retrospective view–the historian has to examine the events of the past *as the only ones possible*:

To evaluate the plausibility of an event means to establish what the chances are for it to occur. If we accept this position, do we have the right to speak of the probability of some fact in the past? In an absolute sense, we obviously don't. We may only guess about the future. The past is something established, which no longer holds a place for the possible.[12]

There is a definite consistency in these opinions: the retrospective view inescapably leads to the conclusion that what has actually happened is not only the most probable, but also the only, event possible. If, on the other hand, one starts from the notion that a historical event always results from the realization of one of several alternatives and that in history identical conditions do not signify equivalent consequences, then there will be a need for alternative methodological approaches to the material. There will also be a demand for a historical approach of a different competence: realized courses will appear to be surrounded by clusters of unrealized opportunities. Let us imagine a motion picture, which demonstrates one man's life from cradle to grave. If we look at it retrospectively, we will say: this man only had one single opportunity and he died with iron lawfulness the way he was bound to die. The falsity of such a view becomes apparent when we use a forward-looking approach to the scenes: then the film becomes a story about lost opportunities and in order to fully display the essence of life, a series of parallel alternative shots would be necessary. And it is possible that in one version the hero will die on the barricades at the age of 16, and in another at the age of 60 write accusations against his neighbours to the organs of state security.

History is an irreversible (unstable) process.

In order to examine the essence of such processes and to understand what they signify as applied to history, it is extremely important to consider the analysis of these phenomena made in the works of Ilya Prigogine, who has studied dynamic processes in chemistry, physics, and biology. These works have a profoundly revolutionizing significance for scientific thinking as a whole: they bring random phenomena into the circle of scientific interests and also find a functional place for them in the general dynamics of the world.

In his examination of irreversible processes, Prigogine made a distinction between different forms of dynamics. In separating stable and unstable structures, Prigogine indicates that in spaces close to these dynamic processes behave differently: "the laws of equilibrium are universal. Matter near equilibrium behaves in a 'repetitive' way."[13] Dynamic processes, which occur under conditions of equilibrium, are completed in accordance with determinate curves. However, to the extent that it distances itself from the entropic points of equilibrium, the movement approaches those critical points where the predictable flow of processes is interfered with. (Prigogine calls them points of bifurcation.)[14] In these points the process has reached the instance when an unequivocal prediction of the future becomes an impossibility. Further development will take place as the realization of one of several equally possible alternatives.

The following is especially noteworthy to us: at the beginning of the book the authors point to the words of Isaiah Berlin, who saw the difference between the natural sciences and the knowledge of the humanities through the antithesis of an interest in the repeatable on the one hand and in the unique on the other. Later on they pay attention to the fact that "when we move from equilibrium to far-from-equilibrium conditions, we move away from the repetitive and the universal to the specific and the unique."[15]

In strongly unstable situations the processes proceed under conditions not of a stable determinate flow but of a fluctuation (from Latin *fluctuare*, to be in a state of excitement, to be excited, and *fluctus*, storm; we may recall that Horace used this word in reference to social upheavals: "O navis, referent in mare te novi fluctus!"). At the moment of bifurcation the system is in a state that makes the prediction of the following state impossible. One can only indicate *one of the states* into which it may transcend. At this point the role of chance may turn out to be crucial, provided we understand chance not in the sense of something without a cause but as something of a different causal order. In this connection it might be appropriate to recall Ross Ashby's not very original definition:

By saying a factor is *random*, I do not refer to what the factor is in itself, but to the relation it has with the main system. Thus the successive digits of π are as determinate as any numbers can be, yet a block of a thousand of them might serve quite well as random numbers for agricultural experiments, not because they *are* random but because they are probably *uncorrelated* with the peculiarities of a particular set of plots. Supplementation by "chance" thus means (apart from minor, special requirements) supplementation by taking effects (or variety) *from a system whose behaviour is uncorrelated with that of the main system.*[16]

The trajectory of movement in space with an uneven distribution of stable and unstable relations is outlined by Prigogine and Stengers in the following way: in the withdrawal from stable space the intensification of a "fluctuation occurring at the 'right moment' resulted in favouring one reaction path over a number of other equally possible paths". And further:

Self-organization processes in far-from-equilibrium conditions correspond to a delicate interplay between chance and necessity, between fluctuations and deterministic laws. We expect that near a bifurcation, fluctuations or random elements would play an important role, while between bifurcations the deterministic aspects would become dominant.[17]

Thus, the random and the regular will cease to be incompatible notions and appear as two possible conditions of one and the same object. While moving in a determinate field, it represents a point in linear development which is falling into fluctuation space; it comes out as a continuum of potential possibilities with chance as a starter.

Prigogine's ideas, which throw light on the general theory of dynamic processes, also seem extremely fruitful as applied to the movement of history. They can easily be made explicit in relation to the facts of world history and its complicated interweaving of spontaneous unconscious and personal-conscious movements. The alternation of determinate periods (or rather, periods which are dominated by determinate processes) and periods in which the role of points of bifurcation increases explains the phenomenon of maintained redundancy on a relatively constant level which we have observed. It would moreover be an impermissible simplification to perceive anonymous processes as the total predominance of determination and individual action as the kingdom of chance. First of all, there are no completely anonymous elements and no elements one hundred per cent determined by personal efforts in history. In both categories one can easily single out either principle. It is simply a matter of their proportions. Secondly, both these tendencies are familiar with periods of a calm, predictable flow and of violent eruptions, when determination and unequivocal prediction recede into the background. More important is what constitutes the specificity of precise historical development – a development whose elements consist of individuals with ability to think and will. Szilard published a work in 1929 with the solemn title: "Über die Entropieverminderung in einem thermodynamischen System bei Eingriffen intelligenter Wesen".[18] History is precisely a process which proceeds "with the intervention of a thinking being". This means that at the points of bifurcation there is not only a mechanism of chance set in motion, but a mechanism of *conscious choice* as well, which becomes an important *objective* element of the historical process. The new understanding of this points to the necessity for a semiotics of history, i.e. for an analysis of how this human individual, in the process of making choices, imagines the world. This is, in a certain sense, close to what the "new history" calls "mentality". The results of research in this field, and the comparison with what has been achieved by the Soviet researchers Toporov, Uspenskii, Ivanov, Zalizniak, Pyatigorsky (who lives in England) and many others in the reconstruction of various types of ethnocultural consciousness, are nevertheless convincing enough to suggest that the historical semiotics of culture is the most promising course in this direction.

When the historical process is examined in the direction of the temporal arrow, the points of bifurcation are constituted by those historical instances where the tension of contradictory structural poles reaches a climactic moment and the whole system leaves the state of equilibrium. In these instances the behaviour of both individual people and the masses ceases to be automatically predictable, and determination recedes into the background. It is then appropriate to regard historical movement not as a trajectory but as a continuum, potentially capable of being resolved in a series of variants. These junctions of lowered predictability consist of revolutionary moments and abrupt historical changes. The choice of that course which is actually realized is dependent upon a complex of random circumstances and, to an even greater extent, upon the self-awareness of those acting. It is no coincidence that words, speech and propaganda find a particularly important *historical* significance in these instances. Thus, if there was a situation of indeterminacy *before* the choice was made, then *after* its realization there arises a principally new situation for which the choice was a necessary precondition, a situation which appears as a given to the continuing movement. Random *before*, it becomes determinate *after* the choice. "Retrospectivity" reinforces determinateness. To the continuing movement the choice is the first link in a new lawfulness.

Prigogine notes that at the moment of bifurcation the process acquires an individual character, approaching humanistic characteristics. It would be possible to make a relative scale of non-predictability: the intervention of chance – the intervention of a thinking being – the intervention of a creative consciousness. If there is a rigid unequivocal determination at one pole of the development, then the other pole is structurally constituted by a creative (artistic) activity. In the real process it is impossible to establish just one of the poles in isolation. However, the fact that the work of art appears unpredictable *before* its creation and a determinate element of regular tradition *after* it demonstrates the isomorphism of processes on different levels.

Let us examine the behaviour of an individual human being. As a rule, it is realized in accordance with certain stereotypical patterns which determine the "normal", predictable course of his actions. But the number of stereotypical patterns, their selection in any given social outlook, is considerably larger than what the individual human being realizes. Some of the existing possibilities are rejected on principle, others appear less preferable, while still others are regarded as admissible versions. In the instance when the historical, social, psychological tension reaches its maximum, when the individual human world view is shifting abruptly (as a rule, under high emotional tension), the individual may abruptly change the stereotypical pattern, and seemingly jump over into a different, under "normal" circumstances totally unpredictable, sphere of behaviour. Of course, if we were to examine the behaviour of a crowd at such an instance, we would then observe a certain repeatability in the way many units of people changed their behaviour, after having chosen a (for them) totally unpredictable "sphere" under the different circumstances. What appears generally predictable to the "crowd" will not seem predictable to the individual personality. As Kant had already observed:

the weddings (and the births and deaths which depend on them) on which human free will has such a great influence, do not seem to be subject to any rule, which could serve as a basis to mathematically determine their numbers in advance. At the same time, yearly statistics about them in the big countries show that they also occur in accordance with the unchanging laws of nature.[19]

From Kant's observation one could draw the conclusion that individual phenomena are characterized by a reduction in predictability and that this makes them different from mass phenomena. Such a hypothesis would, however, be premature. And the historian knows, on purely empirical grounds, that the behaviour of the crowd often is more difficult to predict than the reaction of an individual person. And from a theoretical point of view, the very notion of "individuality" is not primary and self-evident, but dependent on the method of codification. Of considerably greater interest is Prigogine's and Stengers' notion that near the points of bifurcation the system tends to change into a mode of individual behaviour. In conformity with the example cited by Kant, one could say that as a rule individual marriage takes place in a state of emotional tension as the result of a choice between alternatives, of an act of free will. However, for an association of the "population"-type, this is an action that realizes the norm. The closer the behaviour of the system is to the norm, the more predictable it is.

There is still another side to this issue: at the point where one may predict the next link in an event, one can be sure that there has not been a choice of equally possible alternatives. But consciousness is always a choice. Thus, by excluding choice (unpredictability, perceived by the external observer as chance), we exclude consciousness from the historical process. But historical patterns are also distinguished from all others by that fact that it is impossible to understand them, with the exception of the conscious as well as semiotic activity of people.

Creative thinking is particularly revealing in this connection. As we have already said, the creative consciousness is the generator of a text that cannot be predicted according to automatic algorithms. Here we could focus on the fact that certain aspects nevertheless always remain predictable ("traditions") and, if we examine only these, then some processes would appear uninterrupted and even, others predictable with a certain degree of probability, and still others totally unexpected. But the degree of their unexpectedness would also vary, depending on whether we read the order of texts in the temporal direction or against it. Unexpected texts are not impossible but simply less probable. But the lesser probability of, for instance, "Byronic romanticism" occurring without Byron determines the situation only up until the moment of his appearance. Moreover, in the cultural sphere, the more unexpected this or that phenomenon is, the stronger its influence on the cultural situation *after* it has been realized. The completion of an unexpected event (occurrence of an unpredicted text) sharply alters the situation for the following one. The improbable text becomes a reality, and the subsequent development originates from it as if from a fact. The unexpectedness fades, the originality of the genius is transformed into a routine with the imitators, after Byron come the Byronists, and after Brummell the dandies of all Europe.

With a retrospective interpretation, the dramatic discreteness of the process disappears, and Byron emerges as the "first Byronist", as the follower of his followers, or, as it is usually called in historiocultural research, "predecessor". Friedrich Schlegel coined the saying in one of his "Fragments": "The historian is a prophet turned to the past."[20]

This witty remark gives us a reason for noticing the difference between the position of the fortune-teller who predicts the future and the historian who "predicts" the past. No fortune-teller or prognosticator calls the future unequivocal, like something inescapable and singularly possible: a prediction is either made according to the principle of a two-step convention (of the type: "if one does this-or-that, then this-and-that will happen"), or purposely given a vague formulation, in order to necessitate complementary interpretations. In any case, the prediction always retains a scent of indeterminacy, the inexhaustibility of choices between certain alternatives. This is where the constant theme of misunderstood predictions in folklore and ancient texts originates. Thus, for instance, Thucydides relates the following event:

To Chilon, who had consulted the oracle in Delphi, the god uttered a prophecy: to the supreme festival in Zeus's honour Chilon must possess the Athenian Acropolis. At the time of the games at Peloponnesian Olympia, Chilon, intending to become a tyrant, seized the Acropolis together with followers and a detachment of armed men, who had been sent by Theagenos. He proposed that this also be that "supreme festival in honour of Zeus", which the oracle had prophesied, and that he as victor at Olympia was especially justified in interpreting the oracle in that particular way. Did the prophecy imply that the "supreme festival" be held in Attica or at another different place, this Chilon had not thought about, and the oracle not explained?"[21]

As a result, Chilon's scheme led to his death. A special collegium of decemvirs usually gathered in Rome to interpret the predictions of the sibyllic books. Cicero notes in the treatise *On Divination*: "concerning the interpreters of all these oracular answers, their role in relation to those whose prophecies they interpret is akin to the role of the grammarians in relation to the poets."[22] By way of conclusion Cicero wrote:

"Chrysippus filled an entire scroll with his oracular answers, in part fake ones, in part the kind that had come true by chance (as is often the case with all kinds of prophecies), in part such vague and dark ones that they were in need of an interpreter themselves. And in order to understand the meaning of an oracular answer, one has to resort to other oracles (*sortes*). Finally some of them are so ambiguous that one can only understand them with the aid of dialectics. Thus, when the extremely wealthy emperor of Asia, Croesus, was presented with an oracular answer saying that Croesus would destroy a great power during his campaign through Galicia, this emperor thought that he was bound to destroy a hostile power but turned out to destroy his own. (*Ibid.*, Book II, ch. VI, p. 115)

Cicero also recounts the prophecy made by the oracle for Pyrrhus: "Aio te, Aeacida, Romanos posse", which was deliberately formulated to allow two interpretations: "I am telling you, Aeacides, you are able to conquer Rome" and "I am telling you, Aeacides, Rome will be able to conquer."

The historian, who "predicts backwards", is different from the fortune-teller in that he "removes" the indeterminacy: that which had not happened de facto could not happen at all, in his view. The historical process loses its indeterminacy, i.e. it ceases to be informative.

Indeterminacy implies an interpreter. And here a parallel comes to mind: an artistic text, in opposition to a scientific one, also carries a high degree of indeterminacy and is in need of an interpreter (critic, literary historian, connoisseur). Moreover, a scientific text does not need such an intermediary. The difference obviously resides in the fact that the scientific text looks at the world as already structured, completed, and consequently looks at it retrospectively to a certain extent (of course, to a lesser degree than the historian). The artistic text creates a world, a world permeated by mechanisms of unpredictable self-development. This is related to yet another series of phenomena. The very notion of unpredictability is relative and more or less dependent upon the degree of probability of this or that event. The closer one gets to the points of bifurcation, the more individual the curve of events gets. Incidentally, the same thing goes for the degree of predictability/unpredictability in different types of texts at the same historical point. Thus, in science, for instance, we may observe the simultaneous occurrence of even the most unexpected ideas: Newton and Leibnitz were simultaneously working on integral and differential calculus, Darwin and Wallis arrived at the idea of evolution independent of one another, the idea of the theory of relativity was simultaneously hit upon by Einstein and Poincaré; Lobachevski, Bolyai, Gauss, Schweickart and Taurinus independently and simultaneously approached the problem of non-Euclidean geometry. We do not find such phenomena in the history of art. This gives rise to yet another peculiarity: if we were to assume the death of some famous inventor before he had succeeded in making his invention, we can be sure that sooner or later (as a rule within a closely foreseeable future) this invention would be made anyway. In this sense, the unexpected death of this or that scientist does not fundamentally alter the course of the historical process. However, if Dante or Dostoevsky had died during childhood without having written their works, these would not have been written at all, and this would have meant a change not only in the development of literature but also in the general history of humanity; Dante's and Einstein's degree of greatness may nevertheless be considered commensurable.

Thus we may conclude that the necessity of relying on texts confronts the historian with an inescapable double distortion: on the one hand, the syntagmatic linear tendency of the text to transform the event by changing it into a narrative structure and, on the other, the reverse tendency of the historian's glance. Semiotics is knocking on the doors of history. By flinging them open for it, history would be able to transcend the theoretical gap separating it from the other twentieth-century sciences.

Notes

1 Jakobson, Roman (1971) Quest for the essence of language. In: *Selected writings* vol II. The Hague/Paris, pp 350–351.

2 *La nouvelle histoire* (1978) Sous la direction de Jacques Le Goff et Roger Chartier, Jacques Revel, Paris, pp 222–226.

3 See Leo Tolstoy's tale "From the notes of Count Nechliudov. Lüzern"

On July 7, 1857, in Lüzern, a strolling destitute singer sang songs and played the guitar for half an hour in front of the Schweitzerhof Hotel, where the richest people stayed. About a hundred people were listening to him. The singer asked everybody three times to give him something. Not one person gave him anything, but several people laughed at him.

And further:

This is the kind of event historians of our time are obliged to write about in burning ineffaceable letters. The event is more significant, more serious and has a much deeper meaning than the facts which are described in newspapers and history books.

This is a fact not for the history of human deeds, but for the history of progress and civilization . . . Because the entire life of people is not led in the sphere of law. Only one thousandth of a portion of it is subject to the law, the remaining part occurs outside of it, in the sphere of society's mores and views. (Tolstoy LN, *Sobranie soch. v 22-kh tt.*, t.III, Moscow, 1979, pp 27–28).

Any representative of the "new history" could put his signature under these lines.

4 Uspenskij, Boris A (1988) *Istoriia russkogo iazyka* (XI–XVII). Budapest, pp 12–13.

5 *Ibid.*

6 Hegel, GWF (1975) *Lectures on the philosophy of world history.* Cambridge, p 126.

7 *Ibid*, p 65.

8 Poincaré, Henri (1908) *Science et méthode.* Paris, p 68.

9 *Ibid*, p 71.

10 Bloch, Marc (1974) *Apologie pour l'histoire ou metier d'historien*, Paris; Bloch, Marc (1986) *Apologiia istorii, ili remeslo istorika*, Moscow, p 28.

11 *Ibid*, p 29.

12 *Ibid*, p 71. Condorcet, who had been declared an outlaw, worked some weeks before his suicide, while in hiding from the Jacobin tribunal, on a book about the history of progress which embodied the entire optimism of the Age of Reason. Marc Bloch, hero of the Resistance, a fighter of the anti-fascist underground, who was prevented from concluding the work we have cited by the execution squad, completely avoids the issues of personal activity and responsibility as historical categories. This is further evidence of the fact that ideas possess stability and a tendency toward self-development. They are more conservative than individual behaviour and change more slowly under the influence of circumstances.

13 Prigogine, Ilya and Stengers, Isabelle (1984) *Order out of chaos.* London, p 13.

14 From Latin *bifurcus*, two-forked, signifying that this point presents alternative continuations of the curve.

15 Prigogine and Stengers (1984) p 13.

16 Ross Ashby, W (1964) *An introduction to cybernetics.* London, p 259.

17 Prigogine and Stengers (1984) p 176.

18 *Zeitschrift für Physik* 53:840.

19 Kant, Immanuel (1784) Idee zu einer allgemeinen Geschichte in weltbürgerlicher Absicht. *Berlinische Monatschrift* p 385.

20 Quoted in Berkovskii NI (ed) (1934) *Literaturnaia teoriia nemnetskogo romantizma. Dokumenty*, Leningrad, p 470; Pasternak liked this saying and quoted it, although mistakenly attributing it to Hegel.

21 Thucydides, *History of the Peloponnesian War*, book I, ch 126, pp 4–6 (in Russian transl: Fukidid, *Istoriia*, Leningrad, 1981, p 54).

22 Cicero, *On divination*, Book I, ch XVIII, p 34 (in Russian transl: Tsitseron. *Filosofskie traktaty*, Moscow, 1985, p 205.)

Translated by Håkan Lövgren

Chapter 21

Working Memory

Julian Hilton

This chapter discusses the difference between human memory and computer memory, and the effects of this difference. There is a tendency to confuse memory capacity – dramatically expanded in computer technology – with understanding and competence. The latter qualities of the human working memory are connected with forgetfulness and fantasy – two qualities that are often seen as disturbing and potential causes of unreliability. But should they not be seen instead as positive properties of the human active memory?

On the basis of, among other things, Bacon's *The Advancement of Learning* and from the Art of Memory's emblematic relationships between memory and language, the question is posed whether the development of computer memory cannot better approximate human memory capacity. Sophisticated memory has the ability to forget – a characteristic linked to judgement. But present-day computer technology is not solely devoted to the gathering and storing of data.

Humans and computers both depend on a combination of passive and working memory for their operations. But where human memory in all its aspects is defective, forgetful, liable to age and tending to fictionalize, computer memory is accurate to the point of literal-mindedness and reliable to the point of irritation. This fundamental difference needs to be explored since it may be a false presupposition of cognitive support systems that the computer's capacity to support inadequate human memory is necessarily a positive benefit. If it is characteristic of human memory to be defective – to fictionalize, to fantasize, to be forgetful – is it always such a help that the computer is not like this at all?

The Necessary Reconstruction of the Past

In his dialogue *The Critic as Artist – Part I*, Oscar Wilde wrote the following exchange:

Ernest: Gilbert, you treat the world as if it were a crystal ball. You hold it in your hand and reverse it, to please a wilful fancy. You do nothing but rewrite history.

Gilbert: The one duty we owe to history is to rewrite it. That is not the least of the tasks in store for the critical spirit. When we have fully discovered the scientific laws that govern life, we shall realize that the one person who has more illusions than the dreamer is the man of action.[1]

Wilde's remarks on history, particularly with their implicit awareness of the Marxist pursuit of scientifically grounded analysis of historical laws, pin-point the special nature of the work in which human memory engages. That work is the constant, and necessary, reconstruction of history. To remember is to reconstruct, and that is why the writing of history, as indeed the retelling of stories, or the re-enactment of plays, is so compelling. Each such event comes out different. Each must be distinct.

This difference is not, however, confined to the retelling, the history itself, but also concerns the reader in the act of reading, the audience in the act of listening. Rereading the past is as much to reconstruct it as rewriting it. The memory is the work. But what sort of work is it? What status should it have? Is working memory interchangeable with working life?

Wilde makes reference to the incipient study of history as a science and seems to imply that he believes history will be amenable to forensic analysis. There are laws and they will be discerned. Or at least, this is Gilbert's view. If we discover these laws, will we find that the one underlying law is that humans always rewrite their history in the same ways – to justify them-selves, to discredit others or to praise them? Or will we learn that the only law is Hegel's – that the one thing we learn from history is that we learn nothing from history? In the former instance we may have some reason for supposing an analogous relationship between human and computer mem-ory; in the latter we may suppose none.

The Unreliable Instruments of Recall

The principal instrument of human memory is language – symbolic system – in which what we know is stored and through which it is re-expressed. This symbolic system may be linguistic or mathematical. It has been an enduring preoccupation of human history to attempt to discern an exact language in which knowledge can be stored remotely to avoid what are seen as the deficiencies of the internal human memory system that has evolved in the brain. On the one hand, this preoccupation has a Platonic character, the dream of rediscovering the First Causes or Ideal Forms from which know-ledge was derived and knowledge was stored. On the other, it has the hallmark of post-Cartesian science, the positivistic stamp of a culture that believes it can ultimately record accurately everything there is to be known.

Computing memory has in part developed in response to both these historical forces. There is, though self-evidently not universally shared, a belief in sections of the computing community that there may be a powerful universal language – still to be written – in which the problem of the exact storage of data and knowledge can be solved. But the vast difficulties of such an undertaking have tended to generate a belief in the need for ever bigger and ever faster machines, rather than to question whether the principles of computer development are not themselves to some extent misconceived. In other words, computing power is often elided in the engineer's mind with operational competence. It is rather like confusing the issue of how big your car should be with why you cannot map-read. It is not a necessary precondition of getting from A to B that you have a three-litre car generating two hundred horse-power; a smaller car will do if you use it skilfully.

But the problem of confusing memory capacity and power with understanding and operational competence is not the only one that affects the way we understand, and use, working memory. The work of the Swedish Centre for Working Life, however, has reminded us, forcefully, that there are two other, deeply related modes of memory, the tacit and the skill-based, both transmitted more through the senses, especially sight, sound and touch, than through any form of symbolic representation. Who can write down how to build a beautiful dome, a pleasing and comfortable chair? Thus there are two forms of weakness to the case for ultimately discernible laws in human behaviour: the first is that the means of recording and expressing such laws are themselves inadequate, and the second is that the concept of a record as in any way stable – or at least stable enough to be considered a law – is indefensible. Nothing ever happens the same way twice. These weaknesses cannot but impact on computing technology, yet there is not as much evidence as perhaps there should be that the computer technologist is aware of the problem.

This may be restated in positive form: how does the concept of working memory look from the perspective of forgetfulness and fantasy as positive rather than negative characteristics of human memory?

First, here is an example of what I mean. During the heyday of theatre building in Britain, from the mid-seventeenth to the end of the nineteenth century, theatres burned down with remarkable regularity. Fire regulations were inadequate and fire protection systems ineffective. The result was that theatre buildings were constantly renewed and rethought according to the desiderata of performers of their time. The building was as much an integral part of organically developing theatre culture as writing or costume design. The building was in the best sense a concretization of a working memory system. From the moment that, for perfectly good reasons, the problem of fire was solved, theatres stopped being burned down, stopped being rebuilt and became increasingly monuments to past theatre styles and increasingly little places for contemporary work. The result is now plain to see. The great majority of theatres are in the nineteenth-century form and so favour nineteenth-century works and above all nineteenth-century playing styles. They are time-bound, dying memory systems.

Our confidence in computer memory systems may be subject to the same difficulties as Wilde diagnoses in the men of action. We may be standardizing to systems that, like nineteenth-century theatres, increasingly inhibit the dynamic sense of performance – performance as the heightened experience of the present – in favour of performance as an act of historical piety or reconstruction. We may be putting our trust in the phenomenology of action, not the epistemology. Where though is the irony? – in the fact that the real de-skilling of human memory that may be effected by the computer is the fear it generates in us of forgetting, in the pressure it generates to fictionalize and fantasize less. We do less with our memories, we rewrite less thoroughly and, worse, less imaginatively.

This would be a neat way of discrediting computers, but for the fact that the debate on the nature of memory and the risk of de-skilling through inhibition of fantasy is an ancient problem. Greek theories of memory debate the competing merits of memory as defined as a logical, architectural, procedural phenomenon and as an organic process of being, or becoming or imagining. Is memory like a storage system, like a house with many rooms, each room holding a difference repository of known things, and each object in each room defining a sub-set of the whole? Or is memory like a myth of metamorphosis, a phenomenon of changing state through enactment, or work? Horace reflects the deeply problematic nature of such a debate in his famous claim (*Odes Book XXX*) that his poems as memory systems are in fact more durable than bronze, so seemingly implying that the apparent durability of the logical memory system is in fact only truly to be found in the poetic – the constantly remade.

So my case should not be read as a another part of the Jeremiad against computing. Quite the opposite; I am interested in computers prospering because I use them the whole time and would like more from them than they currently offer. What concerns me is whether the development of systems is actually premised on the right questions, and when I compare human working memory with that of the computer I am forced to conclude that they may not be.

Language and Memory: The Art of the Emblem

If the issue can be resolved, it seems to me, and to many contributors to this volume, that language is the key, and a particular type of language – the language of metaphor or of deep epistemological or reflective truth. And by language is not meant merely the symbolic, but also the unspoken languages of craftsmanship, or painting. And because language is the tool and bears meaning only in dialogue with an Other – real or imagined – the true impact of technology on our culture, on our working memory, will be decided by and reflected in language itself. In other words, there is a close relation between language and memory.

Just this point is made by Lord Bacon in *The Advancement of Learning*: "The custody or retaining of knowledge is either in writing or memory; whereof writing hath two parts, the nature of the character, and the order of the entry".[2] Bacon disposes briefly of what he thinks writing to be before returning to the subject of memory. He is not impressed by the mere regurgitation of facts. What matters to him is what we do with memory – memory as an active system:

This art of memory is built upon two intentions; the one prenotion, the other emblem. Prenotion dischargeth the indefinite seeking of what we would remember, and directeth us to seek in a narrow compass, that is, somewhat that hath congruity within our place of memory. Emblem reduceth conceits intellectual to images sensible, which strike the memory more; out of which axioms may be drawn much better practique than that in use.[3]

Bacon's principal point is to make memory the agency which mediates between theory and practice, that which, through the power of emblem, reifies thought into "images sensible". In effect, therefore, memory has a double function of recall and representation, in which it is fundamental to the process of recall that a certain transformation and concretization take place.

Underlying this active view of memory is Bacon's scepticism about the mere act of remembering, what he calls "matters of strangeness without worthiness".[4] He might perhaps have applied the same opinion to computer memory: it is not of any particular significance that a computer can recall vast amounts of data. What matters is what the computer, or the user, can do with the data during and after recall. In the development of computer systems, however, an opposite logic seems to be being pursued. Systems are marketed with more and more memory at less and less cost and the effect is that all users can store and retrieve ever larger volumes of data. What purpose such data serves is less often considered.

Bacon implies a view as to what route the design of systems should be taking in his stress on the power of emblem, which is a figure of expression relying equally strongly on the verbal and the visual, on the symbolic and the iconic. Clearly, the recent success of developments in software such as hypercard stem from the same observation as Bacon makes that emblematic modes of storage and representation are fundamentally more powerful than merely symbolic or merely iconic modes. By the same token, the power of hypertext to suggest, and in a sense, demand, interactive data storage techniques means it has a natural advantage over passive text storage systems.

But when compared with the storage power of, say, a Shakespeare play, with its enormously rich texture of complex emblems, even hypercard or hypertext look exceedingly crude instruments. This is not to try to discredit them. Even most literature looks crude next to Shakespeare. Rather, it is to stress how sophisticated the relation between language and memory can be in the storage of data, as Bacon's remarks indicate and how important artistic forms of knowledge storage are as benchmarks of technological achievement. One of the reasons for Shakespeare's enduring popularity and influence is that he managed to produce in extraordinarily compressed form a complete world picture whose actuality seems undiminished by the gradual evolution of our language away from his. We may activate his memory systems in two main ways: by reading, or by watching performances. If we read, we access Shakespeare through language. If we see a performance we access Shakespeare through emblems, which as Bacon observed have that much more power than abstractions. In either case, it is in the nature of the original that we have to work ourselves to get access to the knowledge stored in the works of art. As Shakespeare puts it in *Henry V*:

O pardon, since a crooked figure may
Attest in little place a million;
And let us, ciphers to this great accompt,
On your imaginary forces work. [Prologue, 15–18][5]

The system depends for its success on the embedded and highly compressed knowledge of the text being recalled and represented in the imagination of the audience.

This raises two further possible lines of enquiry about the nature of the relationship between work and memory, both of which concern the activity itself of remembering. The first is the possibility that the concepts of work and memory are in certain circumstances interchangeable. If, for example, a craftsman makes a table, he is relying on an active memory of how to do it and what a table looks like to achieve his goal. This is not intended as a pseudo-Platonic argument about imitations of ideals. There need be no ideal table predicated in the craftsman's mind for him to undertake a table, rather a deep, partly inherited knowledge of what tables are, what they do and how to form one. The work, therefore, is the function of an activated memory meeting as defined need. An analogy may be drawn here with the performance of a dramatic text. The existence of a text such as *King Lear* does not predicate the existence of an original, ideal Play, of which *King Lear* is a pale shadow. It does, however, enable a potentially infinite variety of representations of the text itself. It is rich in what Keats calls "negative capability". When an actor plays Lear, he speaks words that have been written by Shakespeare for Lear (i.e. he merely regurgitates) yet he aspires to do so in such a way that his audience feels that it is hearing him for the first time – i.e. he is creating emblems as he performs.

The second, complementary to the first, is the possibility that working memory is closely related to the concept of tradition and that to be born into a particular culture is to be born into a particular version of working memory. Here again, Bacon sees language as the agent of mediation. Access to a given working memory is through language, and, quite specifically, through the use of language in what he defines as rhetoric.

Rhetoric and Inexactitude: The Power of Emblem

Rhetoric, as Bacon's rather defensive attitude illustrates, has always been regarded with suspicion. It is viewed as a term as interchangeable with deceit, or illusion at best. Yet Bacon's point is that "the duty and office of rhetoric is to apply reason to imagination for the better moving of the will".[6] Expressed in the language of computing, what Bacon might be interested in suggesting is that the real cognitive support that working memory might offer is that of persuading the user to the right choice, to the right exercise of will, but not making that choice, that act of will on his behalf. Put this way, however, it makes the power of expertise much less that of knowledge or reasoning than that of persuasion. It is not that the expert impresses by his knowledge but by his ability to use his knowledge and the authority it gives him to persuade us first to believe him and second to act on his advice. In such a context, accessing the working memory of an expert may well be to a rhetorical rather than an informational purpose.

This, of course, sits uncomfortably with the technocratic view of the computer as remorselessly logical, tireless and reliable. But it confirms utterly the line of argument in Stephen Toulmin's essay in this volume that it is of the essence of natural language, of any kind, that it be inexact. Indeed, part of the pleasure of using language lies in its inexactitude, the fact that it, often unwittingly, throws up ambiguities, puns, allusions. At one extreme, the principle of inexactitude constitutes, as Bakhtin perceived in his theory of carnival, perhaps the most powerful response humans have developed to the dangers of totalitarianism. No matter how much you blame Jews or Communists for the evils of the world it is very hard to define exactly who these alleged people are, still less what they may have done. At the other, the principle of inexactitude underlies a set of personal and psychological propositions, of which the *lapsus linguae* which so intrigued Freud is one, in which human memories themselves seem to delight in subverting their own apparent function.

We delight in emblems, and hence accord them great power, first because they are integral combinations of symbolic and iconic information – powerful indices in fact which, as Shakespeare indicates, allow us to store knowledge highly efficiently (his ratio is one million bits to each emblem) – and secondly, because they support inexactitudes, and indeed depend on them. Inexactitude from one perspective is user choice from another. We all use a common stock of emblems because, as Wittgenstein reminded us, if we do not have them we cannot communicate at all. They are both memory system and means of expression – *langue* and *parole* – at once. But we use them in different ways, each use bearing a distinct signature. It is because we know as humans that our memory systems are defective that we have to work constantly to retrieve and reconstruct what we know and, while this is at times burdensome, it is also of great practical value in that the emblem stock is constantly reviewed and refreshed by use.

Yet as Jon Cook, in a powerful lecture *One Culture, Two Cultures, Three Cultures . . .* has pointed out,[7] it is not merely Plato who has influenced the Western preoccupation with exactitude but also Aristotle, who makes the capacity to organize knowledge according to taxonomic principles, and to generate powerful abstractions from historically determined data, the fundamental skill of government. From such a case emerges the ascendancy of professional knowledge over artisanal skill, of the text-book over apprentice learning. In other words, it has been fundamental to social organization that we have apparently refused to acknowledge in our social and political structures the way our memories actually function. It is hardly surprising, therefore, that one powerful appeal of computers to governments is the capacity computers give government to increase their grip on the central organization and administration of data.

We may, however, be wrong as citizens to feel threatened by this, for the danger of centralized systems seems to me in the longer term far greater to governments themselves than to individuals. What renders government impossible more commonly and more powerfully than popular resistance is sheer overload. Governments that take to themselves too many decisions, too much control, in the end manage themselves to a standstill. This is the lesson of Eastern Europe since 1945, but the phenomenon is an ancient one. The famous remark by Philip of Spain's ambassador "if death shall come from Spain, I must be immortal" is clearly applicable to large-scale centralized systems of any kind and computers are and will be no exception. This local difficulty of government, however, is part of a much simpler and more powerful aspect of working memory – forgetting.

The Virtues of Forgetting: The Self-maintaining System

The great virtue of human memory is its power to forget. While computers have to be told to forget, humans do so without being asked. Their reasons for forgetting may be varied, from mere lack of interest, to active judgement of value, to the resolution of trauma, but they forget with great skill. The most significant work done by the working memory is forgetting, and the most powerful aspect of forgetting is judgement – judging what is to be forgotten.

My concern about the impact of computer memory systems – which do not forget except by instruction – on human systems is therefore simple: will computers impair our capacity to forget, especially to forget in a judicious manner? At the perhaps simplest level, that of routine office work, the answer seems to be yes. We transmit vastly more information than we ever did before, but the quality of our decisions has probably declined. To improve our decisions, or perhaps just to cope with the sea of paper in which the dream of the paperless office is drowning, we buy more computers. Computers are thus offered a wonderful, circular rationale: how do we cope with organizing all that we are now storing – by using even bigger computers, of course.

At the most complex level, that of cultural epistemology, our inability to forget may be at the heart of the deep uncertainty which seems to beset us. It is in times of certainty that how and what to forget is made simple. Forgetting in the Catholic church, for example, is a fundamental operating principle of religion, as in the ritualized act of forgetting that goes with the processes of confession, penance and absolution. We record the past, judge it and then forget it. But with the passing of conviction in the universal church passed also the institutionalized process of forgetting. In one, historical sense, the rise of science seems connected with this change in that Bacon in the closing years of the sixteenth century writes out of a sense of the collapse of universal Catholic values. Our own times, however, have brought a new variant of the problem, the heritage culture, which is characterized by an apparent inability to throw anything away or pull anything down.

The point at issue is whether computers will ever serve any higher purpose than the mere generation of data if we cannot address ourselves to their epistemological impact, and in particular to the relation between human and computing memory systems, in which issue, I suggest, forgetting is the key.

It will be evident from my earlier chapter in this volume that while I see problems about the development of intelligent systems, I am convinced that in due course such systems will be developed. But in pursuit of such systems very little attention, if any, has been paid to forgetting, except perhaps in the concept of the self-maintaining system. The next step for our dialogue with technology, therefore, should be into the domain of forgetting, which is another way of saying that the epistemological issue which I believe needs most concern us is how to rediscover the metaphysical, equivalent of the rubbish dump.

Notes

1 Wilde, Oscar *The critic as artist – part I*. In: Murray, Isobel (ed) *Oscar Wilde*. Oxford, 1989, p 256. I am much indebted to Allan Janik for drawing my attention to this exchange.

2 Bacon, Francis *The advancement of learning and New Atlantis*. Oxford, 1951, p 156.

3 Bacon, *op cit*, p 157.

4 Bacon, p 157.

5 Shakespeare, William *Henry V*. In Alexander, Peter (ed) *The complete works*. London, 1951, p 551.

6 Bacon, p 168.

7 *One culture, two cultures, three cultures* . . . , lecture given by Jon Cook to the Swedish University Board seminar, Norwich, May 1988, to be published in *Dialoger*, Stockholm.

Bibliography

Abbott EA (1929) *A Shakespearian grammar*. Macmillan, London
Ahlin J (ed) (1985) Konsekvenser för industri- och arbetsmiljöplanering av ny information-
steknologi, Projektrapport 3, Department of Architecture, Stockholm Institute of Technology,
p 9
Aristotle *The poetics*. In: Ross WD (ed) *Works of Aristotle translated into English*. Oxford, 1928

Bacon F *The advancement of learning and New Atlantis*. The World's Classics, London, 1951
Bakhtin M (1984) *Problems of Dostoevsky's poetics*, Emerson, Caryl (ed, transl). University of
Minnesota Press, Minneapolis
Bakhtin M (1984) *Rabelais and his world*, Iswolsky, Hélène (transl). Indiana University Press,
Bloomington
Bakhtin M (1981) *The dialogical imagination*, Holquist, Michael (ed), transl by Emerson, Caryl and
Holquist, Michael. University of Texas Press, Austin
Bassnett S (1980) *Translation studies*. Methuen, London
Bateson G (1973) *Steps to an ecology of mind*. Paladin, London
Berkovskii NI (ed) (1934) *Literaturnaia teoriia nemnetskogo romantizma Dokumenty*. Leningrad
Bloch M (1974) *Apologie pour l'histoire ou metier d'historien*. Paris
Boden M (1977) *Artificial intelligence and natural man*. Hassocks
Büchner G (1972) *Sämtliche Werke und Briefe. Historisch-Kritische Ausgabe mit Kommentar*. Werner R.
Lehmann, Habsburg
Bolton D (1984) *Turing's man: Western culture in the computer age*. Duckworth, London
Bonniers Litterära Magasin (no. 4, 1984) Stockholm

Cattin G (1984) *Music of the Middle Ages I*. Cambridge University Press, Cambridge
Chekhov, A *The three sisters*, In: Frayn, Michael (ed). Methuen, London, 1983, 1985
Cicero, *On Divination*, Book I
Cook J (1988) *One culture, two cultures, three cultures*, unpublished manuscript. Lecture given to
the Swedish University Board, Norwich, May

Dal E (1956) *Nordisk folkviseforskning siden 1800*. Copenhagen
Degerblad J-E (1988) *Planering och yrkeskultur*. Council for Building Research
Descartes R *A discourse on method*, Veitch, John (transl). Everyman, London 1912
Dialoger (eds Florin M, Göranzon B, Sällström P), No. 1 (1985), No. 16 (1990)
Dreyfus HL (1979) *What computers can't do: the limits of artificial intelligence*. Harper and Row, New
York

Eliot TS (1951) *Collected poems 1909–1935*. Faber and Faber, London

Feigenbaum E, Feldman J (eds) (1963) *Computers and thought*. McGraw-Hill, New York

Gödel (1986), *Collected Works*, vol 1, *Publications 1929–1936*. Oxford University Press, Oxford
Goody J (1977) *The domestication of the savage mind*. Cambridge University Press, Cambridge

Göranzon B (ed) (1983) *Datautvecklingens filosofi: Tyst kunskap och ny teknik*. Carlssons, Stockholm
Göranzon B (1991) *The Practical Intellect*, Unesco, Paris and Springer-Verlag, London
Gregory RL, Marstrand PK (1987) *Creative intelligence*. Frances Pinter, London

Hegel GWF (1975) *Lectures on the philosophy of world history*. Cambridge
Hermans T (ed) (1985) *The manipulation of literature*. Croom Helm, London
Holmes J (ed) (1970) *The nature of translation: essays on the theory and practice of literary translation*. Mouton, The Hague
Human Geography No. 50 (1983) Royal University of Lund, Department of Geography

Jakobson R (1971) *Quest for the essence of language: Selected writings II*. Mouton, The Hague/Paris
Janik A, Toulmin S (1973) *Wittgenstein's Vienna*. Simon and Schuster, New York

Kant I (1784) Idee zur einer allgemeinen Geschichte in weltbürgerlicher Absicht. *Berlinischer Monatschrift*
Keats J *The letters of John Keats*, Buxton, Maurice (ed). Foreman, Oxford, 1931
Kenyon Review XXIII (3) Summer, 1961
Kleist H von (1810) Über das Marionettentheater, Berliner Abendblättern 12–15 December *Heinrich von Kleist Sämtliche Werke . . . Mit einer Einführung . . .* von KF Reining, Wiesbaden, n.d.
Kolakowski L (1989) *Tales from the kingdom of Lailonia and the key to heaven*. University of Chicago Press, Chicago

Le Goff J, Chartier R (1978) *La nouvelle histoire*. Paris
Lefevere A (1988) Translation history: mirror upon mirror mirror'd. Plenary lecture at "Beyond Translation", conference held at University of Warwick, July
Leighton LG (transl, ed) (1984) *The art of translation: Kornei Chukovsky's "A High Art"*. University of Tennessee Press, Knoxville
Levy J (1969) *Die Literarische übersetzung: Theorie einer Kunstgattung*, Schaumshula, Walter (transl). Athenäum, Frankfurt

Macdonald D (1960) *Parodies*. Faber and Faber, London
Marlowe C *The tragical history of Dr Faustus*, In: Ridley MR (ed) *Plays and poems*. Everyman, London, 1955

New York Review of Books (1984) 19 July

Pagel HR (1984) Computer culture: the scientific, intellectual and social impact of the computer. *Annals of the New York Academy of Sciences*, vol 426
Pedersen B (1976) *Parodiens teori*. Berlingske, Copenhagen
Poincaré H (1908) *Science et méthode*. Paris
Popovic A (1976) *Dictionary for the analysis of literary translation*. Department of Comparative Literature, University of Alberta
Pratt V (1987) *Thinking machines: the evolution of artificial intelligence*. Basil Blackwell, Oxford
Prigogine I, Stengers I (1984) *Order out of chaos*. London
Printz-Påhlsson G (1984) *Säg Minns Du Skeppet Refanaut*, Bonniers
PTL I (1) January 1976, I (2) April 1976

Rosenbluth A, Wiener N, Bigelow J (1943) *Behaviour, purpose and teleology, philosophy of science* 10
Ross AW (1964) *An introduction to cybernetics*. London

Sällström P (ed) (1984) *Funderingar kring Vetenskap & Musik*. Royal Academy of Music series no. 44, Stockholm
Schiller F Über die ästetische Erziehung des Menschen in einer Reihe von Briefen. *Gesammelte Werke in fünf Bänden*. Reinhold Netiolitzky, vol 5
Shakespeare W *Henry V*. In: Taylor, Gary (ed). Oxford University Press, Oxford, 1982
Shakespeare, W *Henry V*. In: Alexander, Peter (ed) *The complete works*. London, 1951

Shaw GB *Pygmalion: a romance in five acts.* In: Laurence, Dan H (ed). Penguin, London, 1986
Sigma (1965) vol 6, Forum, Stockholm
Sinding-Larsen H (1983) *Fra fest til forestilling.* Magister thesis, Department of Social Anthropology, University of Oslo
Stanislavski C (1963) In: Reynolds, Elisabeth (transl) *Creating a role.* Hapgood, London
Systems Development (1984) A presentation of four different views. Work Environment Fund, Stockholm

Thucydides, *History of the Peloponnesian war*, Book I
Tolstoy L *Sobranie soch* v 22-kh tt, t III. Moscow, 1979
Turing AM (1937) On computable numbers, with an application to the Entscheidungsproblem. *Proc London Mat Soc* 2:42

Uspenskii BA (1988) *Istoriia russkogo iazyka* (XI–XVII), Budapest

Weizenbaum J (1967) *Computer power and human reason: from judgment to calculation.* Freeman, San Francisco
Whitemore H (1987) *Breaking the code.* Amber Lane Press, Oxford
Wiener N (1952) *Materia, Maskiner, Människor: Cybernetiken och Samhället.* Forum, Stockholm
Wiener N See Rosenbluth et al (1943)
Wiener N (1961) *Cybernetics, or control and communication in the animal and machine.* MIT Press/Wiley
Wilde O In: Murray, Isobel (ed) *Oscar Wilde.* Oxford, 1989

Zeitschrift für Physik (1929)
Zuckerkandl V (1956) *Sound and symbol.* Princeton University Press
Zuckerkandl V (1973) *Man, the musician.* Princeton University Press

Name Index